The Way of the Human Being

CALVIN LUTHER MARTIN

The Way of the Human Being

Yale University Press
New Haven & London

Published with assistance from the foundation
established in memory of Philip Hamilton
McMillan of the Class of 1894, Yale College.

Designed by Nancy Ovedovitz and set in Scala
type by The Composing Room of Michigan,
Inc.. Printed in the United States of America.

Library of Congress Cataloging-in-Publication Data

Martin, Calvin.
The way of the human being / Calvin Luther Martin.
p.   cm.
Includes bibliographical references and index.
ISBN 0–300–07468–9 (cloth : alk. paper)
ISBN 0–300–08552–4 (pbk. : alk. paper)
1. Indian philosophy—North America.   2. Indians
in literature.   I. Title.
E98.P5   M36   1999
191'.089'97—ddc21   98–44175

A catalogue record for this book is available
from the British Library.

The paper in this book meets the guidelines for
permanence and durability of the Committee
on Production Guidelines for Book Longevity of
the Council on Library Resources.

10   9   8   7   6   5   4   3   2

Lindsey and Forrest

Contents

Contents

Preface

Deep within *Leaves of Grass* smolders a question we have never answered satisfactorily. "The friendly and flowing savage. . . . Who is he?" asks Whitman. "Is he waiting for civilization or past it and mastering it?" D. H. Lawrence asks it, too, even as he concedes that the native "doesn't believe in us and our civilization," for "the red life flows in a different direction from the white life." Thoreau, deep in the Maine woods with a Penobscot guide who baffles and amazes him, concludes that "one revelation has been made to the Indian, another to the white man."[1]

This book is my response to all three: Whitman, Lawrence, Thoreau, plus Melville, Faulkner, Cather, Hemingway, and more. Perceptive people have been asking the same questions and drawing the same conclusions since the sixteenth century.

They are right: Native America has always posed a challenge to western civilization. The challenge cuts deeply, deeper than we generally care to go: it asks us to examine the fundamental nature of knowledge and even reality itself. "Your idea of reality is too limited," replied Niels Bohr to Albert Einstein when Einstein tried to show that "quantum theory was incompatible with any reasonable idea of 'reality.'" Bohr was right. Just so, I am convinced this is the most disturbing message of Native America, and this book marks my journey into its domain.[2]

I began my academic career by writing a book about Indians and animals (beavers, mostly) and the fur trade. At the time I knew no Indians and had never laid eyes on a living beaver—I had learned it all from libraries. In the twenty years since, I have come to know beavers and I have lived, briefly, with Navajos and spent several years living among Eskimos.* I taught, for no salary, at a prison filled with Yup'ik Eskimos away out on the Alaska tundra, near the Bering Sea. I taught, as well, at a tiny Yup'ik seminary.

Though not for nothing. These men and women and their children taught me the "way of the human being": *yuuyaraq,* as it is neatly put in Yup'ik. I participated in that way in the villages. All the while pondering Whitman's question.

The experience of it has changed me; it changed me as a scholar. I stopped doing "research."

Perhaps it is best explained by my desk, a simple wooden table that I built myself during my graduate student days in Evanston, Illinois. I was broke and needed something to write a dissertation on. A neighbor, a librarian at Northwestern, invited me over to his workshop in his basement and we made it in a week. Over the years I moved that desk from Illinois to New York, to New Jersey, Baltimore, Washington, D.C., New Hampshire, and then to Alaska. In those years I wrote four books on it, including this one.

Academic books, except this one felt different. This one, I believed, seemed to have *yua:* a spirit, a person—to be alive itself. I left Alaska a little over a year ago, and before leaving I gave my desk away to an Eskimo friend, Oscar Active. I asked him to do me a favor: to take it

---

*Eskimos are called "Inuit," incidentally, only if they are Canadian Eskimos.

out to his fish-camp on the Kuskokwim and set it up outside for Margaret, his wife, to use cutting up the king and silver and red salmon. No more rhetoric on Native America to be composed on that board: it would join the power of the fish-camp; it would help feed the people, the people of the salmon.

"And when it gets old and rickety," I further asked, "please don't toss it out. Saw it up and burn it in your steamhouse. Release its spirit to the air, the tundra wind."

Oscar is a large man, in size and spirit both, and he laughs a large Yup'ik laugh. "Ii-i," he said. Okay.

I wrote this book mostly on the Alaska tundra, in the blue, vast arctic light, unlike anything I have seen. My wife and I lived there through the kindness of the Yukon-Kuskokwim Health Corporation. From Alaska we moved to Grand Manan, an old volcano away out at sea off Canada's east coast. I continued writing in a cottage by the sea. Len and June Brierley brought us to this special world, and I thank them for it. I then completed the manuscript in Santa Fe. There John and Edith Pierpont gave us the key to their home in the high desert amphitheater of the Sangre de Cristo.

Sean Kane, God bless him, sustained me throughout with his Irish brilliance and warmth. (Sean, may you remain my companion for the rest of my life.) Jack Goellner and Barbara Lamb of the Johns Hopkins University Press read the manuscript from end to end, as did Mike McGiffert of the *William and Mary Quarterly*, and each improved it. Finally, in a small town on the northern edge of the Adirondacks, as I prepared the manuscript for my editor, a prince of a librarian named David Minnich got me every book I needed.

Charlie Kilangak, Sr., Willard D. Church, Jr., Oscar Active, Joe Kashatok, and John Kailukiak are dear Yup'ik friends whose lives in-form this book. I am indebted to them. The identities of several people in Chapters 5 and 6 are imaginary; nonetheless, they are so.

Nina forever gives me grace, and Lindsey and Forrest, my grown children, have (unknown to them) given me life.

The Way of the Human Being

ONE

Coming to America

He was Eskimo, he was Inupiaq, from the North Slope, and like some other Eskimos I have known he bore one name only: Katauq. And it was his own, original name. "Anyway, Katauq was sitting in his igloo one day when those with him noticed that he moved not a muscle, though he continued to breathe. They knew that he had gone *traveling*, his spirit had left his body to go see how things were at some other place." They knew if they left his body perfectly still, his spirit would find its body mask again when it returned from its journey, and he would be just fine.

Katauq's spirit traveled to a great meeting of bowhead whales. They gave him a parka to wear, and when he put it on, he was as one of them. Traveling with the whales as a whale, he learned their habits and their ways.

As spring came on, the whales informed him that they would be traveling along the coast. When they came to Point Hope, they would be met by whalers. He would notice that some of their umi-aks [whaling boats] would be nice and light in appearance, and some dark, and dirty. If he wished to be caught by a whaler, then he should surface by one of the clean and light boats. These belonged to good people, respectful people. They shared their catch with the children who had no parents, with widows, and with the Elders. They were kind people, with good hearts. Their ice cellars were clean: good places for a whale to have its parka of meat and muktuk stored. The dark, dirty boats belonged to people who did not share their catch, and who were lazy. No whale wanted to give itself to these boats.

If Katauq were to go to the village as a whale, and give himself to the whalers, his spirit could not return to his human body. It could put on another whale parka, but it could never go to the human. He could, however, fly back to Point Hope as an eider duck. Then his spirit could return to his body.

That's what he did: flew right back as an eider duck. "He told the people of his time with the whales, and let them know how the whales felt, and how they respected respectful people."[1]

Be careful what you say of this story. Pull it over you and wear it like a parka for a while, being sure you wear it the way you read it here: without critical analysis, as part of yourself. Hard to do, yes. But if you can manage this, you will hear it as an Inupiaq would hear it. You will hear it as did my Yup'ik friend Charlie Kilangak, whom I watched listen, spellbound, to that master storyteller of the Yukon-Kuskokwim delta, Maxie Altsik. Charlie told me that Maxie's story (which was much like Katauq's) had a spirit, *yua:* the story itself was a living thing. The *yua* ("its person") spoke to him. In some uncanny way, he said, the story was about him. Maxie, he added, was a "powerful man" to know that he needed this story.

Repeat Katauq's story to a few friends, but avoid saying anything about it—just tell the story. Soon you will begin to notice something strange: people will be a bit alarmed at your not commenting on it.

Most people (except for young children, I'll wager) will promptly *measure* it with an opinion, and many will look for confirmation of their judgment by appealing to you for yours. Beware of this—beware of the question. Questions are usually a statement; they generally conceal a set of premises and an agenda. Questions are tricky forms of discourse, which is why older Eskimos take care not to ask them much.

Anyhow, deflect the questions. Merely tell the story.

Something else, too, may happen: the story might seem to be thinking you rather than your thinking it. This is a potent thing and it is a legitimate thing, totally against common sense but nonetheless real. Don't reject it; this is how an Eskimo would perceive such a story: it has *yua*.

So may one begin to perceive "the way of the human being"—the way of the world of those people who beheld the first Europeans splash ashore five hundred years ago, and yet who did not regard time or reality or even words themselves in the way those newcomers did then or we do now, and who have struggled mightily with this strange new western philosophy ever since.

That is what this book is about—about the people who measure this story one way (*yua*) and those predisposed to measure it another way (fiction). Two opposite realities—two stories, really—playing themselves out on this continent.

What I myself have learned to say about both realities I shall say, carefully, in the book that follows.*

* The present book continues the discussion of certain themes that I explored in my last book, *In the Spirit of the Earth: Rethinking History and Time* (Baltimore: Johns Hopkins University Press, 1992). These include my quarrel with history, the meaning of Trickster, the matter of native altruism, and even the story of Japasa. And bears, which have been the linchpin of all my books. I look at all of these issues, now, within a different context that I hope gives them further shape.

The rich smoke from the brier bowl rose, windblown, up the clapboard wall of the house set back in the trees. An autumn night, leaves of ash, maple, beech, and oak beginning their turn to reds and yellows and oranges. Smells of leaf mold on the air. It was a night with a fairy, mischievous wind and broad moon. A listener would have detected faint peepings overhead, wave upon wave, as the birds of the north, great and small, rode a high northwind, answering a call only they could hear. From innumerable scattered lakes and rivers, ponds and marshes and brooding forests, they thronged the great celestial flyways, navigating by stars and river lines and deep magnetic fields. The night breathed and moved and beat its wings with power and magic. Altogether it was an event of ancient meanings, a time to be up and attentive to earth's doings and messages. Snow crickets sang of it, careening bats felt it with their clicks, and the night creatures of the wood with tiny sounds went about their errands mindful that something immense was happening. A shadowed figure beneath the window knew it well, too. Above all, he knew who he was—being all of this that was going on. He knew himself as essential to the event and closed his eyes in that exquisite knowledge, as the night coursed through and claimed him as one of its own.

Upstairs a boy traveled in dreams a child knows on such nights, till touched and awakened by the visitor's reverie and smoke. Curling around the room in the moon's pale light, it began to remind him of something familiar, something so natural that he took it for granted. Softly he crept out of bed and stood by the window. Below was a dark, still figure and a glowing ember.

So begins the night story that I used to tell my son and daughter, sitting with arm around each before a fire, before they went up to bed. It was their very favorite tale, and it always followed the same formulaic journey: the mysterious creature appearing late at night beneath the bedroom window, summoning the boy and his sister to a meeting with the wizard. Down the stairs and out the door they crept, into the tumultuous night. The messenger would lead by lantern along a woodland path till they came upon a huge, ancient oak in whose trunk was cut a cunningly wrought door. Through the door and up a long, spiraling staircase to the chamber excavated out of the core of this immense living creature. Here, haloed by firelight, stood a sage, a keeper of long-forgotten earthly knowledge.

The old man would speak of a world bristling and crackling with power, the power of origination and deepest formation, which cared for everything—took care of everything—even human beings. The earth, he said, is not a place to fear. The problem was that adults had lost their nerve, lost faith in the marrow of it all. Children, he believed, still hold the mighty secret of *trust*. It was the lesson of the child to the adult: absolute trust. Once trust began percolating back into the soul again, humans would behold the liberating of those colossal earthly powers that now lie silent under the spell of our bad faith. The earth would be alive again and human beings would stop living lives of waiting, stop living in the curse of time and history, to live instead in the still point of beauty.

I was a professor at the time and I knew this was the most important lecture of my life. It was, I thought, the real news: the news of our civilization's infidelity toward a powerful, sentient earth, tempered by the conviction that children, and whatever bits of childhood survived the battering of growing up, might help us in finding a lost trust in this planet. Human beings could unshackle the awesome powers of place if we could only find our body and spirit in the *otherness* of this planet, as our ice-age ancestors and their hunter-gatherer heirs did for tens of thousands of years. Distrust of the earth became the cultural norm only within the past eight thousand years or so, when the stories of man and woman began to career away from the authentic ways of the earth and follow a trajectory of terror—what the philosopher Mircea Eliade called the "terror of history."[2]

I offer this book as an antidote: stories out of step with time and history, stories from a realm older than the one that bred our current "news" and "history."

Several years ago I began teaching a seminar entitled, simply, "Time." I typically start the class by describing one of my pet projects: accost any kid and ask how old he or she is. The answer, usually, from anyone under four or five is a number, and nothing more. A youngster will say he's "four," not "I'm four years old." Prod him, "You're four *what?*" and he draws a complete blank. Suggest that he might be four *bananas,* and you get a broad grin and an enthusiastic yes.

I like this little exercise because I get a kick out of showing this nebulous yet powerful thing, time, briefly unhinged and looking ludicrous in the utter innocence of a child. The number is there, but it refers to a void. There is no vast solar cycle or other heavenly wheel, no march of the calendar, in a young child's never-never land. It is mom or dad who keeps the record, who will say, "Next week is your birthday," or "Christmas is coming soon." Growing older, we soon enough find time attaching itself to us, until we feel seized by it, bringing forth from Aldous Huxley, one of the most vehement antitemporalists of this century, the cry, "*Time* must have a stop!" Thoreau, betaking himself to a neighbor's tranquil pond to live there by a tempo different from the frantic one swirling about him, put it more lyrically: "As he made no compromise with Time, Time kept out of his way, and only sighed at a distance because he could not overcome him." Time is evil, snapped Huxley: "the medium in which evil . . . lives and outside of which it dies."[3]

Time is my element. I am a historian, a handler of this serpentine thing. I contemplate the stuff of Huxley's nemesis on a vast scale, as a philosopher of history, in my books and lectures, looking for meaning in the deep past. I brood upon it daily, and nightly, in my own life, searching for meaning in this, too. Time has fascinated and horrified me. Like Huxley, I have felt the rhythmic, fugitive, irretrievable message of the clock on the wall above my desk—"the clock that dismisses the moment into the turbine of time."[4] Its pulse and the beat of my heart are eerily similar and, I sense, piteously joined. Time is the arrow that wounds me, as I watch myself age and decay and know that time's imperious message is never-ending loss.

Our ancestors first became enslaved to the clock when they began systematically enslaving plants and animals in what scholars politely call the agricultural (or Neolithic) revolution. There was no single point of origin, no one Garden, for the Neolithic; we now know that it happened in at least a half dozen separate nurseries scattered around the world over a span of several thousands of years. Archaeology shows these earliest agricultural societies emerging some seven to ten thousand years ago.*

Standing back and surveying the big picture, we see the events that had engaged hunter-gatherers—the unharnessed schedules of the plants and wildlife sought for food and raiment—now usurped in certain quarters by the powers of computed time: the solar, lunar, planetary, and other heavenly engines that the earliest farmers realized

---

* The following section on the Neolithic enshrinement of time and the origin of a historical consciousness is developed in greater detail in my earlier book *In the Spirit of the Earth*, from which these thoughts are taken. See the bibliographical essay there for further sources. Also highly recommended is Anthony F. Aveni, *Empires of Time: Calendars, Clocks, and Cultures* (New York: Basic Books, 1989).

could be put to work to order and rationalize the seemingly capricious ways of the earth. Put more bluntly, with the advent of the Neolithic, plants and animals were stripped of their *will* and *permission* and forced to submit to a schedule that suited one mathematical mammal's sense of thrift.

I had long studied and taught about hunter-gatherer societies, yet it was years before it dawned on me that here were people whose ancestors had avoided or rejected these philosophical terms. The remarkable *courtesy* rendered plants and animals by nonfarming, nonpastoral small-band societies revealed an approach to these beings that was profoundly different from the one my agricultural forefathers conjured up and that I, raised on the agrarian canon, grew up believing was inevitable and privileged. I began realizing that contemporary hunting and gathering economies furnish a window or, more appropriately, a membrane through which we can perceive that preagricultural, pre-pastoral realm—a pre-Neolithic glimpse of the earth and heavens.

Stretch the membrane thin and hold it up to the dancing light of a fire and behold plants and animals before they are disfranchised into dumb brutes and inert vegetables. Look harder and you begin to make out the dim shapes of people: intelligent personalities whom men and women sang and spun stories about and listened to, to learn the full imaginative repertoire of true humanness. Thus hunters and gatherers acquired the powers of the bush, the desert, the plain, the tundra and sea, by sharing the qualities and powers of the creatures who, it was said, owned each distinctive sphere. These nonhuman people (spirit beings) were mentors and benefactors, giving counsel (through visions, dreams, trances, divination, songs, and manner of life) and offering their flesh out of affection, even pity, for the "wingless, finless, gill-less, naked creatures" with such ingenious hands and clever voices.[5] Thus say countless stories collected over the past five centuries. Underpinning the relationship with the spirits of earth was a tenacious confidence that man and woman are taken care of by this commonwealth, through the principle of the *gift:* creatures gave themselves of their own free will.

The agricultural revolution marked the repudiation of all this and the installation of a new conceptual regime. With calendars came gods and their priestly servants, temples and other ceremonial centers (soon cities), sacred texts and liturgy. In sum, the whole apparatus of organized religion. There is now a growing consensus that religion as we know it was invented to legitimate the presumption of the cultivated field and barnyard and shepherd's flock—for did anyone think to ask the permission of these creatures to be so domesticated? To us, born and bred on the gospel (not to mention the cornucopia) of the Neolithic, the question seems ridiculous. Go find a functioning hunter-gatherer society and see what they think; I have. The point being that initially, at the boundary of one type of economy with another—the transition from hunting and gathering food on plant and animal terms to its production, now, on human-celestial terms—the question must not have been silly at all. When we consider the Pandora's box of environmental woe and existential alienation that was opened by this shift, as a growing chorus of scholars now tells us, the question may yet be worth taking seriously.[6]

Accompanying this revolutionary shift from forager to producer mentality is a troubling new image of the earth as discordant, unforgiving, even dangerous, a place removed from human beings, who today refer to it as the environment. Order (cosmos, stability) versus disorder (chaos, instability) forms the conceptual cornerstone of this new mentality. Within this fantasy realm of imagination we see priest-kings ascending the throne to orchestrate the reordering of the earth (or their corner of it anyhow), to carry out a grand design whose signals originate now in the heavens rather than in conversation with authentic creatures of sea and land.

The secret to agriculture, its genius, is *timing*, and the sovereignty of the priest-kings lies in their wielding that temporal sword. Man, literally the male gender, allied with his fabulous gods, now imagined himself in league with the lunar, solar, and various planetary cycles. Once again, the heavens presented a giant clockworks that astronomer-astrologers discovered they could both chart and predict, and join forces with, through numerals—the numbers that were themselves divine beings.

"Can you bind the chains of the Pleiades," demands the whirlwind of that archetypal pastoralist, Job,

> or loose the cords of Orion?
> Can you lead forth the Mazzaroth in
> their season,
> or can you guide the Bear with its
> children?
> Do you know the ordinances of the
> heavens?
> Can you establish their rule on the
> earth?[7]

To which the mind of the Neolithic replies, in effect, yes. And "do you know when the mountain goats give birth?" further probes the cyclonic voice, amazed at man's hubris.

> Do you observe the calving of the
> deer?
> Can you number the months that
> they fulfill,

and do you know the time when
    they give birth,
when they crouch to give birth to
    their offspring,
    and are delivered of their young?
Their young ones become strong,
    they grow up in the open;
    they go forth, and do not return to
    them.

. . . .

Is the wild ox willing to serve you?
    Will it spend the night at your
    crib?
Can you tie it in the furrow with
    ropes,
    or will it harrow the valleys after
    you?
Will you depend on it because its
    strength is great,
    and will you hand over your labor
    to it?
Do you have faith in it that it will
    return,
    and bring your grain to your
    threshing floor?[8]

The questions cut to the heart of the agricultural agenda, and they
are surely tragic. They seem oddly out of place in the generally Neolithic Old Testament. And in the end they seem not to matter, for we
are told that Jehovah "restored the fortunes of Job when he had prayed
for his friends; and the Lord gave Job twice as much as he had before.

. . . The Lord blessed the latter days of Job more than his beginning; and he had fourteen thousand sheep, six thousand camels, a thousand yoke of oxen, and a thousand donkeys. He also had seven sons and three daughters. . . . After this Job lived one hundred and forty years, and saw his children, and his children's children, four generations. And Job died, old and full of days."9

So plant and animal ways became trapped by detached calculation (measurement)—calculation, now, rather than the gift. Meanwhile, the increasingly agrarian, urbanized, and ballooning populations of the late Neolithic found themselves harnessed to the dynastic ambitions and cosmic duties of their kings. The two processes sprang from the same root.

Agrarian civilizations invariably seem to have a burning sense of righteousness and mission: the sense of being *chosen*. Mankind, at least this favored segment of it, becomes defined as a superior creation commissioned by the sky gods to work for the stabilization of not just this world but the entire universe. Again, it is important to appreciate that the matrix for this enterprise is *time*. The new agrarian religions typically had hardwired into them a beginning point and also an end point: that final cataclysm that marked for some civilizations the start of a new eon and for others the final cleansing of sin and end of all counted time in infinity. Launched on their blood-soaked march of history, on a time line cratered and blasted by wars (all, ironically, in the name of order and good and some kind of god), civilized societies would implore the heavens for a savior. For someone who could redeem them and their children—and I am their child—from the unfolding of their own narrative.

One need only to refer to the papal arguments for the Crusades or the authority that Europeans summoned for swallowing up the New World to get the flavor of this temporal chauvinism, which was not unique to the West, I might add.

One sees a number of variations on these basic themes in early agrarian civilizations, though the element they all share is an expansive, human-celestial vision of order wherein mankind assumes an aggressive role. The point is that this seminal Neolithic vision of *time* was nothing less than a bold revisioning of human beingness vis-à-vis the rest of the earth and cosmos, with the story of that new vision and its aspirations and illusions coming down to us as the narrative of *history*. Again, the agency chiefly responsible for managing all of this was the priest-king and his lineage, and it was the record of their efforts that constituted the first real histories. We ought to think of it, not as the *story* of history, but as the *organism* of history, for, contrary to the common view of history as something gathering dust in the remote past, history in fact has a life of its own, and it has a future. History has a trajectory. The life it has is our own: mankind's commandeered collective imagination. The illusion of history thrives and perpetuates itself because we simply cannot imagine any other way of comprehending the human enterprise. Besides, by this point history has built up such an archive of cherished grief and beckoning opportunity that we are thoroughly caught in its logic.

History, in sum, was originally a highly purposeful activity: the cross our forefathers shouldered when they tore time from the soul of the earth and refocused it above, harnessed to a higher purpose. And, marching in time, we now seem incapable of laying the burden down.

The modern environmental ethic warns us that the earth cannot sustain our sense of mission and destiny and that we will increasingly pay a price for enjoying such a self-indulgent narrative. Let me suggest that we will truly begin solving our environmental and other collective miseries only when our appreciation of *timing* becomes disentangled from these fateful celestial fantasies and is restored to the earth and its authentic economies. Not until, in other words, we reconceive ourselves as actors not of history but of the earth. That is the deepest challenge of Native America.

The sorcerer's late-night conversations became a part of my children's mythology: they touched a chord resonating down to the bedrock of childhood and beyond, to wherever childhood comes from and wherever it remains alive. The message, I knew, was borne along largely by its medium: the fabulous story lifting us out of the white clapboard house into the sensuous, voluptuous, numinous realm of an autumnal night where we are prepared to find a message. The imagination is flowing, released by the incantation "Once upon a time . . ." Ironically, we call it a suspension of disbelief when in fact it is the most ancient, most important belief of all beliefs: the power to let go of what our intellects cling to when our souls say, "No, there is something better. The earth is kin, and its ways are grace." When we really, genuinely let go, we discover that the night and its affairs and citizens are not evil, nor is the earth bathed in sunlight malevolent. We discover the earth to be one vast, orchestrated anthem to beauty, and find ourselves participants within that. Even creators of it. For let it be said, as jarring as it may seem, that humans create deep reality. So suggests the new physics. Humans actually reach out in word and artifice, and finger the dance of elementary reality, which in turn shapeshifts its dance according to how we touch it. Thus the universe runs by a strange metaphysical collaboration, an immense ramifying synthesis that humans, it seems, actually assist in bringing to pass. What Loren Eiseley called that "ancient, inexhaustible, and patient intelligence gathering itself into a universe": we are essential to it.[10]

Night upon night I was a navigator of the universe, pronouncing verities for two small creatures nestled briefly within my arms. It was no accident that I conjured a story using images that had likewise attached themselves to me as a child raised on the land, images that would not release me even as I grew into manhood—the man approaching middle age and father in his own right. Now, years later and far away, I sometimes muse whether those imaginations ever catch the faint scent of pipe tobacco outside a white clapboard house on a wind-blown night.

Thanksgiving of my freshman year at college, and I was far from home. A friend had invited me to spend the holiday with him and his family in Los Angeles. I was still getting used to southern Californians. I remember sitting in the family's living room with his grandfather, an old-fashioned, retired doctor. The man said little, and I felt uncomfortable in his brooding silence. At six o'clock his daughter brought him a dinner tray, turned on the television set, and left us alone watching the evening news in the front room.

It was five or ten minutes into the newscast before I realized that the old man was weeping, silently. Tears streamed down his face as he ate and beheld the spectacle of the day's accounting of ourselves. His grandson later told me that he did this every night. A kind of ritual. "He's senile," he added.

That old black-bag healer, watcher over fevered children, the birth-ripped mother, the body that no longer knows how to live, had the courage, the grace, the compassion, to weep at the ill-conceived news we casually tell and accept as our legitimate story. It has taken me this many years to understand the lesson of those tears, to grasp that this monstrous thing is not our proper story at all. The words to be pronounced on *Homo sapiens* lie elsewhere, in a realm whose originating premise is not fear but trust, where the revelation runs not according to time's calculating powers but by the power of aesthetics. Not as swimmers struggling to stay afloat in the dark river of time but as vessels of beauty: let us so imagine ourselves. Beauty has an older claim on us than does time; beauty was there in the beginning before time was conceived; it was inherent in the originating Word, the idea and its pronouncement.

Time is but beauty's scaffolding.

My lungs are burning by the first mile. I'm not used to this altitude. The thin air. Still, I am running in intense beauty and determined to keep going. It's early. The sun has just broken free of the far mountains. Night chill is dissipating. I labor past the big rock with the graffiti and I am on the stretch where the road goes into a series of dips and rises, when off in the distance I spot a plume of dust approaching—a lone vehicle coming my way. At the top of the next rise I see it, a beat-up pickup truck. Closer yet and I see its occupants: three burly Navajos squeezed into the front seat.

Damn! I'm a blond, blue-eyed Caucasian out jogging alone and here come three big Indians in a truck.

As they draw nearer, I worry that I look like General George Armstrong Custer—sort of. I figure I probably look as much like Custer to them as they look like the Navajo freedom-fighter Manuelito to me. Or maybe Kit Carson, the scout who betrayed the Navajos' trust by taking command of the U.S. army that rounded them up and packed them off to prison in eastern New Mexico. The Navajo still loathe him for that—loathe another guy whom I kind of look like, my fevered imagination tells me, jogging out here on this dirt road.

Panicked minds work fast in situations like this. Fears begin to avalanche. Getting closer, like a slow-motion movie—that infernal little voice we all have in our heads reminds me that Navajos aren't joggers. Shorts, T-shirt, expensive running shoes, pounding the reservation roads: the helpful little voice, safely out of harm's way within my skull, says that they're not likely to be charmed. It then further cautions that I not forget all those times I've been honked at, yelled at, thrown at, even swerved at by motorists as they roar by on highway and city streets. Folks with no particular grudge except that I'm a white guy or, if they are, too, that I am a jogger.

Fifty yards ahead of me now, closing fast, expressionless, three of them. Large. Sunglasses. Headbands. Custer—the Little Bighorn— he had it coming . . . They wave and keep going.

They just wave and keep driving. No horn, no jeering. No massacre.

I emerge from a cloud of dust. The sun is a little higher over a high plateau in Arizona on the Navajo reservation. My chest still hurts, legs feel like lead—and I feel like an idiot.

Fear: the little voice that's only trying to be helpful. I will live on the reservation the rest of the summer and I will learn not to fear them. I will learn to mistrust preconceptions, and I will begin to learn who these people really are, the people who call themselves *real*.

Real people: so where does that leave me?

History repeats itself. My European ancestors who sailed over here in the sixteenth century were just as idiotic as I am. You can see it in the small stories of history, the ones the textbooks leave out.

Giovanni da Verrazano says that while coasting the shore of this voluptuous new land which he had just "discovered" (his word) for Francis I, he and his crew spotted some natives making signs for them to land. The Frenchmen were delighted and judged that this might be the right moment to bestow some of the "trifles" (again, his word) brought along for the very purpose of winning their friendship. The natives did seem friendly enough there on the shore, waving. The captain intended to dazzle them with his "sheetes of paper," eyeglasses, and bells. Toward that end he loaded twenty-five marines into the ship's boat and pulled for the beach. Getting closer they realized that the surf was more than they could manage. So one intrepid young fellow was persuaded to dive overboard and swim the trinkets ashore.

Which he did. It seems he made it through the breakers to within several yards of the beach when, alas, courage failed him. Standing knee-deep in the surge, he flung the package on the sand at the feet of a crowd of Indians, turned, and hurled himself back into the waves.

But luck was not with him that blustery March day. No sooner had he turned around than he was seized by one of the rollers and violently deposited up on the continent, next to his package of toys. Such is the inglorious arrival of the man made in God's image, bearing the fruits of higher civilization: the tourist, half-drowned and puking, and his luggage. Indians, I discovered on the reservation (and they do call themselves "Indians" on the reservations I have been on), have a quick and bawdy sense of humor: they must have thought it was hilarious.

We have called them Indians, though there are now better names; Verrazano never learned what they called themselves. The *real people,* very likely. In any event, the young fellow retching on the beach soon felt himself seized and hoisted aloft by a couple of strapping natives (Verrazano's journal reports they were "somewhat bigger then [sic] we") and carried up to the dry sand. Fear—the helpful little voice—now began sounding the alarm. He began screaming. As he screamed they shouted, "to cheere him and to give him courage." Soon they had him on the ground, stripped of his clothes, "marveiling at the whitenesse of his flesh." Preconceptions—that foreknowledge that fear sometimes appeals to—had warned him that all savages are at bottom murderers. These particular murderers were standing about howling, gesturing at his delicious-looking soft white flesh.

They now have him naked. They begin making a bonfire. At this his comrades in the longboat set up a howl. My God, they are actually going to roast him alive and eat him! Five hundred years later I will have to deal with three burly Navajos in the front seat of a pickup about to offer me, too, insult or violence.

Except no one makes a move to cook him; everyone seems to be just sitting around chatting, having a jolly time drying him out. Emboldened by his unexpected good fortune, the Frenchman signals that he would appreciate going back to the boat now, if they have enjoyed his company long enough. "They with great love clapping him fast about with many imbracings, accompanying him unto the sea, and to put him in more assurance, leaving him alone, went unto a high ground and stood there, beholding him untill he was entred into the boate."[11]

Certainly the French were not alone in their preconceptions of savages. Englishmen, too, were steeped in the legend of "the Cannibals, . . . a cruell kinde of people, whose foode is mans flesh, and have teeth like dogges, and doe pursue them [their victims] with ravenous mindes to eate their flesh, and devoure them." Aye, "and it is not to be doubted," stoutly declared one gentleman,

but that the Christians may . . . justly and lawfully ayde the Savages against the Cannibals. So that it is very likely, that by this meanes we shall not only mightily stirre and inflame their rude mindes gladly to embrace the loving company of the Christians, proffering unto them both commodities, succour, and kindnesse: But also by their franke consents shall easily enjoy such competent quantity of Land, as every way shall be correspondent to the Christians expectation and contentation, considering the great abundance that they have of Land, and how small account they make thereof, taking no other fruites thereby then such as the ground of it selfe doeth naturally yeelde.

Those "tyrannicall and blood sucking . . . Canibals" yielded a marvelous image and handy argument for stealing native land—but in fact such creatures were pure fantasy.[12]

What was genuine was the experience of a Master Hore of London, "a man of goodly stature and of great courage, and given to the studie of Cosmographie," who, "in the 28. yeere of king Henry the 8. and in the yeere of our Lord 1536, encouraged divers gentlemen and others . . . to accompany him in a voyage of discoverie upon the Northwest partes of America."

Soon after reaching Newfoundland, the little band of adventurers "grewe into great want of victuals." Which they endeavored to solve by pilfering from an osprey, who "brought hourely to her yong great plentie of divers sorts of fishes." Raiding a bird's nest brought scant relief, and it wasn't long before they secretly resorted to, frankly, eating one another. Master Hore, empiricist that he was, had not failed to notice that the men were slowly and mysteriously disappearing, though he had assumed, naturally, that they were being either "devoured with [by] wilde beastes" or "destroyed with [by] the Savages." The awful truth was revealed when one of the gentlemen "burst out into these wordes: *If thou wouldest needes knowe, the broyled meate that I had was a piece of such a mans buttocke.*" Whereupon the horrified captain "stood up and made a notable Oration" on cannibalism—real, not fanciful.

Meanwhile, the only savages these men had seen was a canoeful gliding toward the English vessels as they lay at anchor, "to gase upon the shippe and our people." To look, merely. The Christians, on the other hand, immediately set up a shout to their mates belowdecks that here, at last, were "the naturall people of the Countrey, that they had so long and so much desired to see," speedily lowering a "shipboote to meete them and to take them." The sight of a boatload of hungry Anglo-Saxons closing fast was enough to "mightily stirre and inflame their rude mindes" to flee "the loving company of the Christians": they "returned with maine force and fled into an Island . . . , and our men pursued them into the Island, and the Savages fledde and escaped."

Cannibalism, meanwhile harangued Master Hore, was an abomination before God and man. Let us repent, he thundered, and he beseeched "all the company to pray, that it might please God to looke upon their miserable present state, and for his owne mercie to relieve the same."

Repentance was brief, for the crew, we're told, was soon drawing lots to determine which of their company would furnish the next meal—this time with the skipper's approval. At which instant the deity did send relief. "That same night there arrived a French shippe in that port, well furnished with vittaile," which the Englishmen "surprised" and stole. "Changing ships, and vitayling them, they set saile to come into England"—victualing them, one hopes, with something other than scraps off an Englishman's backside.

Cannibals, kidnappers, pirates, and two-bit bird-food crooks—altogether, "six score persons, whereof 30. were gentlemen," on a "voyage of discoverie." Wherein was discovered their own heart of darkness.[13]

Preconceptions had a way of backfiring over here, in this strange new land.

Scholars debate the tribal identity of the "people of the Countrey" whom these sixteenth-century explorers were encountering up and down the Atlantic coast. I think they were *real people*. The three large Navajos in the front of the pickup truck call themselves the *Diné:* "the real people." They were all over the continent: the people who waved.

I remember sitting at a stoplight in Window Rock, Arizona, the small town that serves as the Navajo Nation capital, and being the first car in line. I had lived for eight years in New Jersey and hence was educated about being speedy out of the blocks when lights change. But something must have gotten into me that day; as I gazed off dreamily at the landscape, the light changed to green and then back to red.

Nobody behind me honked.

Being properly socialized in the etiquette of driving, however, I confess I did judiciously honk now and then on the reservation when I felt I was being wronged or endangered by another motorist. Over the weeks I got the distinct impression I was about the only person honking. Nobody, certainly no Navajo, ever honked at me. I started feeling conspicuous.

I still remember the day of my conversion: it was in Shiprock, in a shopping center parking lot. An old man driving the customary pickup, with a sizable family and a few goats on board, seemed to be heading straight for my VW bus. I leaned on the horn. He stopped, smiled, and waved.

He figured that I must know him; otherwise, why would I honk?

The logic that had molded and sustained me for years was clearly failing me out here, leaving me feeling foolish. I was in the presence of the unexpected. How could it be that after five centuries of relationship with American Indians, we—I—can be so ill equipped to deal with the truth of their manner? My logic was not theirs. I was off balance. And, moreover, I was behaving badly.

The Navajo live in a beautiful world. I have gone to Canyon de Chelly and crouched down near the edge of its rim and gazed down into shimmering beauty. A shallow river meanders through fields and pastureland, by hogans still occupied by people who still have the imagination for this place. Smooth, bulging sandstone walls streaked in hues of black and red oxides plunge the eye and plummet the imagination a vertiginous six hundred feet. At the bottom stand the silent, sacred cliff villages of the Former People, the Anasazi.

I have walked the switchback trail into this world in a gathering storm. I have looked up from the broad canyon floor to the soaring rimrock, to the clouds and light that move and live up there. Two worlds exist here: one of sky, of swirling movement, color windowed at the top of mighty towering sandstone walls, and below the watered, green, so-still world of this gargantuan rift. Stand before the remains of a cliff dwelling, lean back and run the eye up the sheer rock, scanning hundreds of feet of color and massiveness to the storm clouds in that world above—and ask how a people could ever have thought to live here.

The Navajo will tell you their ancestors emerged from four layers of world beneath this one: the fifth and most beautiful of their journey. Each of the four denominated by a single particular color, whereas the fifth combines the colors of the rainbow, in fulfillment of the previous four.

In the beginning of the world the colored damp mist of maleness moved upon and clasped the moist colored mist of femaleness, creating first man and first woman. Man, they say, embodies the primal thought of the universe. At the same time he is east (white) and he is north (black); he is dawn and the night, birth and death, and both spring and winter. He is sky. A man's power condenses from the rites and ceremonies that were ordained from the foundation of the earth: he performs the daily rituals and other special ceremonies just as they were conducted in the Strong Time. Hence man's power is static.

Woman, it is said, carries the conversation of the universe in her speech. She looks south (blue) and west (yellow); her power is daylight and twilight; youth and maturity, summer and fall, are within her sphere. Woman is earth. Her inherent powers are to create life and grant sustenance; woman personifies the active world of economy.

Complementarity: the Navajo see man and woman intertwined, yin and yang, between them accomplishing the purposes of the earth, housing the powerful events of the landscape and firmament surrounding them. They have no choice but to perform: humans are the earth and the sky aware of themselves. Mankind is recorder and mirror of it all: voice, hands, the fluid body movements, the imagination of it all. Humans keep it in motion, believe the Navajo, who regard the world as utterly beautiful. Yet beauty—*hózhǫ́*, they call it—unravels, succumbs to entropy.

We were created, they say, to restore the beautiful.

Noël Bennett, a weaver and writer who lived on the Navajo reservation for many years, learned the Navajo way of weaving and the Navajo art of the universe at the same time. She tells the story of White-Shell-Woman and her frustrated efforts at the loom. At dawn one morning, the Holy Ones, resplendent in their buckskin and turquoise, visit her hogan with these encouraging words:

> The loom, my child,
> is life itself.
> The weaving-way holds beauty.
> The loom, my child,
> is breath itself.
> The weaving-way holds power.
> Through weaving one can come to know
> the meaning of life and breath.

The weaving-way restores the beautiful. Beauty comes from the act itself; "man experiences beauty by creating it," say the Navajo. Understood is the principle that an event is nothing without human participation: *there can be no beauty without our creative role in it.*[14]

"With beauty before me, I walk," begins the ancient Navajo prayer:

> With beauty behind me, I walk
> With beauty above me, I walk
> With beauty below me, I walk
> From the east beauty has been restored

From the south beauty has been restored
From the west beauty has been restored
From the north beauty has been restored
From the zenith of the sky beauty has been restored
From the nadir of the earth beauty has been restored
From all around me beauty has been restored.

There is no objectivity in this amazing speech; the singer is no mere observer, standing outside things. The singer is at the absolute center of everything, turning to all possible directions to walk in the strength of beauty and, in doing so, recreating the truth of beauty "from all around me."[15]

Humans are empowered to transact this because they *are*, in actuality, the very thing they invoke—a point revealed in yet another Navajo hymn:

The mountains, I become part of it. . . .
The herbs, the fir tree, I become part of it.
The morning mists, the clouds, the gathering waters,
I become part of it.
The wilderness, the dew drops, the pollen, . . .
I become part of it.[16]

Humans breathe into the world the proper, sustaining songs and stories; man and woman keep the world in motion in dance, in ceremony and ritual. All to maintain the luster, the life, of sheer beauty. The anthropologist Gary Witherspoon says that the Navajo define themselves chiefly as artists. Cosmic artists.

An old Navajo walked into the trading post and headed over to the display case where the silver and turquoise jewelry was kept locked up. Speaking only Navajo, he motioned for the Anglo salesclerk to come over and put on a particularly exquisite and expensive turquoise necklace. She demurred, fearful of what her boss might say. But the man was adamant and, by now, was creating a scene. She did as he asked, to his immense satisfaction. Continuing his shopping, he would check on her now and then to make sure she was still wearing it. When the old man's son eventually arrived to fetch him, the puzzled clerk asked why this was such an issue for his dad. "The necklace has been in the showcase maybe four months now," he carefully replied. "Before that, it was in the pawn vault. Maybe over a year. My father's been watching it. Each time he comes in, it looks worse and worse. He's afraid it isn't going to make it."[17]

There is beauty, and, existing outside it, unconscious of it, there is time. Throughout the entire Navajo creation story there is an utter disregard of time. The story they tell is vastly different from the version archaeologists and ethnologists believe.

The academicians say that the Navajo were among the Paleo-Indians who migrated to North America from Siberia in early post-Pleistocene times, settling down in the interior of northwestern Canada. Here they lived for thousands of years till, in the fifteenth century (for reasons still unknown), they pulled up stakes and joined the Apache in a further exodus south, following Rocky Mountain valleys down into the arid lands they occupy today.

Doubtless all very real, but a species of reality that appears to carry no power or interest for the Navajo themselves. It is the sort of story that makes sense and carries value only to the severed intellect of the post-Neolithic—the mind detached from deep participation with the earth. People who can define themselves as cardinal points, primary colors, segments of the day, the seasons, even the journey of life itself—people such as this are clearly engaging a reality different from the usual western points of reference.

This is precisely what was going on throughout North America when Europeans like Verrazano arrived with the intention of inserting the aborigines into a divinely ordered, privileged history. Into time. "Our world has just discovered another world," marveled the sixteenth-century French essayist Michel de Montaigne, "no less great, full, and well-limbed than itself, yet so new and so infantile that it is still being taught its A B C; not fifty years ago it knew neither letters, nor weights and measures, nor clothes, nor wheat, nor vines. It was still quite naked at the breast, and lived only on what its nursing mother provided." "It was," he wrote wistfully, "an infant world."[18]

No, it wasn't. Savages: people still living in the first light of creation, in the infancy of the race. The aborigines are thought to be an anachronism. Alive, yes, standing there before the metaled, gunpowdered, Bible-bearing European and all his "new-fangles," as Montaigne puts it. Alive, yes, but only as a relic, a specimen of humanity from an age long past. The indigenes—the peoples of America, Australia, Polynesia, Africa—are the lost children; they have failed to mature.[19]

"I," recorded Columbus of his first encounter with the people of Guanahani, October 1492, "gave to some among them some red caps and some glass beads, which they hung around their necks, and many other things of little value. At this they were greatly pleased and became so entirely our friends that it was a wonder to see." Soon "they came swimming to the ships' boats . . . and brought us parrots and cotton thread in balls, and spears and many other things, and we exchanged for them other things, such as small glass beads and hawks' bells, which we gave to them. In fact, they took all and gave all, such as they had, with good will." Such as they had: the admiral finds them "a people very deficient in everything," including clothing. "They all go naked as their mothers bore them, and the women also, although I saw only one very young girl. And all those whom I did see were youths, so that I did not see one who was over thirty years of age." Probably he did but simply didn't realize it: what he judged to be youth was more likely good health and good genes. Many a subsequent European would make the same mistake. "They were very well built," he continues,

> with very handsome bodies and very good faces. Their hair is coarse almost like the hairs of a horse's tail and short; they wear their hair down over their eyebrows, except for a few strands behind, which they wear long and never cut. Some of them are painted black, and they are the colour of the people of the Canaries [islands off the coast of northwest Africa], neither black nor white, and some of them are painted white and some red and some in any colour that they find. Some of them paint their faces, some their whole bodies, some only the eyes, and some only the nose. They do not bear arms or know them, for I showed to them swords and they took them by the blade and cut themselves through ignorance. . . . They are all generally fairly tall, good looking and well proportioned.

But the admiral has plans for these manifestly lovely people. With a stroke of the pen he starts them on the road to cultural maturity; he thrusts them into the western historical agenda. "They should be good servants and of quick intelligence, since I see that they very soon say all that is said to them, and I believe that they would easily be made Christians, for it appeared to me that they had no creed. Our Lord willing, at the time of my departure I will bring back six of them to Your Highnesses, that they may learn to talk."[20]

Columbus clearly saw people of remarkable beauty, and said so. But that's not the point. Columbus saw cosmetics—gaily painted children—when in reality there was a life going on there of vibrant participation with the sheer creative force of the place. It was this larger thing that was potent and beautiful, and it was this that lived. This was the vision of these indigenes, whether in the West Indies or the Southwest or the Arctic tundra—that the place was Beneficence itself, teeming with powers that man and woman must treat courteously (for these nonhuman people were wiser, after all), powers that would take care of the *real people*.

Herein lay the fundamental reality of America. And it is going on yet today. Though besieged and discredited by the dominant western mentality, including the scholarly point of view, nonetheless it goes on. And it is this monumental difference in perceiving and hence creating reality that divides the native from the non-native even today. To discern that native reality is to discover, at last, North America.

Like Noël Bennett, I have experienced something of the jarring Navajo reality. I have felt it in deceptively small ways, when jogging and driving reservation roads, or when shopping in Basha's supermarket in Window Rock in late afternoon, at peak use, and noticing the remarkable calmness among shoppers around me. My wife and I stop our cart for a moment to listen, to savor the full effect. The store, though full, is hushed: people are speaking to one another in whispers.

We are not used to this.

Since my first trip there many years ago I have sensed something of vast moment going on in this landscape of the Southwest. Something ineffable yet terrifically potent and numinous. It doesn't surprise me that artists have migrated there in considerable numbers over the years. The place seems engaged in a powerful enunciation of beauty that inserts us into its deepest phrases. Willa Cather certainly knew it in *Death Comes for the Archbishop*.

At one level she tells the story of Bishop Jean Marie Latour and his feisty vicar, Father Joseph Vaillant, reestablishing the authority of Rome in the newly acquired territory of New Mexico and Arizona following the Treaty of Guadalupe Hidalgo. Yet there is a deeper spiritual text: the conversion of the bishop to the strange beauty and enchantment of the place. Cather recognizes the force of landscape joined to amphitheatered sky, of sidereal night and of wind and perfection of light; she seems to be trying to lay hold of the living, uncanny quality of the American Southwest. "This is more than mere place," she whispers between the lines, as do Georgia O'Keeffe and D. H. Lawrence and countless others.

Truly, "he loved the towering peaks of his native mountains," she acknowledges of her bishop,

> the comeliness of the villages, the cleanness of the country-side, the beautiful lines and cloisters of his own college. Clermont was beautiful,—but he found himself sad there; his heart lay like a stone in his breast. There was too much past, perhaps. . . . When the summer wind stirred the lilacs in the old gardens and shook down the blooms of the horse-chestnuts, he sometimes closed his eyes and thought of the high song the wind was singing in the straight, striped pine trees up in the Navajo forests. . . . It was in the early morning that he felt the ache in his breast; it had something to do with waking in the early morning. . . . In New Mexico he always awoke a young man; not until he rose and began to shave did he realize that he was growing older. His first consciousness was a sense of the light dry wind blowing in through the windows, with the fragrance of hot sun and sage-brush and sweet clover; a wind that made one's body feel light and one's heart cry "To-day, to-day," like a child's.

The air "on the bright edges of the world" would become essential to him. "He did not know just when it had become so necessary to him, but he had come back to die in exile for the sake of it," to the surprise of cultivated, urbane colleagues. "Something soft and wild and free, something that whispered to the ear on the pillow, lightened the heart, softly, softly picked the lock, slid the bolts, and released the prisoned spirit of man into the wind, into the blue and gold, into the morning, into the morning!"[21]

That air on the bright edges of the world. The Navajo speak of first man and first woman originating in the writhing copulation of intersecting mist. Navajos still believe in wind-beings—I myself was confronted by a whirlwind alone one day in an arroyo. This, too, given my empirical, rational habit of mind, was alarming—something I was hardly prepared for.

Have you noticed? The artist has given the slip to time. Cather's Latour finds his beloved Clermont melancholy and moribund; "there was too much past, perhaps." In France "his heart lay like a stone in his breast." In New Mexico the true man of God found time ravished and consumed by something vastly more powerful and important. By the event—by what Frederick Turner calls "the joy of full presence."[22] The holiness of beauty. "In New Mexico he always awoke a young man." Here was the wind to make one's "heart cry 'To-day, to-day,' like a child's," the sort of air that "softly picked the lock, slid the bolts, and released the prisoned spirit of man . . . into the morning, into the morning." Redeemed into the beginning of things.

So like a Navajo, the artist has peeled away the vexing layers of chronology, duration, alienation from the still point of creation. And approached nuclear reality. Where the real is fulfilled, shapeshifted, into what is true. Where time of necessity is annihilated. In its place is no void, no cosmic vacuum, no eternity—which is but infinitely whirling time—but something more like a presence, a convergence. An overwhelming and sure sense of consummation.

TWO

. . . to the Skin of the World

"I am interested in the way that a man looks at a given landscape and takes possession of it in his blood and brain," declares N. Scott Momaday. "We Americans need now more than ever before—and indeed more than we know—to imagine who and what we are with respect to the earth and sky. I am talking about an act of the imagination essentially, and the concept of an American land ethic."[1]

In *The Way to Rainy Mountain* Momaday speaks of his Kiowa ancestors possessing the American Southwest in their blood and brain through narratives of extraordinary kinship. They tell the story of the boy born of the sun and a beautiful woman whom the sun had coveted for a wife. One day the child tumbles to earth, to be found by a great spider—"that which is called a grandmother." The ancient arachnid comforts the foundling with the lullaby,

> Go to sleep and do not cry.
> Your mother is dead, and still you feed
>   upon her breasts.
> Oo-oo-la-la-la-la, oo-oo.

Spider will now suckle the infant.

He grows into a sturdy lad, full of beans. When he miraculously twins himself the old woman is annoyed, since she must now cope with the trials of raising two bundles of energy instead of just one. Yet she loves them both. The terrible day arrives, however, when the boys slaughter a large snake that they discovered in the tipi. "When they told the grandmother spider what they had done, she cried and cried. They had killed their grandfather, she said. And after that the grandmother spider died. The twins wrapped her in a hide and covered her with leaves by the water. The twins lived on for a long time, and they were greatly honored among the Kiowas."[2]

A child issuing from the union of sun with woman; the infant boy coming to earth to be adopted, nursed, and lovingly raised by a tarantula—a grandmother—whose husband is a serpent. The story reveals how union with the Powers takes place: through unbounded kinship.

Likewise there were once two other brothers starving in wintertime—the bison had migrated off. One morning one of them awakes to discover a pile of fresh meat lying invitingly just outside the door. Overjoyed, he urges his sibling to join him in a feast and is surprised when he is rebuffed. "This is too strange a thing," warns the other. "I believe that we had better not eat that meat."

But the first brother gorges himself anyway. "In a little while something awful happened to him; he began to change." He becomes "some kind of water beast with little short legs and a long, heavy tail." Sorrowfully he now realizes, " 'You were right, and you must not eat of that meat. Now I must go and live in the water, but we are brothers, and you ought to come and see me now and then.' After that the man went down to the water's edge, sometimes, and called his brother out. He told him how things were with the Kiowas."[3]

The stories are countless, all pointing to kinship, all over the continent.

There is an Eskimo from a tiny village up by the Bering Sea who told me one day that his Yup'ik name means Puffin. He then handed me a slip of paper whereon were penciled these lines, explaining what, exactly, it means to be Puffin.

I am a puffin.
I live on the cliffs or on steep hillsides.
I know and choose to live where my family will be safe.
I love to fish, and know which fish to ingest for my children.
I could both fly in the skies or under sea and master the winds
    and the currents.
I know where to go by looking at the world around me.
I am a puffin . . . from . . . my ancestral tree, and in blood.
I choose to dress in black and white, so my children will know
    who they are too.
I have this wonderful colorful beak. It helps me identify my own
    kind, so others would know who I am.
I am a puffin, and I am what my creator has made me to be.
I am a puffin, and my son is too.

Despite the unsettling changes in his way of life, now, Charlie Kilangak did not forget he was Puffin and descended from a long line of Puffins.[4]

What is it to be an Indian? I shall tell you, said a young Iroquois, rising to his feet at a conference of native scholars at Princeton University in 1970—I shall tell you what it means to me personally, he said. Once, just after graduating from college, he went fishing with his uncle. "He's an old chief from home, and we are out there in a boat in the middle of the lake and talking about this and that." Whereupon the uncle casually observed that, with that fancy degree and all, a young man must know who he is now. When the nephew matter-of-factly replied that he was who his name said he was, the older man was not impressed. "Yeah. That's who you are, I guess." Pause. "Is that all?" Sensing he was being set up for something, the young man expertly traced his parentage on both sides and then ran back through his clan. "I searched, and he chased me all over that boat for two hours. He wouldn't let me out. I was ready to swim. I was getting mad."

When he finally conceded, "Well, who the hell am I, then?" the older man calmly replied, "'I think you know, but I will tell you. If you sit here, and look out right over there; look at that. The rocks: the way they are. The trees and the hills all around you. Right where you're on, it's water. . . . You're just like that rock.' And I listened. He said, 'You're the same as the water, this water.' I waited and listened again, as he said, 'You are the ridge, that ridge. You were here in the beginning. You're as strong as they are. As long as you believe in that, . . . that's who you are. That's your mother, and that's you. Don't forget.'"

"I never have."[5]

I like to have my students read Margaret Craven's popular novel about Mark Brian, the young Anglican vicar sent to minister to the remote Kwakiutl village of Kingcome. Brian has been recently diagnosed with a terminal illness when the bishop decides to send him, paradoxically, to the most difficult parish of all. Here in Kingcome his priest will learn, finally, what it means to truly live and hence will learn how to die. The bishop is a wise old veteran, who sends his priest off with words that bear repeating here.

The Indian knows his village and feels for his village as no white man for his country, his town, or even for his own bit of land. His village is not the strip of land four miles long and three miles wide that is his as long as the sun rises and the moon sets. The myths are the village and the winds and the rains. The river is the village, and the black and white killer whales that herd the fish to the end of the inlet the better to gobble them. The village is the salmon who comes up the river to spawn, the seal who follows the salmon and bites off his head, the bluejay whose name is like the sound he makes—"Kwiss-kwiss." The village is the talking bird, the owl, who calls the name of the man who is going to die, and the silver-tipped grizzly who ambles into the village, and the little white speck that is the mountain goat on Whoop-Szo.

Adding, after a moment's silence, "If you go there, from the time you tie up at the float in the inlet, the village is you." And indeed it is. Brian becomes the Swimmer: the Salmon who returns to die, lacing its bones with the stream that gave it birth.[6]

The bishop's words took on new meaning for me when I visited the Tlingit village of Angoon. I was hoping to meet several of the elders who had sued the Sitka-based native corporation, Shee Atika, when it attempted to log a portion of the island—Admiralty Island, Alaska, renowned for its brown bear population. Someone had told me to go find Matthew Fred.

I went looking for him at the senior center, where an elderly woman nodded toward a nearby table. I walked over and introduced myself, explaining my small role in the case (I had testified on behalf of the village). He listened thoughtfully. Mr. Fred then reviewed the lawsuit, which Angoon lost. In fact they were losers, he said, as soon as they walked into that courtroom—western jurisprudence has no conception of this sort of plea, in his opinion. Even now it breaks his heart to see the vast clear-cut gash.

As we spoke it seemed important to him that I understand who he was—that he was Raven and Beaver clan. Elizabeth, his wife, introduced herself as Wolf and Eagle (as I remember). A few days before, I had met Thomas Guthrie, a Tsimshian councilman from the Metlakatla Indian Community, working as a dishwasher aboard an Alaska Ferry ship. Mr. Guthrie and I would sometimes chat while he was on break, enjoying a smoke. One balmy evening, while gazing out over a sea flat as oil, he informed me, abruptly, that he was Killer Whale.

So he defined himself. More than being the oldest member of the village council, and certainly more than being a pot-scrubber (as he put it), he was Killer Whale. Likewise, Matthew Fred felt compelled to tell me how he was Raven and Beaver, and his wife, Wolf and Eagle—matters of identity I should know if I were to understand them, understand their words, and understand the meaning of Angoon.

Mabel Jack is in her sixties and a jogger. Which means she's often out alone on the dirt roads and trails—this on an island with the largest brown bear population per square mile of anywhere in North America. I guessed she must be Bear clan, since she was obviously unconcerned about an unpleasant encounter with a bear. One day as my wife and I were out jogging (and keeping a vigilant eye out for bears), we ran into Mabel, speed walking with her daughter several miles from town. I asked if she was by any chance Bear. No, she answered, to my surprise, but then added, "My husband, who's now dead, was Bear." Ah, I thought, this explains why she isn't afraid: her husband's people take care of her.

I was beginning to understand Angoon. On the day I met Matthew Fred, Bernice Hansen proudly told me how her dad had been a great chief. He was Bear, she said, and when he died and his body was taken back to Angoon, a half dozen or so bears materialized out of the woods and lined the road from the dock to the village. She swore it was so. As the truck rolled slowly by, some actually stood up. Bernice added that whenever bears came too close to the village, the old folks normally went out and talked to them, asking them to stay away because they frightened the little children. Bears respected this.

I imagine the young vicar would have understood Angoon:

In the last house of the village, Peter, the carver, lay awake also, and he remembered that in the old days when a great chief died, his soul came straight back to the village in the sleek black body of a raven. . . . Peter did not believe this literally. Yet it seemed likely to him that the soul of the young vicar would return to the village he had loved, as would his own, and surely it would be most inhospitable if no one was awake and waiting. Thus he dressed and sat on the top step of his house in the dark night, and hearing the rustle of some small night creature he, too, spoke softly, "It is only old Peter, the carver, who waits here, friend."[7]

Europeans found stories when they found North America five centuries ago, though they seem not to have realized it. Just as I, when I first became a historian, did not realize it. The journals talk of other things: of people "passionately fond of painting their faces and bodies," and "puncturing their skin, on different parts of the body, in various figures representing the sun, stars, eagles, serpents, etc., in the choice of which they are generally led by the virtue of some extraordinary dream." They write in detail about tailored and embroidered skin clothing; of smoky, cramped wigwams "hot as stoves" or spacious cedar-plank lodges or dusty adobe-brick pueblos or what have you. They testify to savages who frequently "gorge themselves like boa constrictors" when animal flesh is plentiful or "transform themselves by liquor into the likeness of mad foaming bears." For centuries, Europeans carefully documented all this and much more like it.[8]

Superficialities are what they saw and wrote about. Meanwhile the white men looked for gold and diamonds, at first; then land to call their own and quarrel over; and always, piously, souls to win for Christ. But rarely if ever did they search for the stories behind the painted faces and tattooed torsos, the exacting mimesis in dance, or the absolute necessity of consuming it all in the bear feast—the stories that explained a way of life incredibly different from the white man's world. Stories explaining a different reality going on over here: that strange process of disappearing into the mysteries of the earth to be reborn back into human shape, knowing now the meaning of kinship. The stories of incarnation, of crossing the boundaries—these would have to wait till centuries later for the most part, when the anthropologists arrived. Nonetheless, the stories had always been there, in 1492 and long before, since time out of memory, explaining how reality truly and properly worked. Explaining *yuuyaraq*—in Yup'ik, "the way of the human being."

"A long time ago there was a couple who wanted their only son to become a great hunter," begins a Yup'ik story, plausibly enough. Then reality seemingly unravels, beginning with the very next line: so "they permitted a powerful shaman to send the boy to live for a year with the seals. At the close of the annual Bladder Festival, the shaman took the boy to the ice hole and let him depart with the seal bladders returning to their home under the sea."[9]

In the Seal Village the lad learns that a truly great hunter is someone who behaves courteously. Not somebody merely expert in stealth or stratagem, or whose hunting tools are especially ingenious or deadly (though all this may be true), but most important of all someone who understands and performs the proper protocols. Surveying his human village through the aperture of the sea, the child discovers that the etiquette surrounding seal hunting is nothing short of a way of life—hunting seals is a matter of character, of moral fiber, as well as technique and skill applied at a particular season of the year. Seals are, like us, people, who even look like humans once they shed their seal coats. And they constantly watch us through the window of reality separating us from them, in this case, the sea. For land mammals, the aperture is the bush.

Robert Bringhurst explains how the Haida of *Haida Gwaii* (the Queen Charlotte Islands), like the Eskimo seal hunters, lived primarily at and on the surface of the sea: in boats and in the inter-tidal zone. They lived in intimate familiarity with that membrane, sometimes savage, sometimes calm, through which grebes and harbor seals and killer whales, harpoons and halibut lines and paddles vanish, refract and reappear. This membrane, called *xhaaidla* in Haida, stretches skin-tight and resonant over everything in the world of Haida myth. It is the surface of the sea, the land, the sky: the skin of the world, through which the black bears pass as they enter their dens, the killer whales as they sound, and the sharp-shin hawks and eagles as they glide behind the mountain.

As soon as they vanish from our sight across the membrane, say the mythtellers, "the animals take off their feather cloaks or skins. There they appear to one another, and converse with one another, just as we do here among ourselves. They too, in other words, are people." In the conversation of the gods, say the Haida poets, humans are referred to as "common surface birds," since "we need animal escorts, nonhuman powers or guides, in order to penetrate that skin between the world we can see and the ones we dream of, sing of, paint and carve." "But the usual name for us wingless, finless, gill-less, naked creatures," reports Bringhurst, "is simply surface people."[10]

Passing through the boundary, one emerges into something else while retaining the essential nature of one's former self. What remains is the beauty and power of what we might call the Common Self: the deepest meaning of kinship, in other words. For, having penetrated the membrane, one now begins living from the vantage point of that other being who is, in the end, one's real self as well—one becomes the Common Self. To learn this is to become a truly genuine person.

"While staying with the seals," the narrator continues, "the boy would sometimes look up through the skylight [of the men's house], seeing the people from his village as the seals saw them. He observed whether they were acting properly—shoveling doorways, clearing ice holes, and generally 'making a way' for the seals to enter the human world. For example, when he heard snow hit the undersea skylight, he knew that hardworking youths were clearing entranceways in the village above. When he looked up at the skylight, he saw the faces of the young men who cleared the ice holes, while those who failed to perform this action were obscured from view."

With spring breakup the boy swims through "the ocean with his host, viewing human hunters from the seals' perspective." The seals are deliberately giving themselves to the hunters, but only to the "good" ones, who know to treat the seal people with respect. Respect involves a covenant not to overhunt game or waste the flesh and to share the meat and oil and skins with needy relatives and neighbors. The boy and his bearded seal companion present themselves to just the right sort of person, whom they permit to take them. "When hit by the hunter's spear, the boy lost consciousness and was taken back to his village." Here, following the end of the Bladder Festival, he becomes visible once more in human form. The seal bladders have been returned to the sea, to be regenerated yet again as seal people, and the covenant is renewed. "When he became a man, he was indeed a great hunter. From his accounts of his experiences, people came to understand how the seals saw humans and how humans must act to please them."[11]

All these stories, of such profound imagination, carry us to the very border of strangeness, to borrow a phrase from Wallace Stegner. And we find ourselves ill equipped to cross over. Time suddenly snaps back to those Christians who first touched upon North America. Frederick

Turner suggests that they were, unknowingly, "beyond geography"; they had reached the "mythic zones." I agree, though I think that it goes even further than he suspected. I think they were at the furthest limit of their conception of the real and, though utterly unaware of it, were fingering the "skin of the world."[12]

"In truth, my brother, the Beaver does everything to perfection. He makes for us kettles, axes, swords, knives, and gives us drink and food without the trouble of cultivating the ground." This feels surreal, preposterous, like the skin of the world must feel, and the canny priest who heard it thought that the Micmac who said it was being a joker.[13]

Maybe he was. But the Ojibwa (Anishnaabe), the Great Lakes people sharing many cultural traits with their coastal Micmac cousins, still, at the turn of this century, remembered the story of the "Woman Who Married a Beaver."

"Once on a time," it begins in quaint translation, "a certain young woman went into a long fast, blackening (her face). Far off somewhere she wandered about. In course of time she beheld a man that was standing, (and) by him was she addressed, saying: 'Will you not come along with me to where I live?'" She did, of course, and they were soon married, and of course he turned out to be a beaver person. "A long while did she have the man for her husband. When they beheld their (first) young, four was the number of them. Never of anything was the woman in want. Of every kind of fish that was, did the man kill; besides, some small animal-kind he slew; of great abundance was their food." Occasionally a hunter would appear outside the lodge, whereupon one or several of the beaver people "would go to where the person lived"—notice the gift, the absence of coercion—"whereupon the people would then slay the beavers." "Yet they really did not kill them," quickly adds the narrator, "but back home would they come again."

Such, evidently, is the dynamic of the skin of the world. Beaver were "very numerous" in those days, we are assured, and they were "very fond of the people." "In the same way as people are when visiting one another, so were (the beavers) in their mental attitude toward the people. Even though they were slain by (the people), yet they really were not dead. They were very fond of the tobacco that was given them by the people; at times they were also given clothing by the people." A gift exchange: we are at the source of Native American relationships.

Gift giving. Whenever beaver people returned from visiting human people, "all sorts of things would they fetch,—kettles and bowls, knives, tobacco, and all the things that are used when a beaver is eaten; such was what they brought. Continually were they adding to their great wealth."[14]

Maybe by some strange logic, some unfamiliar reality that's difficult for us to comprehend, beaver could turn around and produce "kettles, axes, swords, knives," and so forth—maybe the fellow wasn't joking after all. When one takes into account the skin of the world and the Common Self, where beaver *people* are the reality behind the facade of sixty-pound rodents called *Castor canadensis*, perhaps these things add up.

Francis Parkman, that insufferable young Harvard man "on a tour of curiosity and amusement to the Rocky Mountains" in the summer of 1846, got a glimpse of that dynamic when he was entertained one lazy afternoon by an old Lakota shaman.[15] Mene-Seela was telling his yawning guest that beavers and white men were "the wisest people on earth; indeed, he was convinced they were the same," illustrating his theory with "an incident which had happened to him long before [that] had assured him of this. So he began the following story, and as the pipe passed in turn to him, Reynal [Parkman's guide] availed himself of these interruptions to translate what had preceded. But the old man accompanied his words with such admirable pantomime that translation was hardly necessary." Whether Mene-Seela was relating a dream he once had or what we would call a literal experience is immaterial; both would have been equally real and informative to such a person.

Once, when he was a boy, long before ever seeing a white man, he went off beaver hunting with a few young friends. Eventually they came across a particularly large beaver lodge, which he, Mene-Seela, decided to crawl into, "to see what was there." Presumably he knew already that there were beaver there; presumably some other source of knowledge beckoned him in. "Sometimes he crept on his hands and knees, sometimes he was obliged to swim, and sometimes to lie flat on his face and drag himself along. In this way he crawled a great distance under ground"—in shamanic journey. "It was very dark, cold, and close, so that at last he was almost suffocated, and fell into a swoon." Regaining consciousness—perhaps a new consciousness?— "he could see nothing, but soon discerned something white before him, and at length plainly distinguished three people, entirely white, one man and two women, sitting at the edge of a black pool of water."

The vision frightened him, and he fled, back the way he had come: through the aperture, through the membrane of a beaver lodge, back into the world of familiar identity. Though he would never again be the person he was before. "Having succeeded . . . in reaching daylight again, he went to the spot directly above the pool of water where he had seen the three mysterious beings. Here he beat a hole with his war-club in the ground, and sat down to watch. In a moment the nose of an old male beaver appeared at the opening. Mene-Seela instantly seized him and dragged him up, when two other beavers, both females, thrust out their heads, and these he served in the same way."

Borders of identity become difficult to determine in such a world, where an Inupiaq Eskimo becomes a bowhead whale and an eider duck, and a Yup'ik child shapeshifts into a bearded seal. "'These,' said the old man, concluding his story, . . . 'must have been the three white people whom I saw sitting at the edge of the water.'"[16]

At the edge of the water—at the skin of the world. When Frenchmen, Englishmen, and Dutchmen failed to find the wealth of the Indies in this howling wilderness, they turned, in their disappointment, to what became a lucrative and centuries-long trade in beaver pelts. They shipped these back to Europe to be manufactured into a variety of fancy felt hats: beaver hats. The way the fur trade worked was that natives did the hunting, enthusiastically slaughtering beavers by the hundreds of thousands, while the whites furnished them with a steady stream of "kettles, axes, swords, knives," et cetera—all the stuff the Micmac Indian enumerated. Except that he maintained these came from the beaver, not the white man.

But really, was there necessarily a difference? I mean, was there any difference when one got to the furthest limit of appearances—when one crawled and swam and squeezed into the great metaphysical Beaver Lodge to gaze upon the larger dynamic of things? On the other hand, could one actually peer through the membrane, or did one know such an order of truth only by passing through that skin of the world oneself, participating within it and finding oneself transformed by the event?

Old Mene-Seela "was the grand depositary of the legends and traditions of the village," continued Parkman. "I succeeded, however, in getting from him only a few fragments. Like all Indians, he was excessively superstitious, and continually saw some reason for withholding his stories. 'It is a bad thing,' he would say, 'to tell the tales in summer. Stay with us till next winter, and I will tell you every thing I know; but now our war-parties are going out, and our young men will be killed if I sit down to tell stories before the frost begins.'"[17]

Parkman would not stay. He would go back east and write books that would shape how future generations of Americans would view their national origins. Yet here, for a moment, he stood in the presence of something exceptionally powerful—and regarded it as trivial. Mene-Seela's stories were no more "legends" and "traditions" than Einstein's theory of relativity is legend or tradition. His stories were themselves powers, calling forth the truly real. Literally, a call. Hence "it is a bad thing," he would say, "to tell the tales in summer."

"But to leave this digression"—so Parkman abruptly wraps it up and goes on to more important matters. Three years later he publishes his journals in what became that great American classic, *The Oregon Trail*.[18]

No. This was no digression, and it was no silly anecdote. Somewhere within its borders we unveil the very deepest powers of this aboriginal land, of possessing it in one's blood and brain, as Scott Momaday knew we must. Somewhere we must cross over—to where it possesses us. Francis Parkman obviously had no mind for the world Mene-Seela knew, for imagining who and what he was "with respect to the earth and sky." "I am talking about an act of the imagination essentially," interrupts Momaday, "and the concept of an American land ethic."

We are not there yet. Although the stories, with their strange powers, evidently are still there. The man who told the story about the boy who lived with seals is a Yup'ik Eskimo, Paul John, from Nelson Island. From Toksook Bay: a tiny, charming village of simple wood-frame houses gathered behind a bluff overlooking the Bering Sea. Here families are all related to one another, and everyone still lives by the ancient, unharnassed calendar: gathering cranberries, blueberries, salmonberries, birds' eggs, edible greens, and grasses for boot liners; stalking the caribou and the musk ox and, up toward the mountains, the moose; trapping streams and channels for the beaver, muskrat, and other swimmer people; shooting seals and walrus out at sea, and geese and swans and ducks and cranes; drift-netting or seining salmon, herring, and smelt in rivers and ocean.

In Toksook, as it is throughout the Yukon-Kuskokwim delta, the focus on each species defines time itself. When the "geese come" (*Teng-miirvik*) to the Bristol Bay area, our calendar announces April. On the Yukon it is *Maklagaq*, "baby bearded seal" time. May is generally known as the season when birds lay their eggs. What we call October is *Nulirun*, the "mating (of caribou)," along the Kuskokwim. It is this ancient reality that defines them as Yup'ik: "the real people." Except that as the technology has changed so have the deeper mysteries of the land and sea changed, as though technology and its object are tied by invisible cords. With the velocity and impersonality of rifles, snowmobiles, powerboats—with these, joined by federal and state regulatory powers—the powers shared with the animals and the land itself have become ominously silent.[19]

Though some still hear them. Paul John is old now, an elder, a devout Roman Catholic, and widely respected around the Yukon-Kuskokwim delta. His English is patchy, and at public meetings he invariably talks in his native Yup'ik. I first met him when I attended several days of Fish and Wildlife Service hearings in Bethel, a windy, dusty, ramshackle town of five thousand souls (nearly evenly Yup'ik and non-native) in the heart of the vast marshland delta formed by the Yukon and Kuskokwim Rivers.

Before the Moravians arrived a century ago, Mamterilleq, as it was known to the Eskimos, meant literally a "site of many caches," though it seems to have referred as well to "one who built a smokehouse," in order to preserve the multitude of salmon that bless the Kuskokwim in the spring and summer months. None of this mattered one whit to the first missionaries to spot the site, who instead were pleased by its situation on a bank well above the river and, as Brother Hartmann recorded in his journal, were much moved by the scripture verse for the day: "God said unto Jacob, Arise, go up to Bethel, and dwell there, and make there an altar unto God that appeared unto thee."

"It seemed as though the Lord were now speaking to us in these words, and were thereby pointing out the place for our future operations amongst the Eskimoes." A year later at a missionary conference in San Francisco, Mamterilleq, place of the caches, noteworthy for its smokehouse, was baptized Bethel. On that "occasion of great refreshing from the presence of the Lord," nobody present seemed concerned that the place already possessed a true spirit and that not a single Yup'ik was consulted about changing it.[20]

Jacob's "gate of heaven" is now headquarters to a swarm of government agencies ministering to the current generation of lost Yup'ik souls, some twenty-five thousand of them scattered in tiny villages around the delta.[21] Nina, my wife, and I lived there for several years, where she was a pediatrician at the Indian Health Service hospital.

Now and then, the Fish and Wildlife people in Bethel invite their native advisory board (of which Paul John is a member) to attend a bit of bureaucratic theater called a meeting, where the Yupiit are asked if they would kindly advise the U.S. government on wildlife policy. ("Yupiit" is the plural form of "Yup'ik.") This pleases the Yupiit, who are treated briefly like big shots, although they know that their Uncle Sam isn't really listening to what they have to say. The meeting is very decorous and utterly official. There is a long table, a gavel, a chairman, and *Robert's Rules of Order*.

But the language is wrong.

The meeting is barely under way when Paul John (who is being interpreted in English) suddenly delivers a long passionate speech on that problematic word "subsistence," as in that phrase "subsistence hunting." Washington and its bureaucrats in Alaska are fond of the phrase. Paul John says that he thinks "people" (he's being delicate) don't understand what natives mean when they use the word. He relates that when his son was in college he was once asked by friends what all this "subsistence" business was about, anyway. The young man explained and from that day on was ostracized. It must have been a sizzling explanation.

Paul John was struggling to explain something. Here the Yupiit at this table were being asked to approve bureaucratic guidelines for dividing up moose "resources," and some were even haggling over interregional access to these "resources," when, you know, in former times, Paul John reminded, the people were careful to take care of each other. The man who knew about the seal people was boldly trying to engineer a structural shift: to get people to see the whole subject of moose in particular and subsistence in general in an entirely different light. In the old days there was none of this unseemly discussion of mine and thine. Altruism was once sovereign.

It must have been a lovely speech; the English translation was powerful enough. But there was no space for this sort of discourse in the room that day. Paul John's sentiments had no place to stand or maneuver or gain a purchase on Fish and Wildlife imagination. So his words went nowhere.

Then came another report on the dwindling moose population in some lower river drainage. Maps were put up. The biologist explained how the feds were using planes and other data-gathering devices to survey moose populations all along this particular stretch of river. He then dimmed the lights and projected a chart bristling with bureaucratic jargon, outlining how Fish and Wildlife intended to generate a resurgence of moose in this particular region.

Paul John's hand floated up again. He said quietly that this proposal was okay with him . . . but that it should not be talked about loudly, for it was common knowledge that moose could hear these conversations and might take offense at what was being planned for them, possibly even disappearing altogether.

Paul John was dead serious. He reminded the room that experience had confirmed this. Moose owned and regulated themselves. Albert Dreyer, the crusty old zoologist from Eiseley's "Dance of the Frogs," would have cheered. Dreyer would have asked if moose ever danced.[22] Today, however, the government biologist was a man from a different story; he stared blankly at Paul John for a moment, then continued with his plan of action, as though nothing had happened.

But something of huge import had truly happened. Which was that once upon a time a Yup'ik child—"he was a young child like you," said Paul John, with a curious familiarity—had gone and lived in the seals' "*qasgiq* (communal men's house), where an adult bearded seal hosted him and taught him to view the human world from the seals' point of view." From that boy's experiences, "people came to understand how the seals saw humans and how humans must act to please them."[23]

The man from Toksook Bay knew the truly important stories about seals and, evidently, moose as well. The stories of kinship, incarnation, protocol, the gift, and ultimately of beauty. In that windowless government conference room he was appealing to the experience of those founding stories—and a wholly different reality. The biologist, on the other hand, was unencumbered by any such experience, probably would have found the stories charming and irrelevant, and was thoroughly naive about Paul John's way of the human being.

How like a young child the government man must have seemed to Paul John. "He looked upon us as sophisticated children—smart, but not wise," mused a thoughtful scientist about another man and friend, Ishi, the California Yahi who journeyed through the skin of the world into white civilization in 1911 and passed back out again five years later. "We knew many things, and much that is false. He knew nature, which is always true."[24]

Ishi was no scientist, at least not as we commonly refer to such a person. But he did know the "Once upon a time" stories of this turtle-backed island, or his portion of it anyhow, and it was undoubtedly these that made him wise. And a *real person*.

Momaday writes that there was once a boy,

who took up a terrapin in his hands and looked at it
for a long time, as hard as he could look. He succeeded
in memorizing the terrapin's face, but he failed to see
how it was that the terrapin knew anything at all.[25]

THREE

Cartier's Bear

Once upon a time there was a bear "as big as a calf and as white as a swan" who was way out at sea on a small rocky island teeming with nesting razorbills, great auks, puffins, guillemots, murres, gannets "white and larger than geese," terns, and who knows what else. It was spring. The ice pack had broken up in the far north and was on the move, sailing stately bergs and smaller floes down the great sea-lanes. The bear, a formidable swimmer, had navigated his way out from the mainland through all of this to feed on the plump seabirds with their rich eggs.

While feasting he suddenly spotted a boatload of creatures resembling men clambering ashore, and in fright and amazement he sprang into the sea and began paddling mightily for the mainland, which was well over the horizon. The following day our bear was still steaming along and was about halfway across the channel when the same man-beings reappeared, now closing in on him in a much larger vessel. Putting out longboats, they chased him down, captured him "by main force"—and ate him, pronouncing his flesh "as good to eat as that of a two-year-old heifer."[1]

Meanwhile, far to the north, an old man, a man who dares to call himself a *real person*, a *man paramount*, gradually transforms himself into a similar sort of bear. In perfect, ecstatic pantomime he shapeshifts before his enthralled audience. Slowly, hypnotically, he beats a skin drum fastened about his wrist. Possessed by the imagination of the bear, he "bounded, crouched, sprang up again, and then squatted with glazed eyes as if never would he be able to come out of his delirium."

He has changed himself into the amorous, lascivious bear. Inside the igloo, the audience, shouting for him not to stop, is electric with magic and desire.[2]

The reference points for the two stories could hardly be more different. The former comes from the journal of Jacques Cartier, a merchant in his midforties from the fishing village of Saint-Malo, Brittany, who was on the first of what would be three trips to Canada in the 1530s and 1540s in search of a strait to Cathay. Finding himself thwarted by the massive rapids circling the island of Montreal, our Frenchman, keenly aware of the Spanish bonanza in Mexico and Peru and dreaming of similar fortune, will now pursue the will-o'-the-wisp of the Kingdom of Saguenay, "rich and wealthy in precious stones," gold, "clove, nutmeg and pepper."[3]

For Captain Jacques, as some contemporaries referred to him, is to become hopelessly smitten by gold fever after struggling to the top of Montreal's Mount Royal, where his Iroquoian guides gently touch his silver chain and copper dagger handle, and turn and gesture toward the Ottawa River stretching far off into the haze. Cartier is much impressed that they reveal this to him without any prompting. The Hochelagans (which is what these particular Iroquois are called) now carry the Frenchmen down on their backs, piggyback—for the *sauvages* are rather large and the French rather small, and exhausted by all the climbing.

This kingdom up the Ottawa is all sixteenth-century French fantasy. I grew up in Cartier's Kingdom of the Saguenay, the very spot he looked upon and coveted from atop the mountain—Moses gazing upon the Promised Land. Witness the European beginning to compose a story for the place—starting to imagine it, struggling to fit it into his familiar realm of understanding. As with the polar bear the Frenchman had never seen before: he had never imagined such a creature till now, and the best he could do was compare it to a calf in size and a swan in color and a two-year-old heifer in the mouth. For him a bear was a minor curiosity along the way and a welcome meal in a pinch.

Little did the man know that this creature was the spiritual linchpin of this vast new continent. Inherent within it was the answer to the riddle of North America.

When Cartier got down off the mountain and back to France and told Francis about his land of Saguenay, the king, it is said, was close to delirious in his "great desire and longing" for it. A Portuguese pilot whom Francis had hired as adviser in these matters recalled how his lord would talk "of this to me many times until I seemed to see it with his eyes"—till he, too, imagined the "men who dress and wear shoes like we do," till he saw the "men who fly, having wings on their arms like bats, although they fly but little, from the ground to a tree, and from tree to tree to the ground." Till he, too, could give this fishing station—this land of Cod, as it was first called, now rechristened the more regal Kingdom of the Saguenay, and that in turn soon to be named Canada—a story.[4]

And so historians like me have been doing ever since: struggling to give this place a story. We've progressed well beyond the batman scene, and we know, as I learned in my youth, that the Ottawa River Valley is no Mexico or Peru or China, for that matter. In fact we know an enormous amount about this land of Cod, this Canada, this entire place America, in terms of how Europeans gradually took possession of it, reaped its bounty, and swept aside the native peoples.

But I am not moved by this knowledge; something in me says that it's still the wrong story. Not that I dispute it happened—in that sense it surely is the right story. I find myself these days in search of something more fundamental and, shall I say, timeless about this place and its native peoples. I think something else was being consummated here that most of us are not quite grasping. As with the Frenchman's bear: it was more than he thought it was. Like the land itself, that bear already possessed a story—"but he failed to see/how it was that the terrapin knew anything at all." In a very real sense, the story of the bear was the story of the earth. At the same time the bear's story was the story of the people who called themselves the *real people,* the *original people, people paramount.*

"I have often reflected on the curious connexion which appears to subsist in the mind of an Indian between man and the brute creation, and found much matter in it for curious observation." So wrote an especially perceptive observer of the American Indian, the missionary John Heckewelder, after laboring for more than thirty years among the Lenape (Delaware) of Pennsylvania and New Jersey at the turn of the nineteenth century. Though fluent in their tongue and deeply appreciative of their way of life, Heckewelder would still confess, "I find it difficult to express myself clearly on this abstruse subject, which, perhaps," he wondered, "the Indians themselves do not very well understand."

There was a time, say the Lenape, when their ancestors lived "in the bowels of the earth. Some assert that they lived there in the human shape, while others, with greater consistency contend that their existence was in the form of certain terrestrial animals, such as the ground-hog, the rabbit, and the tortoise." What appears inconsistent is actually not: Native Americans universally maintain that humans and animals were made to occupy the same skin—the skin of shared personhood. Here, at creation's origin, there was nothing really to distinguish humans from animals: one lived in human shape and yet was still groundhog, rabbit, tortoise, or what have you. In the native world, men and women existed more broadly as plenipotential people, people who "are themselves—a Clam, a Dog, a Birch Person—yet they take human shape as well. Each form contains the other. In some ways, they are seen as being both at once."[5]

"In the very first times," recall the Netsilik Eskimos, "both people and animals lived on the earth, but there was no difference between them. . . . A person could become an animal, and an animal could become a human being. . . . Sometimes they were people and other times animals, and there was no difference. . . . There were wolves, bears, and foxes but as soon as they turned into humans they were all the same. They may have had different habits, but all spoke the same tongue, lived in the same kind of house, and spoke and hunted in the same way. That is the way they lived here on earth in the very earliest times, times that no one can understand now." The ethnologist Waldemar Bogoras found that "the same being, human or animal, . . . is represented as having two or several forms, separate and coinciding. The being, however, does not assume these forms in turn, at first one, then another. It possesses all of them simultaneously. The forms are like the right side and the under side of the same cloth, like the face and the reverse of the same superficies. Men are animals and animals are men." The Trumai of Brazil, he observes, "live by fishing. For their Bakairi neighbors the Trumai are simply water animals. They sleep on the bottom of the river, they feed on fish."[6]

So begins the sociology of creation: outward forms blurred in the time of origin, where "all things . . . crouched in eagerness to become something else"—a reality that Heckewelder, trained in the Christian and classical Greek tradition, had difficulty comprehending. Boundaries between human and animal quite simply did not exist. "That the Indians, from the earliest times, considered themselves in a manner connected with certain animals, is evident from various customs still preserved among them, and from the names of those animals which they have collectively, as well as individually, assumed." A name like Blackfish, for instance. "If we pay attention to the reasons which they give for those [animal name] denominations, the idea of a supposed family connexion is easily discernible."[7]

Heckewelder illustrates with a vivid anecdote about rattlesnakes. "One day," he remembers,

as I was walking with an elderly Indian on the banks of the Muskingum, I saw a large rattle-snake lying across the path, which I was going to kill. The Indian immediately forbade my doing so; "for," said he, "the rattle-snake is grandfather to the Indians, and is placed here on purpose to guard us, and to give us notice of impending danger by his rattle, which is the same as if he were to tell us 'look about!' Now," added he, "if we were to kill one of those, the others would soon know it, and the whole race would rise upon us and bite us." I observed to him that the white people were not afraid of this; for they killed all the rattle-snakes that they met with. On this he enquired whether any white man had been bitten by these animals, and of course I answered in the affirmative. "No wonder, then!" replied he, "you have to blame yourselves for that! you did as much as declaring war against them, and you will find them in *your* country, where they will not fail to make frequent incursions. They are a very dangerous enemy; take care you do not irritate them in *our* country; they and their grandchildren are on good terms, and neither will hurt the other."

"These ancient notions have, however[,] in a great measure died away with the last generation," Heckewelder notes sadly, "and the Indians at present kill their grandfather the rattle-snake without ceremony, whenever they meet with him."[8]

The delicate web of kinship between man and animal would collapse before the eerie logic and unearthly power of the hand—the technology—of rattlesnake killers. The deep sociology of place would become unstitched by diabolical forces like the white man's liquor: "calculated to bewitch people and make them destroy one another." Such was the Lenape explanation for the bottle. "I once asked an Indian at Pittsburgh, whom I had not before seen, who he was," recalled Heckewelder. "He answered in broken English: 'My name is *Blackfish;* when at home with my nation, I am a clever fellow, and when here, a *hog*.' He meant that by means of the liquor which the white people gave him, he was sunk down to the level of that beast."[9]

And what is the power of a name? For North American Indians and Eskimos a name was a house in which one lived with the power of the earth; a name pronounced kinship with one's place. As with my Yup'ik friend, Puffin. Blackfish knew that he had forfeited his cohabitation when drunk. He sensed himself orphan. Call me Ishmael—call me a hog.

Five centuries have passed, and I am confident that the man so detached as to kill a bear by "main force" alone, without ceremony, on a sunny day out at sea, never reached the place—the *real* America, the continent borne by "the great Tortoise" upon its back.[10] Jacques Cartier reached the end of a story already lodged in his brain before he weighed anchor and set sail: the phantasmagoric Kingdom of the

Saguenay. And when, on the third voyage, the *sauvages* finally threw him out, slaughtering a good many of his hopeful colonists, and he sailed home for the final time, confused and angry—when they did that, the people really living here demonstrated the point precisely: that the man never reached the story of this place, and that his outlandish stories were not appropriate here. They had welcomed him initially with an enthusiasm and joy that literally nearly knocked him over. Yet within just several years they were ejecting him.

But the strangers, speaking not just French this time, or Basque, but English and Dutch and other tongues foreign to this power, would return—for there was no stopping them now—and successfully impose their story of *history* on the land, uncoupling the real people from the other persons. Pulverizing kinship.

But not, I think, irrevocably. Not as long as a fragment, a mere bone even—a story—of shapeshifting survives and is told.

Back when the world was young, when there was still great power sparking at the surface of things, we find our story (or its beginning, anyhow) in the archetypal shape-changer, the Trickster-Transformer, the centerpiece of creation stories throughout aboriginal North America. Traveling under the name Hare (or Great Hare: upper Great Lakes), Coyote (Southwest), Raven (Pacific Northwest), Kluskap ("Liar": maritime Canada), or some other, usually animal name, Trickster is eager to adjust this bright new world to make it congenial for his human cousins—"teach the people . . . a better life." Such is Earthmaker's task for this odd little creature, or so Hare announces himself—though one can never be sure. Trickster is a consummate liar and confidence man. Robert Bringhurst, poet and scholar from the Pacific Northwest, warns that "his agenda, if he has one, is secret even from himself."[11]

Trickster's fundamental problem is that he doesn't know the stories—any stories. Thus, whether intentionally or not, Trickster will set the course of relationships among humans themselves and between humans and the nonhuman people round about them; he draws man and woman out into the world through the vital power of the stories he is willy-nilly creating. All done by a screwball and hopeless bungler.

"At the heart of the Haida intellectual world," writes Bringhurst, stands Raven:

> In his usual incarnation, a songless yet sonorous, polyglot bird. But he is more protean than that. He is bluegreen, white, or black, as occasion may require; he is male or female, human or avian, or if need be, mineral, vegetable or fish. He is beautiful, shameless, lazy, vain, yet incessantly active, curious, hungry, salacious, quick to disinterest, yet for preference monogamous. . . . As lovely as the night sky, as immortal as the cockroach, he finds his way to everything worth having, but his greed is our gain, for when he has stolen it for himself, he will lose it or tire of it soon, or in a fit of generosity, he will deliberately give it away. One way or another, it will be shared. This is how sunlight, moonlight, dirt, trees, fish, fresh water, good weather and sexual pleasure came to be spread throughout the world.[12]

We would be wise, however, not to let ourselves become too amused by this clown; the danger is that one might take him too lightly. His significance for human consciousness throughout the ages is incalculable. Paul Radin, in his classic *The Trickster,* sees a phenomenon who is "at one and the same time creator and destroyer, giver and negator, he who dupes others and who is always duped himself. He wills nothing consciously. At all times he is constrained to behave as he does from impulses over which he has no control. He knows neither good nor evil yet he is responsible for both. He possesses no values, moral or social, is at the mercy of his passions and appetites, yet through his actions all values come into being."[13]

Pressing the issue further, Stanley Diamond regards Trickster as the personification of cosmic ambivalence and ambiguity: the point where good and evil embrace, as do justice and injustice, the moral and the immoral—where each becomes thoroughly amalgamated with its seeming opposite, thus rendering these principles meaningless.[14] The notion of God and Satan—a split consciousness of the universe—will not emerge until urban, agrarian (or pastoral) societies successfully cleave Trickster in two, with staggering implications for our understanding of the world, of ourselves, and of others, as we are beginning to see in the behavior and rhetoric of the early European visitors to these shores.

On one hand, Trickster embodies the hidden, secret urges of us all: the feelings and wishes and thoughts we are ashamed of, even terrified to admit to. Trickster boldly and loudly gives expression to it all. It is not for our entertainment only that Hare introduces himself to us with his "intestines wrapped around his body, and an equally long penis, likewise wrapped around his body with his scrotum on top"—the creature seized by cravings for food and sex and letting it all hang out. It is monstrous. He admits to neither shame nor propriety; he speaks to mankind's deepest anxieties and ambivalence on these most delicate subjects. Perhaps Trickster is archetypically infantile. He will try anything; no urge, no enterprise, is too outrageous for his curiosity and vanity and pleasure. That he is mutilated and humiliated and otherwise chastened, or hated, by his victims in the experience is our gain, our lesson. He seems to signal to humans that despite his negative example we, too, will fall victim to folly: "If we laugh at him, he grins at us. What happens to him happens to us."[15]

Through all this astonishing display Trickster sets the limits of proper behavior with the larger world and maybe even within ourselves. He shows how it is a conscious, intelligent world, a landscape of kindred, and through his adventures and reversals humans learn the proper protocols and etiquette to follow in gaining a living in cooperation with these other sentient beings. One learns how to approach them properly. Greed, disrespect, vanity, and arrogance are guaranteed to upset the apple cart, as Trickster's career amply demonstrates. In a lifetime spent fashioning disequilibrium and personally suffering the consequences and at the same time bequeathing the charter of those consequences to his human cousins, Trickster is really telling humans that equilibrium is the goal. In a world where everything breathes with life, has motion, is intelligent with thought, and is kinsman, equilibrium can work only when everything is exchanged as a *gift*, rather than through theft, stratagem, or "main force." As, for instance, when an animal-being gives itself freely, with full permission, to needy human brethren. And where humans keep their demands on these other beings modest, approaching them in ceremony that speaks of the original and everlasting kinship.

The Winnebago Trickster cycle contains a wonderful lesson on the need for courtesy and balance. As we read along we come across Hare in an uncharacteristically repentant and reflective mood, having just suffered a sound thrashing by his (human) grandmother for his latest misadventure. Composing himself, Hare resolves to begin the sober task of finding animals "for the human beings to eat." And so he decides "to ask the animals themselves." Which is surprising: one would expect Trickster to use some clever ruse to achieve his ends. In any event, the element of a request, of permission, will define the protocol of the hunt from here on out: Trickster is setting precedent.[16]

The animals are all convened, large and small, and Hare asks each, "How do you wish to live?" Elk replies first. "I wish to live by eating human beings"—an injudicious reply, showing no compassion for the needs of human people and threatening disequilibrium should there exist a creature who constantly preys on humans. So Hare tricks Elk out of his menacing teeth, and Elk learns his lesson. "Hare, I take back what I said for I was wrong. Your uncles may kill me and eat me at all times." "It is good," says Hare in thanks.[17]

Death, by the way, is not the end but a transformation, "for the first law of this universe says, 'Everything is eternal, yet nothing is constant.' Form is continually changing. The entire landscape . . . is a nexus of Power moving beneath the outward appearance of things . . . : of Persons shifting in and out of form, of patterns recombining. Life is a kaleidoscope of Power, and Death is just a shifting of the glass." Hence, as we have seen, animals slain by humans were believed to continue living as People, spirit people; the hunter is left with merely the fleshy coat that the spirit person has put on solely for human benefit, both to be visible and to be given as a gift.[18]

The principle is as ancient as the Pleistocene and is universal among Native Americans. "It is true that man kills the animals for his food and clothing," confirms Ruth Murray Underhill, discussing the O'odham (Papago), "but this is only with their consent. They are willing to offer their bodies for death—which is not real death, because after it they go back to their secret kingdom and take bodies again. In fact, the animal body is put on at will in order to be more comfortable in the world."[19]

Hare discovers this when he visits an elderly beaver and his wife and children, and spends the night. At dinnertime "the old couple said to their children, 'Which one of you shall our grandson eat?' 'Me,' they all shouted in chorus." Selecting a medium-sized volunteer, the parents boiled him up and served him to their guest. "Grandson," cautioned the old man, turning toward Hare, "do not separate the bones but pick the meat off very carefully and leave all the sinews attached." Hare, however, was ravenous and predictably clumsy. At meal's end all the bones were carefully gathered and deposited in the water—and another precedent was born. "Soon after, a beaver came in crying, and when his parents looked him over they noticed that the sinews in his forepaw were broken and that he was crying for that reason. And this is why beavers' paws to this day are drawn together."[20]

Unlike Hare, however, one need not have all the bones for the fleshy person to come round again. Among native peoples in the past and among the more observant today, only the long bones and skull are preserved and deposited back in their natural element or, as often happens with the skull, especially a bear skull, placed up in a tree overlooking some pleasant view. The preserved bone becomes the essential "channel" for the spirit person to "come once more into matter." The principle is one that Ruth Holmes Whitehead calls the second law of the Micmac cosmos, though it applies throughout aboriginal North America: the part encapsulates the whole. "And as long as a piece of it survives, the whole can be read out, reborn."[21]

The Trickster story has taught the human audience the origin of a custom, while emphasizing that beavers and humans are, in each case, people—a related people. Hare is called grandson. Beavers, and bears for that matter, are always grandmothers or grandfathers: spiritually more powerful, more sagacious beings who figured prominently in the aboriginal diet because, as we now begin to see, they were so immensely fond of their human relatives. Such would be the natives' logic, if they were pressed for an explanation, yet how antithetical this is to western reason.

And so when Hare asks Bear, "How do you wish to live?" Bear replies that it is fine for humans to eat him, provided they fast beforehand. "If anyone tried to find him without having fasted, he would not be successful for he would hold his paw in front of the opening of his cave." Bear's reply speaks at several levels of meaning, including an intriguing physiological allusion about both bears and humans (on the ability of bears, Amerindians, and Eskimos to both feast and fast on a heroic scale). "Bear, you ought not to have said that," responds Hare, "because my uncles have medicine that is hard to overcome and they have dogs that can find anything."[22]

Still, Bear said it, and it has deep meaning.

Having gone around the assembled group and questioned them all, Hare invites everyone willing to give himself to humans to "take a bath in this oil. You will be fattened thereby." Bear plunges in first and rolls about, "and that is why he is so fat" to this day. Mink jumps in next, but he's deemed not "fit to be eaten so they fished him out and wrung him dry and that is why is he so thin and lean." Skunk suddenly dives in uninvited, amid noisy complaints that he's too stinky for anyone to eat. But Skunk promises that if anyone who is sick eats him, he will be cured. "So Hare told the people to let him alone if he kept his promise to prolong their life."[23]

And so it was that all the animal people whom humans would eat acquired their fat, the most highly prized and significant item in the native diet. Trickster, that rascal, knew his physiology.

The animals have all gone home, but the story is not over—not for Bear, with his great medicine and uncanny resemblance to humans themselves. Grandfather Bear calls for a unique ceremony. Hare boils a kettle of corn and takes it into the sweat lodge, where he will now demonstrate how humans must approach these special beings. As the stones in the hearth begin heating up, they begin to reveal Bear's location.

Hare, we are told, now concentrates "his mind." "In the vapour-bath he communed with all the trees and with all the grasses and weeds, with all the stones and even with the earth. Then he poured tobacco as an offering and began the ceremony." He sings and asks his grandmother to sing with him—song is always the voice of power. Humans, natives have always maintained, sing their way to the soul of animal persons. "He began with blackroot songs," and as he sang, "the bear was seized with a great desire to look towards him." When Bear can no longer resist, and turns and gazes in his direction, Hare cries, "Grandmother, someone's mind came to me just then!"

Someone's mind: the People were careful not to refer to the bear by his generic name, as I have injudiciously done. So as not to offend and risk rejection, it was thought proper to use an honorific title or leave it vague—as "someone," for instance. A man returning from a successful hunt might enter the lodge and sit and smoke for a while before casually and quietly mentioning to his wife, "I saw Someone Dark in the bush today." She understands his meaning.

Hare's grandmother exclaims, "Try harder!" And the Old One in his cave, who "could hear all that was said . . . regretted what he had said on the previous day." Hare now starts singing his dancing songs. And "again the bear was seized with a strong desire to dance. Finally he was seized with the desire to come over to where Hare was singing[,] for the savour of the food was so enticing that he wished to have some of it. Thus he could not keep his mind off Hare and the things Hare was doing."

Behold the power of hunting magic: irresistible, ecological, courteous.

Once Bear's mind has come to him repeatedly, Hare quits, knowing the Old One is now within his power. Setting out the following day with his dogs, Hare instructs them, "In this direction there came a mind to me last night." It isn't long before one of the dogs spies the den, even as Bear tries to conceal it by blocking the opening with his paw—for Hare had not fasted, as Bear had stipulated. Frantically, Bear pleads with the dog to hush up, bribing him with a piece of fat. But the dog barks ferociously anyhow, and the secret is out.

Hare, much pleased, prods Bear out of the den, notches one of his supernatural arrows, and aims it at the creature's side. "The bear looked askance expecting to be shot at any minute." But Hare lets down the bow and allows the dogs to chase Bear, who, in his confusion, merely runs right up to Hare again. "Again Hare pointed his arrow at him," this time "right at his heart." And Bear, we are told, "now stopped running and simply walked."

But once more Hare does not shoot. The next time Hare pointed the arrow at the bear "he began to cry. . . . 'So you are not as strong-minded as you thought?'" chides Hare. "'Why do you cry? This is what human beings could do to you even if you did put your paw in front of the opening of your cave. If I had been one of your uncles you would have been killed by this time.' 'Hare, . . . you were right. From now on the people will be able to find me whenever they hunt for me.'" Whereupon "the bear gave himself up, and the people to this day do as Hare did when they want to hunt bears."[24]

First, however, the people have to entice Bear's spirit (mind) to come to them.

And we now begin to see the full dimension of the hunt. The physical hunt—the act of going out into the bush—has a prerequisite: the medicine hunt, the fusion of minds, the hunter's and the hunted's. Mankind's message is always a *request,* not a demand: "Will you permit me to take your flesh?" The answer, when affirmative, is always a *gift.*

The Cherokee tell numerous stories about bears, two of which are particularly appropriate here. The first describes how bears once met "in council in their townhouse in Kuwa'hi, the 'Mulberry Place' [one of the high peaks of the Smoky Mountains], and the old White Bear chief presided. After each in turn had made complaint against the way in which man killed his friends"—without even asking the bears' "pardon" before he "devoured their flesh and used their skins for his own adornment"—"it was unanimously decided to begin war at once against the human race." But their claws, they quickly discovered, made it impossible to use the bow and arrow effectively. "It is evident that man's weapons were not intended for us," counseled the old White Bear. And so they changed their minds, withdrew the declaration of war, and resolved to live with the consequences.[25]

The second story speaks of a clan, the Ani´-Tsâgûhi, "who voluntarily abandoned the life and form of human beings and became a company of bears. To accomplish the transformation, these people abstained from food for seven days and had the will to live in the woods as a 'drove of bears.'" Before leaving, they comforted their relatives by saying: "We are going where there is always plenty to eat. Hereafter we shall be called *yanu* (bears), and when you yourselves are hungry come into the woods and call us and we shall come to give you our own flesh. You need not be afraid to kill us, for we shall live always."[26]

Even though one may hunt bears successfully all one's life, every time it is mythic. Every time is First Time. There can be no expectations except for the confidence that one is always taken care of, by bears especially, who will see to it that the people are fed. Still, there is a certain etiquette to follow, which includes the understanding that one must not ask for more than is needed, nor waste flesh or bones, nor treat any part of the body with disrespect. The hunter knows that the animal spirit accompanies the carcass and watches the entire proceedings.

When the narrator, above, says Bear "was seized with the desire to come over to where Hare was singing[,] for the savour of the food was so enticing," what he fails to disclose, and other sources make clearer, is how Bear in fact *does* arrive in spirit to dine and listen and even dance—to be entertained. Hare and his dogs follow the trail of Bear's spirit from its visit the night before. So with our Inuit bear-dancer at the beginning of the chapter: Bear is actually there. Polar bear has entered him. Mimicry is no mere impersonation; it is possession—always unnerving to the Christian European mind.

What the hunter draws on in the medicine hunt is the common origin, a shared Personhood, that only *real people* can know: the people who know the stories and, in telling and dreaming them, inhabit them; the people who understand how human beings can also be bear beings, beaver and caribou and loon. In the dreams of maturity, confirms Robin Ridington, a Beaver (Athapaskan) Indian "sees himself as a child living in the bush and knows that the stories he has both taken for granted, and taken literally, are about *him*. When he entered the world of animals as a child he also entered into the stories. The animals he knows and *is*, are the animals of the creation."[27]

Jacques Cartier, of course, sees none of this when he sees the bear. Not knowing the story, nor evidently inclined to, he cannot possibly know that Bear arrives first in the spirit, then in the flesh. He does not realize that being a properly discharged human in this place refers to being Bear as well. He does not fathom the sociology of the gift.

And because of all that, the Frenchman will never solve the riddle of what he witnesses: why these people, these *sauvages*, are so well fed and clothed and housed, and so well spirited, and live for so long. They are all of this because they think to live in the very atomic structure of the place, allowing *it* to enter *them* (the direction is significant), possess them, on its terms. Mankind's conversation with a world approached in trust is, at its core, aesthetic. Reciprocally aesthetic, it seems. We detect this in our own biblical story of first man and first woman in the Garden. Beholding the earth unself-consciously, the people here sang to it, danced, drummed, played the flute, clothed and decorated their lithe bodies to impersonate it, feasted and even dreamed it. "Because he who comes looks so fine," runs the caribou lure song of a man, a Naskapi, who lived in that trust. "And now surely we and the good black things, the best of all, shall see each other," likewise sings the jubilant Cherokee hunter as he strides off into the wilderness.[28]

In the Micmac story "The Child from Beneath the Earth," the old woman feasting on oysters suddenly stands up, for "the need to dance is filling her. She begins to move. She dances around those oysters, those *mn'tmu'k*, back and forth, winding around and around them. She dances faster and faster. The dance is filling her with something; she has the Power in her. Power is filling her, and as it does, one of those oysters begins to change its shape. This *Mn'tm*, Oyster Person, it begins to grow. . . . It fills the whole space of a whale, *nusknik ika'luj.* . . . This oyster is shaping itself into a whale. The old woman's dance is calling it."

She and her husband and son butcher the Gift, "eat whale blubber and rejoice. There is enough food for the whole winter."[29]

Meanwhile, the man who has dined with Old Beaver Person, Kopit, "is feeling something." He perceives that it's the "right moment" to hunt whales and invites the other men of the village to join him. "But the wind is all wrong," they object; surely one would be foolish to put out to sea in this kind of weather. No, he persists, canoes—even the harpoon—won't be necessary. "I am telling you. I am feeling whales." Though skeptical, they follow him down to the seashore, where immediately the wind dies and "the sea becomes as smooth as the oil on top of soup."

He takes out his alderwood flute and begins playing "the music of whales calling to one another." Still, nothing, and his grumbling friends turn for home. "But this hunter has eaten with Kopit, and he knows. He has Power. He stays playing his whale-music on the shore." In the fullness of time, away out at sea, a whale person pulls on a coat of meat and blubber and breaches the surface, announcing itself with a powerful jet of spray. Whale has felt the Power, and, I would add, is compassionate. "It listens to the pipe-music, the whale-music. It thinks it hears the singing of its kin-friends, the Putupaq, and so it comes. Closer and closer . . . , under the Power of the music," till it grounds on the shore. The flutist sprints home to tell the others, and they all come rushing down to see. They take the Gift: the fleshy coat of whale. "For days they are cutting up the meat and the rich blubber, and carrying it home to eat and to cache. Piles of it are sent round to all the families."[30]

And that night, say Micmac storytellers even now, there is a man somewhere singing and drumming, as he does every night, in the lodge where he has lived "since the world began." "I am Man Singing for Animals," he explains to guests, "singing for the animals, for all the animals, the *waisisk*, to come alive, to come back to life, from all those parts of them, all those wings, heads, feet, all those bones, meat, marrow, all those parts of them that have not been eaten by the People, all those parts of them that have not been eaten by other animals, all those parts of them that have been thrown away."

"He puts out the fire, and he sings in the dark. He takes out a moose bone and sings over it. The moose jumps out of the bone, and runs away." He does the same with a caribou bone. "The caribou leaps up and runs away. He takes out the bones of mink and beaver and bear, and while he is singing, these bones burst into animals, and the animals run away. All of them come back to life. This man . . . , the Man Who Sings for Animals, the Man Who Brings Back Animals, he makes them all live again."

"I do not like to see the People waste anything, any part of the animals," he tells his visitors in the morning. "They should treat those things with respect. They should save everything, they should save eel skins. They should save all the parts of the animals. What they cannot save and use, they should bury with respect."[31]

People lived bountifully on this turtle-backed continent because the other People and Powers here were fond of them—an idea we find absurd, as Jacques Cartier undoubtedly would have, too, had he been apprised of it. The western intellect seems to have no room for this sort of reality and almost no imagination for it; like Trickster's, our arrangements with the earth do not run this way. We, like those early European visitors, remain prisoners of our own thoughts, our own rationality, and our nightmares. We invoke God and the persuasive powers of our hardware—Cartier erected large crosses, read to the uncomprehending natives from the Gospels, and kept his powder dry. We detect no will, at least none that journeys with us, in the plant and animal kingdoms about us.

I recently ended a book I wrote with a troubling remark by Albert Einstein, who, when asked his thoughts about the ultimate nature of the universe, said that he wondered if it was *friendly* or not.

I can imagine an Ojibwa answering Einstein's famous question with the story of the boy whose father beat him—an unfriendly beginning indeed. Yet immediately the trained ear detects something wrong, for Indians and Eskimos were notorious for *not* punishing their children, either verbally or physically. "They seldom wean their young ones before the age of three or four years," reported Peter Grant of the Ojibwa at the turn of the nineteenth century, "unless they happen to have another in the interval; this no doubt proceeds from their uncommon tenderness and affection towards their children. I have always observed that any particular kindness conferred on these young favorites never fails to ensure the affection of the parents, and, on the contrary, should any one abuse their children, it would most certainly lead to a sullen hatred which would never be forgotten." As with the Ojibwa, so, too, with the Micmac. "One cannot express the tenderness and affection which the fathers and mothers have for their children," marveled Father LeClercq. "I never saw a Scold amongst them," declared John Lawson of the Carolina natives, "and to their Children they are extraordinary [sic] tender and indulgent; neither did I ever see a Parent correct a Child, excepting one Woman, . . . and she (indeed) did possess a Temper that is not commonly found amongst them."[32] More than a few Europeans, especially missionaries, disapproved, on the "spare the rod, spoil the child" principle.

Yet such a beginning is common to Native American stories: the introduction warns against abusing a child, while on the other hand it sets up a situation of disequilibrium requiring great power to correct. All this reminiscent of the Trickster stories. In any case, the boy flees into the woods after one such beating, running blindly hither and thither until he runs right into something large and dark—that grabs him.

The bear is waiting for him. As he screamed in fright—"Iya!"—he lost all memory of his parents and "instead," it is said, "became fond of the bear that had come to take pity upon him; he was not slain by it. Thereupon he was carried away into the forest, very much was he loved (by the bear). 'My grandson,' continually was he called."

The story goes on to describe their adventures together and the bear's tender attention to the child's welfare, taking special care, in typical bear fashion, to keep him well fed.

"Come," said Grandfather one day, feeling winter seeping into his bones, "let us seek for a place where we are to stay!" Whereupon he "rolled over upon his face and belly, in order to find out in his mind how many people would be passing by during the winter." Thus they found the perfect den, where "all winter long slept the Bear," and "with him slept the boy."

Still, now and then a hunter did come perilously close to the cave. But Grandfather, with mighty clairvoyant powers, always knew it and would fling a smoked fish out the door in response. Gracefully arcing through the air, the fish would transform into a ruffed grouse and take wing—and the man-being would go chasing after it, no doubt well pleased with his good fortune.

Meanwhile, whenever the youth was hungry during those long, dark months, the Old One would simply say, "Look there at my back," and would roll over slightly. "And when the boy looked, very nice was the food he saw. Everything which they had eaten during the summer before was all there," ingeniously stored in the mysterious larder of that massive body. "'Do you eat, my grandson!' he was told. Truly did the boy eat. So that was what (the Bear) did throughout the winter when feeding (the boy)." Occasionally, remembered the narrator, his grandfather would say: "Even though I take pity upon people, yet I do not (always) give them of my body. Too much harm would I do you if I should be killed"—a puzzling yet provocative statement.

So the two of them passed the cold, brittle winter, cozy and amply fed within the womb of sheer grace, which is the deepest meaning of all.

When the snow began to glisten and drip and run away singing in tiny rivulets, the redwings and curious jays returned from their southern journey to join the chickadees and juncos and grouse. Amid this swelling chorus of birdsong and snowmelt, the rivers boomed and cracked their armor of ice and sent it off. Somewhere deep within his millennial soul Grandfather heard it all and one day arose, renewed.

The Old Fisherman now took his eager young grandson to the choice spots along the river, where the trout, delicious and firm-fleshed for that icy water, were sure to be had—and where the People had set their ingenious deadfalls for bears. But Grandfather knew all that and easily avoided the man-traps: there were other things on his mind besides feeding his human brethren.

They lived happily and well, Grandfather and the child, until the day when the Old One said that it was time for the boy to go back to his other parents, who, he confided, were grief-stricken over the boy's loss. Slowly walking him back to the edge of the lake where his other family lived, Grandfather embraced him for the last time, promising, "If at any time you are in need of food, then do you call upon me. I will feed you." As he turned for home, the child unwittingly passed through the mysterious skin of the world and lost, we are told, all thought of his grandfather.

It was a joyous reunion back home for parents who perceived that something other-than-human, something immensely powerful, had taken care of their young son—a son who, like Mabel Jack's husband and Bernice Hansen's father, had become kinsman to Bear. Like the man who had feasted with Kopit, the lad now had Power and, by the way, would never be thrashed again.

It happened one day that as the boy was out playing his mother overheard him boldly shout, "My grandfather, I wish to eat, do feed me!" She gave it little thought, till her son suddenly burst through the door, shouting, "Look! yonder swims a bear." Sure enough, "when they ran down to the water, they saw a bear swimming along." As if on cue, "the boy hurried over to get his little war-club, he too got into a canoe.

"And when they got near to where the bear was swimming, slower then went the bear as he swam along; lower he bowed his head. And the boy said: 'I myself will strike him.' . . . And when they drew up to the bear, the boy picked up his tiny war-club, whereupon he struck him but once, and then (the bear) was dead."

"Such was what always happened to the boy"—are we surprised? "Whenever he was heard saying, 'My grandfather, I am hungry, feed me!' then there, wherever they were living in the winter-time, would he obtain a bear, near by the wigwam. . . . That is the end (of the story of the) Bear."[33]

It is, however, the proper beginning of the story of North America. Long before there was a Columbus or a Cabot, or fishermen jigging for cod off Newfoundland, there was a Bear living here who stood in good relation to the people of the land. "Sometimes they were people and other times animals, and there was no difference," they say.[34] Jacques Cartier and the host who came after him were not prepared for such terms. Not that we should fault them; they dutifully believed what western civilization had drilled into them. What saves us now from the philosophical repercussions of Cartier's perception is the fact that the organic meaning of Dark One remains alive—all Cartier made off with was a fleshy coat, not the spirit. We are capable of appreciating this now, perhaps even knowing this now.

No, the stories and their unfamiliar reality are not dead on this continent. American history is radically redefined when it begins with the shape of a bear.

FOUR

Einstein's Beaver

Or maybe the shape of a beaver.

Consider the shape of things in the Micmac story with the opening line "The Old Ones of the People are camped in the forest by the sea." This marks it as the original time. Strong time. Yet the People are starving: "They cannot find the moose. They cannot find the caribou or the beaver. No one has seen bears, or any little animals like rabbits or partridges."[1]

Partridges.

Consider grouse. We have already been thrown off balance by the proposition that a ruffed grouse might be a smoked fish flung into the air by a denning bear attempting to divert the attention of hunters. Grouse/fish: what is the shape of this thing? Can something occupy several shapes at once? The question is not trivial, as we shall presently see.

Notice, it's not that these animal beings don't exist, and it's not necessarily that these animal beings don't exist in the vicinity of the People. The problem is that the People cannot find them. The People cannot *see* them, cannot connect with them. It's wholly a problem of Perception. But what is Perception here? It is, as we will soon see, per-

ception of an utterly fundamental sort; it is, I am proposing, essentially the vision of quantum reality.

"There is a woman living in this camp of the People, and she says to her husband, 'Go out once more. Maybe you will have good luck if you try just one more time.' So he puts on his snowshoes and goes out into the snow." And gets lost. Except that one never gets lost in this realm of Perception. In fact, just when you think you're lost is when interesting things begin to happen, and they emphatically won't happen until you lose your usual frame of reference. When you're lost is actually when you are opening yourself up to being found by a different reality.[2]

It is in this state that "he sees something"—the wording is noteworthy. The narrator, I should add, has become the snowshoed hunter himself. The speaker is not telling someone else's story; he speaks his own. Being a myth, the story is alive, and whoever says it enters it. "He sees something": each time in this living narrative when something powerful is introduced, it is referred to by this nebulous word "something." The reason is that "something" powerful is "plenipotential" (if I may borrow a term from embryology). It is full of potential for being a number of things at once. In fact, it *is* a number of things at once. It is like the embryonic cell, a germ cell, a stem cell, which can differentiate into several cell lines, hence forming several quite different sorts of tissue. As the stem cell develops through the stages of maturation along a particular cell line, it will lose (relinquish?) those plenipotential powers. At some point it will assume the character of a single sort of cell: nerve, gut, integument, bone, or what have you. And it can never go back, it seems. Yet, back in the strong time (indeed, the embryonic time), that cell had special powers: it was, potentially, many things. In a sense—may we call it a quantum sense?—it is all of these things at once. In a mythic sense it might be at once grouse and fish.

"He sees something": the narrator signals that the shape of things to come might be fluid. Plenipotential. At the same time, since the narrative itself is alive, it is always prudent to introduce the powerful thing in an ambiguous yet courteous way to preserve its sanctity.[3]

"He sees something" means that he sees *what he wishes to see*—and that is more quantum reality. By that I mean that he helps create what he sees. "He sees the tracks of other snowshoes." At first he is alarmed, fearing that there must be lots of other hunters around and hence game is probably scarce. But then he remembers the principle of altruism (the Gift): "but perhaps they have something to eat."[4]

He follows the tracks in the hope of the Gift, eventually coming "to a lake, and at the far end of it he sees something." Deepening plenipotentiality. A lodge with smoke wreathing up from it: somebody must be home. He approaches, calls hello, and enters.

An old man is asleep by the fire, where a caribou head slowly roasts over the coals, dripping delicious-smelling fat. "The old man wakes. 'Greetings,' he says, 'come in and welcome. Did you see any young men in the forest?'" The old man is confirming the man's consciousness: snowshoes = hunters. Let us put this another way. I said that the hunter saw what he wished to see (snowshoe tracks)—that he helped create what he saw in the land of the plenipotential. Now the mysterious old man is confirming what the hunter created, while at the same time the hunter is assisting in creating this scene, too: the hunter is utterly immersed in the power of the plenipotential.[5]

Soon enough the man's sons return, dragging "great sled-loads of caribou meat." The father wonders what has taken them so long, implying that game in these parts, contrary to the hunter's perception, is plentiful. So why on earth are the People starving? Again, animal abundance is not the issue, Perception is: the Power to see what is in fact there and to participate in the conversation of the Gift. The hunter, now, personally experiences all of that: he is seeing what is there and he is participating in the dialectic of the Gift. Yet, curiously, he helps to create it all, too.[6]

Soon they are all, including their guest, dining on the roast caribou, rounding off the feast with a smoke—a courtesy to the animal's spirit. Whereupon "the old man asks politely where the stranger is from," and the latter relates "a little of his camp: how the hunting had been so bad, and how all the people were so hungry. 'We are in great trouble,'" he admits.

"We must help our friends back there in the forest," exclaims the old man. Notice "friend": animal beings always regard humans as *friends,* unless the latter have somehow offended them. "You boys tie up . . . a good back-load of meat for him to take home."[7]

They do, and the happy hunter sets out for home.

"When he reaches his own wigwam, he drops the load of meat outside, as is the custom, and goes in. His wife is sent out to fetch it in."

"'There is a small bundle of something outside,' he says quietly."[8]

There are several things to notice here. First, the male brings animal flesh from the bush to the hearthsite. This is traditional for North American peoples. It is males who have the spiritual identity and even responsibility to go out into the bush, that domain of animal spirits, and translate Animal Spirit to Animal Flesh. Sacred flesh. There is a spiritual geography (cosmography) here that welds landscape, animals, and the male hunter into one coherent structure. The Chipewyan explain it with the following story, as recorded by the arctic explorer Samuel Hearne.

> They have a tradition . . . that the first person upon earth was a woman, who, after having been some time alone, in her researches for berries, which was then her only food, found an animal like a dog, which followed her to the cave where she lived, and

soon grew fond and domestic. This dog, they say, had the art of transforming itself into the shape of a handsome young man, which it frequently did at night, but as the day approached, always resumed its former shape; so that the woman looked on all that passed on those occasions as dreams and delusions.

And soon the woman was pregnant.

Not long after . . . a man of such surprising height that his head reached up to the clouds, came to level the land, which at that time was a very rude mass; and after he had done this, by the help of his walking-stick he marked out all the lakes, ponds, and rivers, and immediately caused them to be filled with water. He then took the dog, and tore it to pieces; the guts he threw into the lakes and rivers, commanding them to become the different kinds of fish; the flesh he dispersed over the land, commanding it to become different kinds of beasts and land-animals; the skin he also tore in small pieces, and threw it into the air, commanding it to become all kinds of birds.[9]

Here woman comes first, while man, her shapeshifter consort, is born anew as the Common Flesh.

Woman, with her more earthy, seemingly more original powers of creation and procreation and nurturing, houses within her body the intense power of the domestic landscape. Her power lies in translating Animal Flesh to Animal Food. Sacred food, naturally. Woman, the home, the children, food, and plants all form a separate yet complementary realm to that of maleness. Hence the hunter "drops the load of meat outside, as is the custom," and "his wife is sent out to fetch it in."

"'There is a small bundle of something outside,' he says quietly." So deceptively simple a statement. How often Europeans heard this refrain over the centuries: "We have had but modest success in the chase." The hunter takes pains to understate success. Typically, whites judged Indians and Eskimos to be deceivers for that very reason, since later inquiry generally proved the fact of the matter to be quite the contrary. Fact, however, is fact only within a certain paradigm of reality, and, as we are seeing, there were two very different realities (perceptions) now percolating in North America: one western, one aboriginal. One historical, the other mythic. The western perception took it as "a general rule . . . not to believe the first story of an Indian." So declared George Simpson, redoubtable governor of the Hudson's Bay Company. For the Indian "will tell you on arriving that there are no deer, and afterwards acknowledge them to be numerous; that he has been starving, when he has been living in abundance."[10]

Likewise Gontran de Poncins, the French ethnographer who camped with Inuit one winter on the rim of the world, recalled in his memoir a man named Angutjuk, "one of the most impressive specimens of pure Eskimo" he would ever lay eyes on. "Here was a man" whose "glance . . . seemed to come from a great distance, from another world." Watching him, admiring him, sitting there in the room with him one day, de Poncins blurted out: "Angutjuk, . . . have you trapped many foxes?"—which was about the worst question one could ask such a person, as de Poncins himself admits. "It is not good form to ask this question. It is an infraction of a man's individual rights, which is to say, it concerns nobody but himself. A shadow of ill-humor passed across his face and was gone. He waited a moment, smiled, and then said slowly: 'I am not much of a hunter.'" Followed by the inevitable correction: "I did not need to wait until the next day to be sure that he would produce more foxes than all the others together."

"His record is curious," de Poncins went on. "Two hundred and twenty-six foxes in one year; and nine in the next. Obviously, trapping had not interested him the second year." Or perhaps this native, like his hunting brethren throughout aboriginal America, sought animals within a totally different domain of perception from the one our Frenchman was familiar with. "I do not believe that I was inordinately slow to learn something of the Eskimo mentality, but I must say that the more I learnt the greater seemed to me the difficulty of penetrating it. Everything, presumably, has a logic of its own; and certainly if the Eskimo mind operated in accordance with a species of logic, that logic was not ours."[11]

"There is a small bundle of something outside," he repeats, quietly. *Something.* Plenipotentiality. What the quantum physicists call *superposition:* matter (which, as Einstein perceived, is itself energy) exists in many states at once. The Micmac hunter has left the Gift in the plenipotential realm; he has not *measured* it as meat, but left it unspecified, capacious, full of potential—as *something.* When his wife unwraps it, however, "behold! It is not meat at all. It is *mitiey maskwi,* poplar bark! It is food for beavers, not for humans."

This hunter has not been with People at all—he has been in a beaver lodge. He has been visiting Kopit.

Kopit. Old Beaver Person.

This man has seen Kopit.

Kopit has Power. He has shown this man his human shape. He has shown him a wigwam of the People. He has shown him his children hunting, and shown him a caribou head to eat.

This man has eaten with Kopit. And Kopit has sent food home with him.[12]

What transpires now is extremely interesting—and here we must remember this is a foundational story, designed to instruct. Often in these founding stories there are glaring inconsistencies with normal experience, as with the Ojibwa parents who beat their child, who was rescued by the bear. Whereas here the story begins with game being utterly unavailable in the winter months—something any Micmac would realize is peculiar, since winter is generally a splendid time of year to find game. Except that the purpose of the story is to show how human beings gain the Perception to hunt, and so it posits scarcity.

The hunter's wife unwraps the package and identifies poplar bark. What seemingly started out as caribou meat has shapeshifted into poplar bark. Poplar bark / caribou meat: notice the shape of this thing. We must understand, however, that it is metaphysically *both* poplar bark and caribou meat. And it could emphatically remain both were it not for the sad fact that, now, the hunter breaks faith with superposition: he flashes anger, betraying a sense of expectation. "*E'e,*" storms the man, "'I have eaten poplar bark, and brought it home to my family; I think next time I will eat BEAVER.' He says to his kin-friends, he says to the hunters of the People, 'I have found a beaver lodge.'" Witness the string of specifics that now pour forth from him: (a) "I have eaten poplar bark"; (b) "next time I will eat BEAVER"; (c) "I have found a beaver lodge."[13]

Gone is the Power of *something;* in its place are rigidly measured shapes: poplar bark, beaver, beaver lodge, with no room for being anything other. A great cosmic door has slammed shut; reality itself has moved over a notch. A beaver is now a beaver is but a beaver. Our hunter is now thinking as an empiricist; he has doubted his role in the "participatory universe."

In sum, he's wrong, and that's exactly why the Micmac, the *real people,* tell these didactic stories: to maintain a grip on *true* reality.

If the vexed hunter had thought to remember another Micmac tale, "The Child from Beneath the Earth," he would have realized his blunder. "Out in the forest, all by themselves," this one begins, "an old man and an old woman are living." The old couple keep hearing "a Noise"—*something*—"a sound of knocking, a sound like the birchbark drum makes. It is a sound like the beating of a heart." Perception is moving into superposition. Drum/heart: same thing. Finally they perceive it's coming from underground, so they begin digging and there, behold, "is a small boy. He has come to them from the World Beneath the Earth." From the farther side of superficial appearances, rather like the Kiowa child tumbling to earth to be adopted by Grandmother Tarantula.[14]

As with Tarantula, this old couple consider themselves blessed by the gift of a child, and they take loving care of him. He grows swiftly, and soon, we're told, "he is helping. He hunts for them. He fishes for them."

But curious things now begin to happen—strange powers of perception. One day, late fall, the boy comes in and announces he's going fishing, which seems straightforward enough. And he does, soon returning with the stunning news, "I have caught a whale." Remember, he said he was going to *fish*, not *hunt* a whale (mammal, after all); the two acts are seemingly very different things—empirically, are shaped differently. Whales are not generally considered fish, except that here, in the plenipotential, they are. So "the old man and the old woman rush down to the shore to see this whale. There it is on the shore: it is a large pile of *mn'tmu'k*, oysters."[15]

Whale/fish/oyster: reality drops its mask further.

Unlike the hunter whose anger precludes possibility, the old couple continue to affirm the plenipotential; they detect no contradiction whatsoever. "They sit down, all three of them. The old man takes out his knife. The old woman takes out her knife. The child who has caught this whale takes out his knife, and they all have a feast. These are very big oysters." One wonders what might have happened had the hunter and his wife gone ahead and cooked the poplar bark as caribou meat, and eaten it—I think we know that answer by now.[16]

Suddenly, as they gorge themselves, "the old woman stands up. The need to dance is filling her." We have encountered this remarkable passage in a somewhat different context, above; let us consider it anew in this one.

> She begins to move. She dances around those oysters, those *mn't-mu'k*, back and forth, winding around and around them. She dances faster and faster. The dance is filling her with something; she has the Power [Perception] in her. Power is filling her, and as it does, one of those oysters begins to change its shape.
>
> This *Mn'tm*, Oyster Person, it begins to grow. It grows high. It grows wide. It fills the whole space of a whale, *nusknik ika'luj*, thirty widths of the elbows-placed-on measure. This oyster is shaping itself into a whale. The old woman's dance is calling it.[17]

An old woman's dance asks Oyster if it is not, surely, also Whale, and it answers, "I am." The woman, her husband, and their perceptive son are living "out in the forest, all by themselves," though evidently not all by themselves: they are alive to the teeming presence of the Common Flesh. So long as there is allowance for the plenipotential, oysters will be danced into "the whole space of a whale." Somehow we humans clearly have an enabling role in this very earthy transaction; somehow, it all depends on the question we ask the universe. A universe where Grace abounds; a universe where we live, always, in the strange reality of the Gift.

This, surely, is the story the hapless hunter should have brought to mind in his outrage. Instead he and the other men set out the following morning "to hunt those beaver"—except that there has been a reality shift. "This man has eaten with Kopit. Now he has Power." Grace has come to him in an epiphany, despite himself—remember, this is a didactic tale. And it has *yua:* spirit.[18]

As they retrace his journey, step by step, the hunters stumble upon a bear's den. They take the bear—Perception is coming to them. Still, they cannot fully see that Bear and Kopit are the same thing now, and in their metaphysical blindness they continue in hot pursuit of Kopit—absurdly pursuing what they have found already. "This hunter has eaten with Kopit," warns the narrator a second time. "And now Kopit," who seems to have a lot of patience, "will show him something."

Something. Kopit will insist on living in the plenipotential, while, in grace, he will bless the hunter with the fact of that reality until eventually this stubborn man perceives it. "Kopit makes them walk for a long time through the white forest": Old Beaver is in charge of true reality. They reach the spot where the man originally encountered the other snowshoe tracks, "but these other tracks are no longer there. Before them, still clear, lie the tracks of the man, but the other snowshoes' marks are gone. That Old Beaver has Power. Kopit is going to show that man something."[19]

Something. They reach the lake. The beaver lodge has vanished. "Kopit is gone. He has been there, he has not been there. Kopit has Power." Kopit is in perfect superposition: he has been there, he has not been there. The disappointed men trudge back to their village, empty-handed, they believe. Theirs is a perceptual problem; they have not found *Castor canadensis,* true enough, but they have found *Ursus americanus,* which is but Old Beaver Person, Keeper of the Game, in another mask.[20]

Kopit is teaching deep reality, not superficiality. A man, a hunter, launches himself out of despair into the spirit of the earth. Navigating now, not so much by the terms and tools of the chase as by the hope that "good luck" (his wife calls it) exists. He is looking for a principle, in effect asking the universe, "Are you Grace?" (Einstein's question, too). So disposed, he crosses the skin of the world to the realm where deepest reality abides—in a beaver lodge, full of good smells and good prospects.

The answer is affirmative.

Yet as the true nature of Nature unfolds, we see how this man with no name does not grasp the answer even as he literally holds it in his hand. He sees deceit. He has not submerged his own identity within this larger domain of being; he remains, in a word, *self-conscious*. Self-consciousness being, by definition, a consciousness separate from common consciousness: the realm of Old Beaver Person.

Kopit is going to show this man something: that self-consciousness must yield to common consciousness. The shift occurs when, finally, we are told, "the man who was shown things by Old Beaver Person has Power." Notice him now acquiring an identity that breaks his isolation, his own specificity: he is acquiring a name. Not just any name, but a power, like Blackfish, that draws him out of his isolation, out of his lack of perception—a veritable rebirth. A few lines later the flux—"the man who was shown things by Old Beaver Person"—has solidified into "The Man Who Visited Kopit." Such a person can now "feel" whales, and we have watched him in the last chapter calling one in on his alderwood flute.[21]

Alderwood: beaver food. We're back to the poplar bark, the caribou flesh—the extraordinary dialectic of an Old Beaver Person.

Nâlungiaq, the Eskimo, offered an explanation for all this metaphysic by saying that "in the very first times," when "both people and animals lived on the earth, . . . a person could become an animal, and an animal could become a human being. . . . Sometimes they were people and other times animals, *and there was no difference.* . . . All spoke the same tongue. . . . That was the time when magic words were made" (my emphasis). Which Nâlungiaq, perhaps eyeing her white listener, volunteered was a difficult matter to grasp. "No one can understand now," she muttered, or "explain how it was."[22]

And so it was. And still is in aboriginal America—if the stories survive and are believed.

Nâlungiaq's houseguest, Knud Rasmussen, found her analysis ethnologically charming. I can imagine certain twentieth-century physicists finding it a good deal more interesting than that, however. Consider quantum mechanics, quantum reality—the "metaphysical bomb" that began as heady speculation in the 1920s and 1930s and today is the driving force of theoretical physics.[23] Except that no one really understands what it means. Or how it works. (It is said that Enrico Fermi once exclaimed that anyone who thinks he understands quantum mechanics doesn't know what he's talking about.) Here, in this strange, fantastic universe of the subatomic particle, we approach the reality spoken of in the myths—that reality invoked by an old Yup'ik man who somehow knew that moose surely hear us, of the hunter quietly telling his wife that he saw "something dark" in the bush today, the world of an old woman dancing an oyster into the shape of a whale.

Visualize a simple physics exercise: imagine an opaque screen with two holes in it, one above the other. Electrons are fired at the screen from an electron source. Some of the electrons pass through the top hole and some through the bottom hole, and on passing through the holes their pattern is registered on an electron detector, similar to a television screen, set up behind the screen.

"Now, when the top hole in the shade [screen] is covered," continues MIT professor Alan Lightman, "a certain pattern of light is seen on the television screen, and when the bottom hole is covered another pattern is seen. We may interpret the first pattern of light as that produced by electrons traveling through the bottom hole, and the second pattern as that produced by electrons traveling through the top." Simple enough. "When we uncover both holes, however, the pattern of light is *not* the sum of the first two patterns, but a completely different pattern. In fact, the new pattern is what we would expect if each electron could divide itself into many pieces and *simultaneously* pass through both holes."[24]

The metaphysical bomb begins to tick.

We now install an electron counter behind each hole, a device that merely clicks when an electron passes through the hole but does not obstruct the passage of the electron on its journey. We are now able to see where electrons land on the television screen and can tell which hole they pass through on the way there. The result is unnerving. "What we in fact find is that the two new detectors [counters] never click at the same time. One clicks, then the other clicks, but never two clicks together with the same electron. None of the electrons passes through both holes at once." What's more, "when the two new detectors are in place, the pattern of light on the television screen *changes* to the sum of the two one-hole patterns, as we would expect from a situation in which some electrons travel through the top hole and some through the bottom."

"To sum up, when we don't measure which hole each electron goes through, each electron behaves as if it subdivides on the way to the shade and passes through both holes at once; when we do measure, each electron behaves as if it stayed whole and passed through only one opening."[25]

There are variations on this experiment, which has been repeated many times in laboratories all over the world. In fact, pick up just about any introductory physics textbook and it's there. Sometimes it is described as the double-slit experiment, as here; at others, the beam is split using mirrors. But the results are essentially the same. The point is that what we choose to measure somehow determines the performance of the electron. "Somehow," says Lightman, "the properties of the electron depend on the mind asking the questions." At extreme conditions of reality and matter—the microcosmic (the subatomic world) and the macrocosmic (the universe itself)—objectivity seems to vanish and the observer becomes, literally, a part of the experiment, determining the outcome. "The observer," in the words of Princeton physicist John Archibald Wheeler, "is inescapably promoted to participator. In some strange sense, this is a participatory universe."[26]

Mankind, it seems, has an unavoidable role in creating the reality of the universe. There was a time, continues Wheeler, when scientists imagined the universe as something outside them, amenable to inspection "without personal involvement," as though one were looking at it through a glass window. "The truth, quantum theory tells us, is quite different. Even when we want to observe, not a galaxy, not a star, but something so minuscule as an electron, we have, in effect, to smash the glass, to reach in, and install measuring equipment." And when we do we inevitably change the reality of what we are observing.[27]

Hence the chief stumbling block of quantum mechanics is *measurement*. For whenever one measures the performance, or the nature, of elementary particles, one inevitably changes their behavior in generally unpredictable ways. This poses a serious philosophical challenge for physics, whose whole thrust has been to predict with certainty. Whereas classical physics believed it could guarantee this outcome, quantum physics denies it to us. Newtonian physics enunciated principles that were deterministic: it is possible to predict precisely the behavior of, say, billiard balls struck at a particular angle and with a particular force. Quantum mechanics, however, rests on principles that are strictly probabilistic: there is no telling where an electron will go until we've seen it get there.

The problem of measurement becomes surreal, and totally counterintuitive, when we move into the realm of simultaneous knowledge (Niels Bohr's principle of complementarity). Let's say we know the color (white or black) of a certain electron. It then turns out we cannot know for certain any of its other properties, such as whether it's hard or soft. The weird thing is that quantum experience shows us that subjecting a white electron to scrutiny for hardness in fact results in some of those white electrons changing from white to black. The hardness measurement ("hardness box") evidently has a transforming effect on the outcome. All we are allowed to say for sure is that our white electron exists in a "superposition" of being hard and soft.

What superposition actually means is that our white electron "can't *be* a hard one, or a soft one, or (somehow) both, or neither," writes the physicist and philosopher David Z. Albert, in *Quantum Mechanics and Experience*. Notice that "it isn't *at all* a matter of our being unable to simultaneously *know* what the color and the hardness of a certain electron is (that is: it isn't a matter of *ignorance*). It's deeper than that," warns Albert. "It's that any electron's even *having* any definite color apparently entails that it's neither hard nor soft nor both nor neither, and that any electron's even having any definite hardness apparently entails that it's neither black nor white nor both nor neither." According to this, the Copenhagen interpretation of quantum mechanics, "talking or inquiring about the color of an electron in such circumstances is . . . like talking or inquiring about, say, whether or not the number 5 is still a bachelor . . . : superpositions are situations wherein the superposed predicates just don't apply." "Asking such questions," he emphasizes, "amounts to a misapplication of language, to what philosophers call a category mistake."[28]

"Of course," Albert goes on, "once an electron has been *measured* to be white or black, then it *is* white or black (then, in other words, color predicates surely do apply). Measuring the color of a hard electron, then, isn't a matter of ascertaining what the color of that hard electron is; rather, it is a matter of first changing the state of the measured electron into one to which the color predicate applies, and to which the hardness predicate cannot apply . . . , and *then* of ascertaining the color of that newly created, color-applicable state." We must realize that "measurements in quantum mechanics (and particularly within this interpretation of quantum mechanics) are very active processes. *They aren't processes of merely learning something; they are invariably processes which drastically change the measured system*" (my emphasis).[29]

Reading this, one begins to feel the familiar, safe foundations of knowledge start to loosen and threaten to vibrate—or worse. This is not comfortable news.

Measurement becomes even more profound when we realize that the person observing the experiment—that is, the scientist or technician scrutinizing the measuring apparatus for electron hardness or color, who is forming an *opinion* (a *belief*) about the outcome of the experiment—is *also* behaving as a measuring device, and so affecting the experiment's outcome. The observer has walked into the very dynamic of the experiment. As the observer (Albert calls her Martha) regards the pointer on the measuring device, she now enters a "superposition of one state in which Martha thinks that the pointer is pointing to 'hard' and another state in which Martha thinks that the pointer is pointing to 'soft'; *it's a state in which there is no matter of fact about whether or not Martha thinks the pointer is pointing in any particular direction.*" "This isn't anything like a state in which Martha is, say, *confused* about where the pointer is pointing," clarifies Albert. "*This* (it deserves to be repeated) is something *really strange*. This is a state wherein . . . it isn't right to say that Martha believes that the pointer is pointing to 'hard,' and it isn't right to say that Martha believes that the pointer is pointing to 'soft,' and it isn't right to say that she has *both* of those beliefs (whatever *that* might mean), and it isn't right to say that she has neither of those beliefs." In fact, it isn't until the observer *specifies* in some definitive, concrete fashion her belief in where the pointer is pointing that the event is actually born as an outcome.[30]

Back to the double-slit experiment for a moment. Here, we now know, the electrons passing through the screen are behaving either as a wave or as a particle—the decision (wave or particle) being up to the experimenter and his apparatus for taking measurement. Time is a problem here: it's as though the electrons know, in advance, what measuring apparatus will be installed (that is, what question will be asked). "How could an electron passing through a hole," wondered Einstein in the 1930s, puzzling over a slightly different version of the experiment, "possibly know that another hole has been made some distance away?" The answer, apparently—and it is a most disturbing one—is that the *experimenter* knows it. "In some strange sense, this is a participatory universe," reminds Einstein's colleague John Archibald Wheeler.[31]

Like Moses standing before the Almighty, we should perhaps remove our shoes. We are standing, Wheeler tells us, in the presence of "a mysterious new entrant on the stage of physics," something that "may someday turn out to be the fundamental building unit of all that is, more basic even than particles or fields of force or space and time themselves." Wheeler christens it the "elementary quantum phenomenon"; most physicists now refer to it as "superposition." Here at the very heart of what is *real*, the deepest question one can pose to the universe, we are ushered into the presence of a smiling, sublime paradox: "No elementary quantum phenomenon is a phenomenon until it is a registered phenomenon—that is to say, brought to a close by an irreversible act of amplification such as the triggering of a photodetector or the initiation of an avalanche of electrons in a geiger counter, or the blackening of a grain of photographic emulsion." Or the word, spoken or written, of a sentient observer. "When we change the observing equipment," cautions Wheeler, "we do not learn more about that phenomenon. We have instead a phenomenon that is new and different. *The observer's choice of what he shall look for has an inescapable consequence for what he will find*" (my emphasis).[32]

Superposition is "above all . . . untouchable, impenetrable, impalpable," and, even more alarming, "it is non-localizable." Einstein's reaction to all of this unfolding mystery: "God does not play dice." Einstein, who had helped midwife the new physics, ultimately could not abide the deepening uncertainty of reality, or outcomes, that his colleagues in Copenhagen, led by Niels Bohr, were acknowledging. That "Bohr-Heisenberg tranquilizing philosophy," Einstein dismissed it. The great man would devote the latter years of his life trying to refute its Ouija board implications, judging quantum theory "incomplete." Together with colleagues Boris Podolsky and Nathan Rosen (in the famous EPR experiments), Einstein assumed that measuring the spin orientation of one electron would have no effect whatsoever on the spin orientation of a second electron that at one time had been in contact with the first electron. "That," says David Z. Albert, "seemed almost self-evident."[33]

Yet they were spectacularly wrong, as the work of John Bell would prove definitively. "The assumption that the physical workings of the world are invariably local must (astonishingly) be false": a measurement on electron 1 invariably produced an immediate effect on electron 2, regardless of the distance separating them and whatever obstacles might intervene. Nonlocality (that is, the repercussions of "measurement"), concludes Albert, "may be something we need to learn to live with, something that may simply turn out to be a fact of nature"—precisely what Paul John was trying to say to the Fish and Wildlife biologists. Each time Einstein tried to scuttle quantum theory as "incompatible with any reasonable idea of 'reality,'" reminisces Wheeler of the two old friends now moving rapidly in opposite onto-logical directions, Bohr would reply, in essence, "Your idea of reality is too limited."[34]

John Archibald Wheeler, hailed by Alan Lightman as "the greatest living expositor of quantum physics," is a courageous man, the sort who contemplates, "What is the right idea of 'reality'?" Nobody can safely say just yet, he admits, "but, Bohr tells us in effect, no one can take even the first steps of the way who is not guided by the lesson of the quantum." With superposition, the elementary quantum phe-nomenon, Wheeler feels we have moved tantalizingly close to un-derstanding ultimate reality. "Are we destined some coming cen-tury," he asks wistfully, "to see all of existence derived out of this utterly primitive unit? And on the way, are we not surely destined to find some single simple idea that will lend itself to statement in a sin-gle sentence, so compelling that we will all say to one another, 'Oh, how simple!' and 'How stupid we all were!' and 'How could it have been otherwise?'"[35]

Superposition. Does the answer to all of reality lie within its ghostly, cosmic ganglia that are somehow our own? Wheeler, following on Bohr and his group, clearly thought so. And are we to believe that this quantum reality is the invisible glue of our everyday, common rela-tionships and experience, the deceptively straightforward realm of ta-bles and chairs, of trees and mountains? Or of bears, say—or beavers?

Nobel laureate Eugene Wigner drew the line here. "For us," insisted Wigner in debate with Wheeler, quantum mechanics "is not valid."

Unless one happens to be the Man Who Visited Kopit. Or the old woman who danced an oyster into a whale. For both stories speak unambiguously of superposition to people who believed that the world they inhabited worked that way. And what did I hear Paul John from Toksook Bay describing if not nonlocality? Moreover, it seems unlikely to me that something that works at the subatomic level and also, apparently, at the macrocosmic level would not be valid at our mundane level, too. Yet Wigner remained adamant that the "transition," as he called it, between quantum reality and our experiential reality "is not contained in present day physics."[36]

I, however, see a remarkable transition in the "physics" of mythology. I think this is precisely what pre-agrarian mythology is talking about. Paleolithic mythology, being the language of native philosophy, understands the universe very differently than the Newtonian mechanical model does. Such mythology attends to what Einstein called the "spaces" between objects; it emphasizes relationships, taking a relativistic view rather than insisting on the absolute standards (as in absolute time) of classical physics. Such mythology knows that matter (what physicists call "mass") is a field and that this field can shapeshift. It knows that mass is energy and energy is mass.

"What impresses our senses as matter is really a great concentration of energy into a comparatively small space. We could regard matter as the regions in space where the field is extremely strong. In this way a new philosophical background could be created. Its final aim would be the explanation of all events in nature by structure laws valid always and everywhere."[37] Those are Einstein's (and a colleague's) prophetic words, written fifty years ago. All this strangeness of perception began dawning on western science only within the past century and a half, with the great conceptual breakthrough being Maxwell's equations on electromagnetism followed soon thereafter by Einstein's revolutionary theories on light and spacetime and the geometry of gravitational fields. With that, reality now seemed to come in two forms: one three-dimensional (the conceivable universe, operating by Newtonian principles), the other four-dimensional (the inconceivable universe, working by relativistic and, we might now say, mythic principles).

Mythology, however, has never thought to imagine itself in such sterile scientific terms. The literary scholar Sean Kane puts it better when he says that myth, "in its most ecologically discreet form, among people who live by hunting and fishing and gathering, seems to be the song of the place to itself, which humans overhear." As with Australian Aborigines, who join "their songs with vast, intangible vibrating fields of energy in which they . . . narrate the form—or one of the changing forms—of a particular supernatural being who . . . appear[s] variously as human, plant, star, mountain, or animal." The Haida have a word, *sghaana,* to describe a power "greater than human power." "According to an element that can be suffixed to the Haida agglutinative verb," continues Kane, "such powers can be named as being about to become or capable of becoming something or someone else. It is like being able to name energy in a state of transition."[38]

Witness the perception of Uncle Bul, a contemporary Australian aboriginal elder, who declares that he can tell "where the animals are by dreaming them. He joins his dreams to theirs." In his trance visions he sees the animals in their spiritual rather than physical forms, "hanging on a 'web of intersecting threads.'" Other elders say "they perceive the animal ancestors as fields of resonance or vibration"—as "a kind of music." These animal ancestors "are thought to speak their dreams of the plants or animals by naming the specific vibratory pattern of each. That is how they create life. Drawing vibratory energy out of themselves, they name that energy—the inner name is the potency of the form or creature." What these people hear, in Kane's elegant phrase, are "the acoustic signatures of each of the animals."

> Uncle Bul says he sees . . . the life of the landscape interwoven in a web of threads. His unconscious (if we can use that term) is continuous with nature's. In some way, *he is so open to the various signs and songs of the world that he is aware of them in their simultaneity as pure abstract pattern* [my emphasis]. Aboriginal visual art shows this abstraction. A painting of the Dreaming of a kangaroo—that is, the energy field out of which an actual kangaroo emerges to the human eye—is like a dance of colored pattern. There may be nothing resembling what we know as a kangaroo in the painting at all. . . . Instead, there is in the patterns emerging out of fields of energy a quality of *vibration*—vibrations that represent the original Dream-songs of the animal-being on the day the world was made. [39]

One can imagine such a person being effectively aware of superposition and nonlocality.

Consider the stunning opening lines of the Haida story-poem "Sapsucker," as translated by Robert Bringhurst: "Grass surrounded something round, they say. / He travelled around in it, Sapsucker did." Something so common as a bird's nest is brilliantly recast into superpositional shape by the turn-of-the-century Haida poet John Sky. Think of Niels Bohr's complementarity, of Heisenberg's uncertainty: one might perceive (measure) either the nest or something round bounded by the nest, but one cannot participate in both realms at the same time. But it is *not* a nest, insists John Sky, correcting us. This is grass surrounding *something* round, and this is Sapsucker, traveling around "in it"—unspecified, immeasurable. This is the state Sapsucker travels around in: the plenipotential. Here, in two gloriously spoken lines, is a mind that surely knows reality in superposition.[40]

Superposition, Wheeler reminds us, is "above all . . . untouchable, impenetrable, impalpable," and "non-localizable." Myths "are about 'something mysterious,' intelligent, invisible and whole," harmonizes Kane—"the song . . . which humans overhear."[41]

The beautiful thing about superposition and nonlocality is their uncompromising insistence that humans are fundamental participants in creating the event. Nor will it do to hide behind our consciousness, claiming for it the sovereign power of detached observation, and so saving ourselves from tumbling into the Event. No, responds the spectral voice of superposition, we are participants before consciousness is even awakened—we have no choice in the matter. Humankind lives in the world in a way that few of us reading this page have ever dared imagine. Truly this is a metaphysical bomb. It is a reality starkly antithetical to the objectified vision that grew up on the shores of the ancient Aegean and Adriatic—the controlled, manipulated, materialist world that the Greek and Roman philosophers enunciated and bequeathed to modern civilization. A world of mankind apart.

There are those, like Wigner, who cannot imagine quantum reality corresponding to normal, mundane reality. Or the late theoretical physicist David Bohm, who forty years ago proposed a deterministic counter-thesis to the "metaphysical perplexities" of superposition. In Bohm's view, all subatomic particles are moved around by actual, physical wave functions that follow completely deterministic physical laws. In the inimitable language of David Albert: "What God did when the universe was created was first to choose a wave function for it and sprinkle all of the particles into space in accordance with the quantum-mechanical probabilities, and then to leave everything alone, forever after, to evolve deterministically."

> Therefore, the positions of all the particles in the world at any time, and the world's complete quantum-mechanical wave function at that time, can be calculated with certainty from the positions of all the particles in the world and the world's complete quantum-mechanical wave function at any earlier time. Any incapacity to carry out those calculations, any uncertainty in the results of those calculations, is necessarily in this theory . . . a matter of ignorance and not a matter of the operations of any irreducible element of chance in the fundamental laws of the world. Nevertheless, this theory entails that some such ignorance exists for us, as a matter of principle. The laws of motion of Bohm's theory literally force this kind of ignorance on us. And this ignorance turns out to be precisely enough, and of precisely the right kind, to reproduce the familiar statistical predictions of quantum mechanics. . . . The theory describes a real, concrete and deterministic physical process—a process that can be followed out in exact mathematical detail—whereby the act of measurement unavoidably gets in the way of what is being measured. In other words, Bohm's theory entails that this ignorance—although it is merely ignorance of perfectly definite facts about the world—cannot be eliminated without a violation of physical law.[42]

Bohm invites us to exchange what he considers the mystification of particles for what some of his critics consider the mystification of wave functions. Yet what is surely most interesting here is the mighty effort to winch the imagination back into the familiar, deterministic, fully objectified world of classical physics once more—the Aristotelian world of mankind apart and its terrible "beauty of understanding."[43]

Early one autumn evening years ago, a little cool and just-gathering dusk, my wife and I were on a walk around the Institute for Advanced Study (in Princeton). We lived in the neighborhood. Up ahead there materialized a dark figure with flashlight, clearly looking for something lost—short lunges to and fro, bent over slightly. We startle the man. "Ah, Professor," I exclaim, recognizing the eminent physicist. I remind him who I am, for we know each other only slightly. He is pleased to see me, and I introduce Nina. Eugene Wigner is always charming. But this evening he is preoccupied. I switch on my own flashlight and begin to hunt. "What are you looking for?" "A certain crack in the pavement," he explains in his familiar Hungarian accent. "The one I walk to each evening. It marks the end of my walk, and I seem to have lost it." "What does it look like?"—playing the light around our feet. Like all the other cracks hereabout, it sounded to me. Not having a clue what we were looking for, Nina and I joined in nonetheless, every now and then suggesting this or that might be the one. No, he would say on close examination: not it. Two or three minutes of fruitless searching and we wonder if one crack might not be as good as another. Oh no, he replies; only that one special rift will do.

That would be the last time I saw Eugene Wigner, though not the final time I spoke to him. We left him there, on the road, lost. I recall turning around and seeing the lonely figure still searching for—something.

The man is now dead and the road repaved, I see. In the years since, I have lived far away, except for one autumn when I moved into the old neighborhood once more. I walked over to the institute just as it was coming on dark, just when I knew I would meet Professor Wigner on his customary walk. I stood where we three had convened that evening and pondered the message of the quantum. As I walked away, I wheeled around and called back into the silence that superposition is real for mankind, too.

So confident was I, I didn't wait for his answer.

FIVE

Raven's Children

I have never seen an Eskimo perform the dance of the lascivious bear, as Gontran de Poncins did in the high Canadian arctic. Although shortly after moving to Alaska I did see a large, dead, stuffed bear locked behind glass in the lobby of a fancy Anchorage hotel. He certainly wasn't dancing. "Polar Bear," read the sign, like a gallows notice, followed by a list of particulars:

> Taken in 1971 on the ice pack west of Shishmaref, Alaska. This large boar (male) measured 10'6", weighed 1500 lbs. and was shot with a .338 Winchester mag.
>
> On display compliments of ———.

Something stood there, locked in measurement. I think of Noël Bennett's story of the old man in the trading post, insisting that the young sales clerk put on the silver and turquoise necklace. "The necklace has been in the showcase maybe four months now. Before that, it was in the pawn vault. Maybe over a year. My father's been watching it. Each time he comes in, it looks worse and worse. He's afraid it isn't going to make it."[1]

Afraid it's not going to make it: my fear, too. There were days, years ago, when I would visit the Kodiak bear in the Baltimore zoo. A vast,

potent being. Solitary in his concrete prison, technically alive, I suppose, yet somehow not really, not any more. I preferred cold, rainy days, knowing there would be no hordes of schoolchildren—to be alone.

> From seeing the bars, his seeing is so exhausted
> that it no longer holds anything anymore.
> To him the world is bars, a hundred thousand
> bars, and behind the bars, nothing.
>
> The lithe swinging of that rhythmical easy stride
> which circles down to the tiniest hub
> is like a dance of energy around a point
> in which a great will stands stunned and numb.
>
> Only at times the curtains of the pupil rise
> without a sound . . . then a shape enters,
> slips through the tightened silence of the shoulders,
> reaches the heart, and dies.[2]

—Rainer Maria Rilke

He would watch me, slowly swinging his massive head side to side. I came out of compassion, such as the old man felt for the necklace. I came to learn something larger, more mysterious, than I could put into words at the time. Perhaps I came to learn to dance.

Maybe it was that memory that compelled me to visit Kodiak Island recently. I stayed at a bed-and-breakfast run by a pleasant young Christian couple. The husband said he was a subsistence hunter and fisherman. When I spoke of bears he told me a story.

He said he was out elk hunting on nearby Afognak Island several years back, and as he rounded a bend in the trail he suddenly came upon an enormous bear burying an animal kill on a small knoll no more than twenty yards away. Bear and man locked onto each other at the same instant.

... then a shape enters,
slips through the tightened silence of the shoulders.

The man was utterly terrified, literally weak-kneed. The bear but turned its massive head, slowly, side to side, trying to get a better look at him. The man still remembered seeing into those two black pools of eye.

As time held its breath the angel of death came and spoke to him, reminding him how bears are dangerous when burying their kill, and not to forget: these monsters can move like lightning when they have a mind to. Fear now screams at him to strike first. He brings rifle to his own eye and squeezes off one clean, ear-splitting shot—

reaches the heart, and dies.

Fear defeated him. It wasn't Bear that defeated him, that is certain—the bear had done nothing but look at him. Remember Hare concentrating his mind: "In the vapour-bath he communed with all the trees and with all the grasses and weeds, with all the stones and even with the earth. Then he poured tobacco as an offering and began the ceremony." He starts to sing, beginning with "blackroot songs," and as he sings the bear is "seized with a great desire to look towards him." When Bear can no longer resist and does look his way, Hare cries, "Grandmother, someone's mind came to me just then!"[3]

My friend surely did not know what this story catches. Indeed, that Grandfather, swinging its head from side to side, had the power to be any number of things to that young man. For somewhere, wherever it is that truth dwells, it lived (and lives on, I am certain) in superposition. Except that the man, long before he rounded the bend in the trail, long before he was even born, had already measured it in fear.

A young Eskimo in jail explains to me after class that the old people, when they used to go out berry-picking, if a bear showed up, would speak to it. "We're here just picking berries"—soothing, even, confident, spoken to *something* powerful right there. "Leave us alone; we're not here to hunt you." It hears. Understands. And leaves. My host on Kodiak never knew this and, moreover, I suspect if he were told it he wouldn't believe it.

He told me he believed in Jesus Christ, yet he could not bring himself to *believe* Jesus Christ. Who said (didn't he?) that we must live as he did: in superposition. "For I was hungry and you gave me food," said he. "I was thirsty and you gave me something to drink, I was a stranger and you welcomed me, I was naked and you gave me clothing, I was sick and you took care of me, I was in prison and you visited me." But Lord, protest his incredulous listeners, when did we see you hungry and thirsty, or the stranger, or see you naked, sick, and in prison? "Truly I tell you, just as you did it to one of the least of these who are members of my family, you did it to me."[4]

Walt Whitman never called himself a Christian, but he nonetheless understood Christ's sermon on superposition better than most certified Christians I've met. "I am the man. . . . I suffered. . . . I was there."

> Agonies are one of my changes of garments;
> I do not ask the wounded person how he feels. . . . I myself
>   become the wounded person,
> . . . .
> I become any presence or truth of humanity here,
> And see myself in prison shaped like another man,
> And feel the dull unintermitted pain.

The message is riveting and is fundamental to our own cherished religious tradition: offering a civilization strangled by fear, measuring everything in fear, the "chance to love everything."[5]

Even before reaching Alaska, as I packed to move there for the next few years, I had read about the Interior Department's controversial bear-collaring project up on the Yukon-Kuskokwim delta. Increased sport hunting (of brown bears in particular, for trophies) had driven the biologists to conclude that it was time to measure the bear population in the vast Yukon National Wildlife Refuge, to get an idea of how well they were reproducing and what their foraging behaviors were like.

Measurement consisted of biologists traveling upriver into the foothills, where bears, once spotted, were shot with a tranquilizer dart. Down and drugged, each was branded, suffered one of its teeth being pulled, and was fitted with a collar carrying a small radio transmitter. For the next several years that radio would send out a signal revealing the bear's whereabouts to listening biologists.

But bears are not a thing to be measured, I quickly learned. The Yup'ik Eskimos were incensed. Normally a pacific, agreeable people, resigned to being deceived or steamrollered by *kass'aq* (white) laws and programs—this time they drew the line.* At bears. They took their complaint to the highest levels of government, where the project was put on indefinite hold.

What was the problem? The scientists running the survey could never quite figure that out. I visited one of them in his office in Bethel one autumn day, a man with a Ph.D. in wildlife biology. I can still see the heavy metal desk littered with scientific reports. "We're using the very best scientific techniques," he says plaintively, with a sweeping gesture of the hand. Radio-tracking: state of the art.

Yet the Eskimos still say no.

I try to explain that bears are special, that they've been sacred as long

* Yupiit call all white people *kass'aqs* (pronounced "gussuks"), since the first whites they saw were Russians who called themselves Cossacks.

as humans have been humans. How bears, more than any other thing, form the spiritual center of gravity for traditional people like these Eskimos. I can see from his blank look that he's uncomprehending. I gather he thinks it's an interesting anthropological story, but certainly not science. (I sit there thinking about a button a student once handed me: "Your theory is interesting . . . but stupid.") He keeps telling me he needs empirical data. Numbers. When I suggest that he ask around and find some Yup'ik elders who—how should I put it?—"know" bears, who "feel" bears, to get their advice on how to proceed, he is mute. This isn't science at all, I can almost hear him thinking. I sense I don't belong in this man's office.

Soon thereafter the U.S. Fish and Wildlife Service held its fall meeting with the Yup'ik advisory group, the one where Paul John reminded everyone that moose can hear us talking about them. I found it odd that nobody, either on the panel or in the room, said a word when the government delivered its report on the state of the bear census.

The next day was different. As the reports from the day before were summarized, an elderly Eskimo asked to speak. He spoke out passionately against the mistreatment of bears, warning that it was like "playing" with them and worrying that the biologists were hurting them. He said the same thing about reindeer. He had friends who had been out hunting when they heard a wheezing sound nearby. Searching around, they discovered a reindeer and realized that it was gasping for air because of an ill-fitting radio collar. They shot it, out of compassion—afraid it wasn't going to make it.

That was all he said.

That evening I sat down at my desk and wrote out my frustrations. Sixteen months earlier, when the bear project was still steaming along, an article had appeared in the local newspaper condemning it as "culturally insensitive." John W. Andrew, a Yup'ik from the native village of Kwethluk, had written the article in his capacity as natural resource specialist for the Association of Village Council Presidents. "Brown Bear Study a 'Slap in the Face,'" was the title of the first in a three-part series. "Regional leaders and elders consider this plan culturally inappropriate and a sign of utmost disrespect"—the prose was bracing. A week later, part 2 appeared, as promised. Once again the government biologists took a pounding, as Andrew outlined the care with which Eskimos had traditionally approached the whole matter of hunting bears. It was an interesting article, especially the publisher's notice at the end: "John W. Andrew is the former natural resource specialist for the Association of Village Council Presidents . . . and now works for the U.S. Fish and Wildlife as a regional subsistence coordinator."[6]

Part 3, of course, never appeared. Strange things happen in bush Alaska.

I had noticed at the meeting how several times either a Yup'ik panel member or someone in the audience had made an earnest plea that the old ways be honored. When it came time to hear general testimony, the chairman invited Joe Chief, Sr., to please come take the microphone. Joe, like Paul John, is an elder esteemed throughout the delta, and I watched with fascination how the older councilmen fixed their attention on him as he spoke, as though he were saying something sacred and somehow fragile—like a spider's web in its inclusiveness.

The old man's voice rose and fell as he talked long and solemnly about the necessity of following tradition. He didn't seem to want to argue specifics, such as the bear project, but instead addressed the whole problem. The old ways of conduct, he said, almost desperately, must not be allowed to die. He began by explaining that what he was going to say he had heard from elders. This is common among Eski-

mos: the oldest person, generally the oldest man, will summon the
wisdom of the elders from the generation gone by, who doubtless had
done likewise in their time. Eskimo authority derives from the accu-
mulated wisdom of the ancestors.

But it is largely for naught. The Yup'ik have been robbed of a proper
forum in which to discuss their relationship with the land. I could detect their frustration in having to meet this way: as a *kass'aq* corporate
board, following *Robert's Rules of Order*. We straitjacket them with our
language (as in our gloss on the word "subsistence") and our structure
of discourse. Their call for respect for old ways has no soil, in our reality, to take root and grow. Their words seem quaint in our western
empirical, utilitarian, marketplace way of seeing things. I sense a re-
ciprocal frustration in the Fish and Wildlife officials I have talked to:
they seem to genuinely want to work with the Eskimos but are intractable in their scientific superiority.

I witnessed this one evening as my wife and I entertained a biologist friend for dinner. The man had worked for Fish and Wildlife for
years and was a formidable bird ecologist. I noticed a curious way of
knowing (epistemology) during the course of the evening—an epistemology of nature, as it were. Our friend had entered the field of ecol-
ogy because of his profound love for the subject. This is what keeps
him in Alaska: his immersion in the habitat of these birds. He is hap-
piest when with them, he said, as he rhapsodized about one glorious
day, sitting perfectly still in an alder thicket watching thrushes. The
changes in light, sometimes creating a dappling effect on the feathers
and other times, especially in late afternoon as the sun beamed directly
into the bushes, showing them in a wholly different aspect—how
magical they seemed. He had joined them in the joy of full presence.

His desk job was nowhere near as charming: the tedious hours of producing reports and grant proposals and scientific papers. I winced when he added, "But I don't know the high-powered math required to do my job well." So he planned on spending several years away at some university, learning statistics. There was a woman who had worked with him on a project—absolutely brilliant, he exclaimed. She had managed to subject the data, fragmentary as it was, to a statistical model that boggled his mind. He was envious.

There is, I think, a crazy objectification going on here. Thrushes, harlequin ducks, eiders are removed from the individual's experience with them into "resources" or "objects" to be "managed" or "studied" (terms used liberally throughout the evening). Here is the man who sits for a day in an alder thicket, bathed in "thrushness" and its un-measurable meaning, and likewise the man who is the (unwitting) agent for the delaminated view of the earth that characterizes western science. A powerful and dangerous epistemological shift is transpiring here. On one hand there is the reality of linkage, we might call it, and on the other the reality of separation. The latter troubles me. It results, I believe, in a kind of cultural vertigo: we don't know who we are or where we are.

That evening around the supper table we talked as well about the Yup'ik hostility to much of this research, including the bird studies. Our guest tensed up. I was alluding to a native's account of a bird study he had helped with near Hooper Bay, where there is a large and mar-velous breeding site. This is native corporation land controlled by the Hooper Bay traditional council. Tom Ayagalriak had described how the biologists had put flags by the nests of certain breeding birds and had handled the eggs. Tom declared that where this had occurred the parents had abandoned the nest.

Our biologist friend protested that Fish and Wildlife research might often *appear* intrusive, but in fact it does not endanger activities like breeding—the allegation was simply not true (he had zeroed in on the oft-expressed native charge that research threatens wildlife well-being). He said Eskimos are invited to visit the sites to see for themselves that wildlife are not being damaged, which strikes me as being akin to flying them to Bethel for a corporate-style meeting with Fish and Wildlife officials to gaze at the charts and listen to the statistics on how the animals are being well treated throughout the Yukon National Wildlife Refuge. While in the company of biologists they appear convinced, he went on—but did he realize that Yupiit, like all Eskimos, are unlikely to contradict someone to his face? These are people who prefer to say no through a third person, a trait long entrenched in this culture. Anyhow, they get back to the village council meetings—and out of range of *kass'aq* logic—and change their story. The consensus from the council meetings is that the biologists are tampering with the welfare of the birds and should be stopped (one is reminded of the man's complaint about "playing" with bears). Our friend conceded that Yupiit are tenacious in their conviction that all this research is strange, discourteous, and vaguely dangerous. At the same time it was evident he regarded all this as superstition and nonsense.

However inadequately they may explain it in *kass'aq* terms, this is nonetheless Yup'ik epistemology. "He plainly points out"—the room full of elders is hushed as Maxie Altsik speaks, barely above a whisper. Charlie Kilangak later translates from my recording: "He plainly points out that whatever is on the land or in the water, in our custom it's not a playful thing to play with an animal spirit, or animals that are in the water or under the water. That's what he's saying. That's our custom, that's our tradition."[7]

The aboriginal view simply cannot pierce the armored chauvinism of western science. Moreover, the natives know that with these supposedly innocuous studies come regulations from both federal and state agencies about hunting for birds and eggs. Restrictions and guidelines—a language and power that redefine the ancient relationship between these things and with this place, redefining their very selves. At what point in the process do they stop being the *real people*, one wonders? All this is intolerable and frightening to them.

When making preparations for going out hunting, the man won't tell people he's going hunting. In the old days he would not assert he was going to get such-and-such animal. There was no bragging. It was more a case of his wife or mother saying, "We're out of seal oil," say. The man draws on experience; it's what we are given.

Even if there are many game he may not catch anything. The animal doesn't want to give itself to the hunter on certain occasions. If he can't catch the animal, even drawing on all his skills, it's because the animal doesn't want to surrender itself. If the man needs, say, more sealskins to re-cover his kayak, he may catch one or two, though he needs seven. He can catch just a few. That's all he was given and the time ran out. He's disappointed. That's all he gets; he will have to make do. If there's lots of seals, yet he may not get as many as he wants. This is all he's given.

My dad, when I was growing up, used to say, "Don't be stupid. Don't say you're going to catch things when you go out. Don't think you're—don't specify, don't say you're a great hunter, 'cause you catch a small duck."

There is a certain hour near dawn when the animals are not scared, and it's easy to take them then. This was before there were guns. Nowadays with snowmachine or plane and gun with scope—we can kill far and instantly. Now the hunter doesn't have to rely on the animal's lack of fear. We lost that instinct of being spiritual, respectful, motivated. The old hunters knew how to read the weather, the terrain, and the animal's habits and ways.

"I have the spirit of some ancestor," continues Charlie Kilangak, "and that's what gives me the ability to hunt." Adding, ruefully, "it's harder [to hunt] today than formerly, because we have lost the spirituality, the respect in hunting. Animals' lives are being wasted: skins thrown away, joking and laughing. Animals are diminishing fast with the great bang of whites arriving with their technology."[8]

Charlie is in his midforties, I would guess; he's from the native village of Emmonak, on the Lower Yukon River. He calls me Doc, and he thinks I have an inordinate interest in bears. He tells me that when he was still a baby he contracted tuberculosis, so he spent the first few years of his life in a hospital in Sitka, I believe, where he was raised by the nurses. They thought he was adorable. One day he was bundled onto a plane and whisked off to another world, actually to his home village out on the endless rolling bog called the Alaska tundra. He still remembers being terrified and in culture shock, going around the village informing people that they stank (they smelled of fish and seal oil). This greatly amused everyone, and friends and relatives to this day call him Stinky. And we are friends. "I hope my ancestral spirit will survive and pass into my son," he confides, "so he will hunt and live as a Yup'ik. This, when the oil runs out. I hope to pass it on to my son. My son carries the name of a deceased hunter, and when he killed his first beaver we gave it all to the daughter of the man after whom he was named."

There are those who say the Yup'ik have only shreds of their former sense of themselves and the meaning of place and their role in it. But surely their hope for the future lies not in wholly capitulating to our western objectifying of it all, and the silent loss of self-respect and self-perception as the people of the trumpeter swans, host to the bearded seals, the *tuntu* (caribou), and the *tuntuvak* (moose). Right now that relationship is best witnessed by the outsider in the Eskimo dances performed in the long dark winter season, like the bear dance that de Poncins described. There, on the dance floor, holding owl-feather or caribou-fur fan, is where a congress with Fish and Wildlife should be taking place.

Or at the Bethel Senior Center, where I spent several winter afternoons asking elders what they thought of the bear project. Though the first afternoon I asked merely about bears in general. Probably a dumb question, kind of like de Poncins's to Angutjuk about how many foxes he had killed. Only later was I to learn, in Charlie's broken English, that "there used to be sayings of the animals: they got ears on the tundra. Bears got ears that they could hear through the grasses, or bush, or any kind of vegetation there is. They could hear us through maybe what they eat or maybe what they live with, or maybe they would sense something of . . . Gee, that guy, you know! And that bear would know which person it is [who said something]. The animal would hear what that person said." It's "a very important rule," confirms Alma Keyes. "My late father used to caution us about them [bears]. And since I wasn't always cautious and timid, I would go hunting and berry picking by myself. I would be out there by myself all day and would talk to them. And they say that if you talk to them they will hear you even though they are out in the distance. They would tell us not to make fun of them out there or in our homes. They say they can hear you, saying they can hear you through the ground."9

So what I heard was mostly silence. I felt conspicuous—kind of like I did honking on the Navajo reservation. Then an old lady took pity on me, God bless her, perhaps because she used to cook at the Moravian seminary in town, where I now taught. Carrie Anvil rescued me—was I to be surprised?—with a story. She emphasized that it was true.

There was a man and his wife and son who lived in a sod house over yonder in the mountains. The man was a hunter, and his wife couldn't help but notice that he was often gone for many days.

One day while her husband was away on one of his lengthy trips a robin flew into the camp, in fact right up to the woman, and blurted out some disquieting news: that her spouse was keeping two other wives down along the coast. [Robins occasionally still seem to be speaking alarming news, Carrie added.]

The woman pondered this, and finally decided to investigate. So off she went in the direction of the coast, and eventually she spied a house. Entering it she found, sure enough, two women. Ah, thought she to herself, these must be the ones my husband is fooling around with! The two unsuspecting women, on the other hand, seeing their visitor's marvelous tattoos, curving up from the corners of her mouth, became filled with envy.

How might they get tattoos like hers? they eagerly asked. Glancing around the room, the cunning woman noticed two large cooking pots bubbling away over the fire. If they would each bend down and but touch their cheeks to the rim of the pot, she instructed, why they, too, would be gaily decorated. They did as told, whereupon the woman sprang upon them and pushed their heads down into the boiling cauldrons—killing them.

She now took their dead bodies and propped them up on the beach, placing dance fans in their hands, to make them appear to be dancing. That done, she pulled over herself, as one would an overcoat, a bear skin she found hanging out to dry. But first she shoved a wooden board—actually a cutting board, the sort women commonly use to cut up meat—under each armpit, down each side of her torso, before hauling on the skin.

Thus masked, the bear-woman concealed herself to await her

philandering husband. Sure enough he eventually appeared in the distance. As he approached the shore he was amazed and puzzled by the sight of his two mistresses dancing, it seemed, there on the beach. Beaching his kayak, he went up close to investigate. All of a sudden his wife, clad as a bear, rushed out and killed him, too.

Thus avenged, the woman made her way back into the mountains.

Meanwhile the boy, the story goes, was sitting on top of the house anxiously awaiting his parents. When his mother appeared, still wearing her bearskin, he was terrified, and promptly turned himself into a jaeger and flew off—which is why the jaeger's call sounds so much like a child's cry of alarm.[10]

Why was this woman telling me this story? Actually she had done more than speak it; she had virtually danced it with her hands, so exquisitely expressive were they. Much of what she said I couldn't understand, it being almost entirely in Yup'ik, with English interjections shot in my direction from time to time. Yet I found (when my interpreter later translated it) that I had understood a great deal from her hand gestures. It used to be that Yup'ik girls and women told stories through "storyknives" carved of ivory or wood. Kneeling down on the ground as they spoke, they would carve each scene in the sand or dirt or snow. Each story was thus reborn from the girl-with-storyknife. And so did this one issue from Carrie Anvil's hands and voice that day.

But why this story? I wondered.

I think I know the answer: because it's true. Carrie had prefaced her performance with this assertion, and now that she was done she added a postscript. A few years ago a group of hunters had shot and killed a bear up on the Yukon River. Nothing remarkable in that, certainly. But when they skinned that bear they were surprised to find her carrying two rotten wooden boards.

Superposition.

Recall Old Ben, the "shaggy tremendous shape" in William Faulkner's "The Bear."[11] Bear knew that the power of myth was over now; the people of historical errands were ascendant, and it was time to begin his journey back into the earth, although the Dark One would orchestrate this final rite of passage. I wonder if, somehow, Carrie's Bear-Woman also knew it was time to die and give up to the new world order that was suffocating the spirit of the land and its human and animal people. I try to imagine Carrie's Bear-Woman being darted and tranquilized, branded, and mutilated of a tooth, and finally radio-collared by a team of efficient scientists. Would that radio and those wounds—for that matter, the entire experience—transmit any story remotely like the one Carrie Anvil storyknifed for me that wintery afternoon: the parable of the wife / Old One who killed her husband for abandoning the family of things, for breaking trust?

Two incommensurate worlds, two different stories, two utterly different ways of measuring reality. Where does this leave the people of myth today? What good can Carrie's story be for Raven's Children, the Yup'ik, when the Bear-Woman has been shot by a couple of hunters up on the Yukon River? Or when a *kass'aq* has his name and numbers attached to the polar bear in the lobby of the Regal Alaskan Hotel? What does it mean when her body mask hangs, now, crucified to the wall of the prison warden's office in Bethel, Alaska? Surely it means Raven's world is now being calibrated differently for the *real people*— and they are suffering for it.

"And it *hurts* us, you know!" Elsie Active glares at me through her remaining eye as she hurls her anguish and frustration across the room at the senior center. "Even when they have meeting and people talkin', they don't listen to us." "I do not ask the wounded person how he feels," spoke Walt Whitman for Elsie Active. "I myself become the wounded person, / My hurt turns livid upon me as I lean on a cane and observe."[12]

First Sergeant Warren Tanner of the Alaska State Troopers is not a typical police officer. Earlier in the month, when my driver's license expired, I had discovered to my dismay that the local licensing bureau would be closed for a week. The clerk's teenage daughter had attempted suicide. It meant that if I drove, I would be doing so illegally till the clerk came back (life in bush Alaska is very human). I called the state police and spoke to Mr. Tanner, barracks commander, and asked if he could help somehow. He invited me right over: he said he would administer the test personally.

Commander Tanner spoke at the seminary, at my invitation. He's *kass'aq;* the students, all Yup'ik. I had asked him to probe the deeper reasons for the stunning alcoholism, child abuse, suicide, and other mayhem among the Yup'ik Eskimo of southwestern Alaska.

He began by telling them he was frustrated; he needed their help. There was something wrong in the lives of many Yupiit, and he was stymied over what to do about it. He illustrated with a small story.

Just the other day in one of the villages there was a Yup'ik man whose wife informed him that she wanted a divorce. He told her he couldn't bear the thought and would shoot himself if she left. Holding a loaded gun to his head, he dramatized his point. He did this repeatedly over the next several days, in front of his wife and children, whenever the topic came up.

She called the state police to have him arrested. But he wasn't breaking the law. She next called the village magistrate to have him evicted, but the man was in his own home, after all, not trespassing. The magistrate counseled that if she filed divorce papers he could then be served notice to vacate the premises. She did.

And he blew his brains out, just like he said. Right in the living room.

Warren Tanner is a humane man. The sort who recognizes the obvious and is quick to implement it. When the license clerk returned from medical leave sooner than anticipated, he called to let me know. And when I went and picked up the license, he called again to make sure everything had worked out. Mr. Tanner and his wife had adopted, the year before, two teenage native children from a Siberian orphanage—they picked them up personally.

The story Warren told was extremely difficult for him. I watched him closely as he spoke; beneath the splendid uniform I saw a man in anguish. Someone who was himself shot in Vietnam—leg shattered, he nearly bled to death as he maneuvered his gunship. Perhaps these experiences clarify the obvious and leave us skeptical of bureaucratic reasoning. Even when the bureaucracy is one's own.

I heard that man apologize for another man's death. "I failed him," he said softly though firmly.

"We all failed him." It's good he added that: I wanted these men and women to see how their theology was quackery if it couldn't heal this wound. One in a multitude of mortal wounds. My wife, a pediatrician, not infrequently examined molested native children at the local hospital. The prison is overflowing with Yup'ik men, mostly, who are lovely and sweet people who got drunk and blacked out and did something awful.

They are sad, orphaned from their old world, and what they have now is a hybrid that doesn't work. They are a people who've lost the story. Or had it drowned in bootlegged vodka or watched it perish from diphtheria or influenza or tuberculosis—or put a bullet in it. Starting with the Russian fur merchants in the eighteenth century and continuing with missionaries a hundred years later, then the teachers and government bureaucrats, all the while battered by appalling epidemics, a tidal wave of alcohol, and now the din of television sets switched on all the time, plus snowmobiles and powerboats and rifles and videos—with all this, the moose don't dream themselves into people any more. At least, not many people. Nor do salmon, caribou, or bears or seals or walrus. I doubt the blueberries and cranberries and salmonberries give their spirit to many Yupiit, either. The other day a young seminarian announced in class that he had spotted a snowy owl while zooming from Kwethluk to Bethel on his snowmobile, adding with a flourish, "I wish I had had my gun!"

Why? I wondered. What sort of story did he intend to insert that creature into? A man blows his brains out because his wife doesn't know how to deal with her wounds, nor he with his; a young man claiming an interest in Christ wants to blow an owl's brains out—and doesn't know why.

Perhaps because of his own wounds.

The old fellow was jovial as he introduced himself to Nina and me on the boardwalk one sunny afternoon. He laughed, saying he had just one name. He was Inupiaq, living in Bethel. He was intrigued by Nina's hat, so we got into conversation.

The man volunteered that he was an alcoholic, as are, he claimed, 98 percent of the other Yupiit in Bethel and throughout the delta. He reeked of booze yet seemed in control of himself. He said he enjoyed binge drinking from time to time and would furnish alcohol to friends and relatives out in the villages as an act of generosity.

He is a tundra walker and proud of it. He spoke of grandparents who could run down reindeer.

As he realized who we were, he nudged the conversation in another direction. He had something on his mind; he wanted to talk about being punished as a boy in school for speaking his native tongue: beaten on the hand with a wooden ruler or at times forced to drop his pants to be struck on his buttocks. He began drinking at fifteen, and it's been his habit ever since. "Freud was wrong," he suddenly blurts out, angrily; "a man cannot get into the mind of another man. Nobody can know the pain and suffering I've witnessed and experienced." He recalled being in Vietnam during the war. Withal, alcohol gave him solace. The men in the prison tell the same story: alcohol gives them relief from manifold fears, leaving them feeling strong and capable, in control of their lives.

He said he didn't have much formal western education, but, by God, his traditional knowledge was every bit as valuable as a western education—this, too, angered him, as though we might imagine otherwise. He declared he could repair any engine, from motorboat to airplane, all without instructions.

When I asked if anyone had ever apologized for the things he had endured from *kass'aqs,* he was stunned. No, he said, nobody had.

So we did. We held out our hands and he shook them. "Apology accepted." He was touched. "You know, I have never said these things to a white man before. It feels kinda good."

Or there is Robert Alixie. Robert is from a village of three hundred souls amid ponds and sloughs by the Bering Sea, a place of human conversation with the sea and tundra that goes back thousands of years. The people here still feed themselves almost exclusively from the abundance of salmon, tom cod, various species of seals, walrus, beluga whales, caribou, ducks and geese and tundra swans, and the small furbearers that share this space with them. Here in our own time is a functioning hunter-gatherer economy. The tiny general store in town is noteworthy for selling very little western food.

Robert is from this place. Except that he will live, till his sentence is up, in the Spring Creek Correctional Center on Resurrection Bay, down on the Kenai Peninsula, hundreds of miles from the tundra and visits from family. "I talked with my Mother at home," he wrote in one of his letters. "They are all doing great and are catching walrus, seals and such. I wish I was home because I would be out in the sea where I do consider Heaven. It is heaven to me because it is also among the ice floes, seals to look for in calm weather, and the sun bright outside."[13]

I met Robert at the Bethel prison when he was beginning his lengthy sentence. In July the prisoners held a potlatch and all the families were invited. I spotted him among the kitchen crew as things were being set up. He was obviously distressed. He told me he's a sensitive man, maybe the most sensitive man there, he said: it was terribly difficult for him to see guests arriving and know his family could not come. He wished sometimes he could just disappear into "someone nothing." As he said it he closed his thumb and forefinger down until they met.

White smoke.

Annihilation. His grandfather told him long ago that he could learn the white man's ways and language, but could never become a white man. The Eskimos, warned the old man, would eventually become a "spot," a dot, to the whites. Irrelevant.

Robert reached for a paper napkin to wipe his eyes. He walked away to the chain-link fence, beneath the sign that says the guards can shoot anyone standing that close to the fence—to weep in private.

Alcohol put him here. He drank and lost consciousness (yet kept functioning, which is a neurological mystery and yet common with natives) and did something frightening. He had been in prison some years back, he added, also for something alcohol-related. Liquor scared him, that it could do this to him. He has a wife and children back home.

I asked if he's an artist. "Oh yes, somewhat." He told me how he once carved an Eskimo hunting a seal out of *pure ivory* (he emphasized). Robert put his right hand up over his head and assumed the hunter's waiting posture as he described the piece: the patient hunter poised above the breathing-hole. Robert, I realized, had carved himself. I marveled at how long one must wait, totally motionless, and asked how long this might be.

"As long as it takes," he rebuked me, irritated at such a dumb question.

I liked hearing him talk of animals. He said bears were not fearsome in the old days; if someone suddenly encountered one, he would talk to it respectfully, assuring him that he had no wish to do him any harm. The bear would not attack. In yet another conversation Robert said with vehemence that hunting and gathering were the Eskimo's *religion*, not *subsistence*.

Words. Our words. Their words.

He told me his grandfather had warned him not to speak too loudly when out hunting, as this offends the animals. Robert vividly remembers the day he ignored this piece of advice; as he walked along he suddenly heard the flapping of enormous wings coming up behind him—vast wings beating the air. They nearly brushed him and then, suddenly, disappeared. He never saw what it was. He assumed it was the Spirit Bird, or Great Spirit, telling him to "hush," just as his grandfather had warned.

He has always believed in the Great Spirit ever since; he thinks it nearly touched him.

Robert's cellmate is an older man who each night begs Robert to tell him a bedtime story. Robert puts him off, but the fellow insists, and Robert obliges as best he can. Robert then gets him to reciprocate. I later noticed them sitting together at the potlatch, horsing around. I walked over and sat with them. Robert introduced me. I remarked on their storytelling, and the older man, very Yup'ik and barely fluent in English, chuckled. "Ii-i."

A few days later, in class, Robert talked of being stripped of one's culture. Like the Inupiaq on the boardwalk, he described being forbidden to speak Yup'ik in school. He had not been physically punished (as children of his parents' generation would have been) but was threatened with having certain privileges denied him, such as snacks and recess. This was crushing, he said. Other men in the room confirmed the experience. Robert's problem was that he kept saying a native word that was the equivalent of "oops" whenever he made a blunder. And of course that landed him in trouble. He reached the point of walking to school each morning reminding himself over and over not to say that confounded word.

Oops. The stories are so poignant.

Once, when I had made a particularly stirring point in the prison class, Charles Wasilie, from Tuntutuliak, asked if he could address the group in Yup'ik, in response, explaining that he wasn't sure he could convey his thoughts properly in English. I said sure. At the start of class a few weeks later, I was, as was my habit, going around the room repeating everyone's name, writing down those who were new. Charles was the last man in the large semicircle, and when I spoke his name he quietly said, "Qavcicuaq." He had introduced himself as this a few weeks ago, and I had ignored it: I called him "Charles," as the guards did. There it was again; he was correcting me.

I stopped, looked at him, and asked him to repeat it. "Qavcicuaq," he said again in his hoarse whisper. I tried to excuse myself, saying the name was too difficult for me to pronounce. But he was relentless. "Learn it anyway," he firmly replied. I asked if he would repeat it again.

I squirmed, saying how difficult Yup'ik is for me, with its guttural and gurgling sounds at the back of the throat. Yes, he agreed—but he insisted. I sought help from another quarter: "How do you spell it?" pen poised. "I don't know," he answered, truthfully.

There was no escape; I was going to have to plunge in, navigating solely by his terms. I took a stab at it. He corrected me.

After I had tried it, he said he's sometimes called "Qav" for short.

We have even taken away their names. In prison he's Charlie Wasilie, shuffling about in blue pajamas and slippers, eating weird food, in a building not his, conforming to a calendar not his, visited by the Assembly of God missionary (who conducts a hymn sing-along) and the likes of me. But today he wanted his name back. "Qavcicuaq," he said softly, in a whispered growl, when I said, "Charles." Surely I must return it to him. He comes up to me after each class and ceremoniously shakes my hand. "Thank you for coming," he always says.

I happened to run into Qavcicuaq the day he was released from prison. A Saturday. He had told me on Monday that he would be getting out on Saturday; he was eager to get a certificate for the course. The thought of getting out made him happy. He said he would not be going back to Tuntutuliak, however; he lives in Bethel now. In any event, Nina and I were walking into the Alaska Commercial Company store early Saturday afternoon when I spotted him talking with some Yupiit sitting on the bench out front. He saw me approaching and stepped back from the group. We shook hands. I asked how he was doing. He seemed intense, wary even. Boldly he replied, "Not well!" Here I had congratulated him for being out of prison, shaken his hand, and asked how he was: "Not well." He said he had been drinking (already), that he didn't want to mislead me: he definitely had been drinking. He appeared mildly intoxicated. He said he was from a culture that believed in honesty. He also seemed to be trying to explain that alcohol was a permanent part of his life, and he didn't feel like apologizing to me for it. I did not comment. He walked away.

The day before, Friday, I had seen him when I visited the prison for an open hearing with some prison officials. Qavcicuaq was one of the first men I spotted as I entered the lock-up. As usual we had shaken hands. I had asked him how he was doing. He said he was doing very well. (He was of course sober.) He said that today he liked his Story. Qavcicuaq had told the class earlier in the week how I had taught him the concept of living by a Story—that we all live a certain Story.

On Friday, in prison, sober, about to go free, he said he liked his Story. Saturday, a free man, and drunk, he said the Story was "not well."

The man who has best analyzed this long spiritual nightmare is from Hooper Bay on the Bering Sea, in a powerful essay titled *Yuuyaraq:* "the way of being a human being." Harold Napoleon wrote it from his prison cell in Fairbanks. Harold, like so many Yup'ik, is notably soft-spoken; when my wife and I met him in Anchorage, Nina had to ask the coffee-shop manager to turn off the background music so we could hear him.

Harold blames the epidemics at the turn of this century for the profound despiritualization not only here, in southwestern Alaska, but throughout the state. "As a child I heard references to *yuut tuqurpallratni*—'when a great many died,' or the Great Death. . . . I heard references to *yuut tuqurpallratni* from three men, my granduncles, all of whom are now dead. . . . In almost every reference to the experience, they used the word *naklurluq*, or 'poor,' referring both to the dead and to the survivors, but they never went into detail. It was almost as if they had an aversion to it."

The suffering, the despair, the heartbreak, the desperation, and confusion these survivors lived through is unimaginable. People watched helplessly as their mothers, fathers, brothers, and sisters grew ill, the efforts of the *angalkuq* failing [*angalkuq*: shamans, who served also as "village historians, physicians, judges, arbitrators, and interpreters of *Yuuyaraq*"]. First one family fell ill, then another, then another. The people grew desperate, the *angalkuq* along with them. Then the death started, with people wailing morning, noon, and night. Soon whole families were dead, some leaving only a boy or girl. Babies tried to suckle on the breasts of dead mothers, soon to die themselves. Even the medicine men grew ill and died in despair with their people, and with them died a great part of *Yuuyaraq*, the ancient spirit world of the Eskimo. . . . Too weak to bury all the dead, many survivors abandoned the old villages, some caving in their houses with the dead still in them. Their homeland—the tundra, the Bering Sea coast, the riverbanks—had become a dying field for the Yup'ik people: families, leaders, artists, medicine men and women—and *Yuuyaraq*.[14]

"Despiritualization": Harold told me he had never heard the word before, but said it fit. He wrote what has to be one of the greatest prison tracts of all time, confronting a profound spiritual void while pondering his own. He thinks Alaska natives suffer from post-traumatic stress disorder, just like war veterans. The shell-shock and disease-shock are the same.

The problem was that survivors wouldn't speak of the memory. It was too searing. In villages where everyone is either your cousin or auntie (as they put it) or uncle, or even nearer kin, the death of half, two-thirds, or nearly everyone must be close to unthinkable. Survivors covered it up in horrified silence. They invoked *nallunguaq*: they pretended it didn't happen.

"To this day *nallunguaq* remains a way of dealing with problems or unpleasant occurrences in Yup'ik life. . . . They had a lot to pretend not to know. After all, it was not only that their loved ones had died, they also had seen their world collapse. Everything they had lived and believed had been found wanting. They were afraid to admit that the things they had believed in might not have been true."[15]

But the sorrow within was more than the spirit could bear. Fathers were angry with sons, calling them failures as hunters and as men. The living brooded, souls snatched away with the departed loved ones. The talking world of spirits was repudiated and lay silent; the myths and stories, even the admonitions for correct behavior, lost cogency. Harold said certain words passed out of the language, words of the spirit, since they no longer carried the weight of meaning. When children uttered them they were reprimanded.

Words themselves had died in the great die-off.

"In the very first times," at the beginning of things in the Eskimo universe, "a person could become an animal" if he wanted to, reminds Nâlungiaq, "and an animal could become a human being. . . . Sometimes they were people and other times animals, and there was no difference. . . . All spoke the same tongue. . . . That was the time when magic words were made. A word spoken by chance would suddenly become powerful, and what people wanted to happen could happen, and nobody could explain how it was."[16]

The Children of Raven became spiritually inarticulate, the pain inaudible. "In their heart of hearts the survivors wept, but they did not talk to anyone, not even their fellow survivors. It hurt too much. They felt angry, bewildered, ashamed, and guilty, but all this they kept within themselves." Except when drunk. Those elders who tried to go back were ignored. They still are.[17]

Harold thinks that the Yup'ik must talk about it now, finally, even though the plagues are long gone. Plagues are past but the mourning continues—the grieving and its psychological and spiritual hammerlock on succeeding generations. We read of the elderly Yup'ik woman who was invited to comment on Harold's essay but declined. "She has suffered the grief of her children dying of old age before her and the suicides of her grandchildren with the quiet dignity and understanding that reveal the true meaning of the term 'elder,' yet when asked about the epidemics she said, 'Too much hurt. I don't want to remember.'"[18]

Perhaps Harold Napoleon is right. Perhaps this is what was going on in that living room where the gunshot shattered the argument—didn't end it, just made it worse. The wounding, I mean. Not a bullet, not a binge on 40 percent alcohol, not a child- or wife-beating will suture such an embedded wound. Anger and more pain are no prescription for even deeper anger and pain.

It has been hard living here, in the presence of abiding sorrow. As I walked over to the prison one lovely winter afternoon, something drew my attention to the fine Yup'ik sculpture outside that grim entrance. A kayak, mere frame and ribs, cast in metal, standing on end. In the spot where the cockpit would be is carved a broad Yup'ik face peering out at the world. Something caught my eye that afternoon, sun low but intense on the horizon, striking it full on. Walking closer and inspecting it, I realized the face had been weeping. A frozen rill had formed below the right eye. Water had likewise gushed from the nose and mouth, all of it now frozen. There it glistened in the January sun.

So like a child, the face was weeping. Silently. Two days before I had met with one of the inmates in the cramped attorneys' conference room, a man I knew well. As he described his hopeless life he wept, quietly, brushing away tears as he continued—he and his wife had both been molested as children. I thought of the prisoners who wept openly when I lectured on alcohol a few months before. I could imagine the children of these men who must weep at home over the drunken anger and rage of fathers or mothers now in jail.

Perhaps I, too, should have wept, as this mute, inert statue somehow knew to do.

SIX

Oscar

Talk to Louis Chikoyak for a few hours and you begin to understand Perception.

When I met Louis he was working as assistant curator at the Yup'ik museum in Bethel. He told me that Mary, the museum curator, had walked over to his table at the Mink Festival, knelt on the floor, placed her elbows on the table, and simply marveled at the things he had made. She asked if he had done all this himself. Indeed he had, he replied. Mary hired him on the spot.

Louis designed and drew the poster for the museum opening: a masterful interpretation of John Kailukiak's haunting mask, "Ocean Bird." Louis has juxtaposed Kailukiak's carving of the Cormorant Spirit with a draftsmanlike rendering of the new Yup'ik cultural center in Bethel. The execution, the contrast of these competing realms of reality, these two powers of spirit, is subtle and brilliant. The amazing thing is that Louis, like nearly every other Eskimo I've met, never took an art class beyond elementary school. As I admired his poster he offered that he makes jewelry, too, and carves ivory and bone and wood boxes and statues and other figures, builds three-dimensional greeting cards, and plays guitar and acoustic piano—all, naturally, without human instruction.

All of it art, he emphasized. It interested me how he pantomimed the piano and guitar as he said their names. I began to detect an extraordinary level of awareness of the life of the thing being touched by his hands.

Louis was eager to show me the original of the poster; he took me into the back room where he had it unceremoniously rolled up. He unearthed his sketchbook, brimming with ideas for carvings. He then hauled out a wooden "spotted seal" box he had started carving, next a T-shirt he had once decorated, wildlife cards with the birds actually flying off the page, and the neat little jeweler's box he had made for carrying the tools and ivory for earrings. Rummaging through a cardboard box he extracted carefully wrapped pieces of wood and walrus ivory and short sections of antler, addressing each lovingly as he removed it.

Louis "sees the life" in a scrap of wood or antler or ivory; he hears the music inherent in the instrument.

I once knew a woman in Maine who was a weaver. I slept one night in the room with her looms. The next morning I told her how in my sleep I kept hearing a strange sound, though I could not now identify it. She said she thought her looms were alive; sometimes she could hear them. As she said that I remembered that the sound in the room was a gentle clattering noise: the loom at work. So Navajo, I thought.

Oscar Active (Elsie's son), from Kongiganak, gave me this marvelous expression: "seeing the life" in something. Oscar said one must have the power to do this in life.

Louis talked by his hands. Spoken words were articulated by dancing hands and intricate finger movements. He said he normally draws with the right hand, particularly when he wants precision. But for something more rough-looking (as he put it), more primal-looking (how I would put it), he uses the left. Thus he drew the tiny animal and human figures at the bottom of the poster with the left. While he speaks of his earrings he absentmindedly sketches them on a handy scrap of paper.

What Louis was really telling me is that Yupiit "feel" the life, the power, inherent in a thing—it seems to enter them. I thought of Oscar repairing a blown head gasket on a snowmobile away out on the tundra with a patch of aluminum foil from his sandwich—it worked. Oscar will repair an engine without benefit of manual. "Manuals are for *kass'aqs*," I have heard him bellow as he works on his boat engine. The first thing a Yup'ik does when he unpacks a brand-new engine is toss the manual in the trash—a bit of an exaggeration, though I swear the manual is usually ignored. I had a young man in class declare that there isn't an engine alive he can't fix—again, doubtless an overstatement, but the point is well taken. I remember Bernice Andrew learning to play a song so readily, so naturally, when I showed her how on the piano.

Or the masks: each tells a story. But there is more here than meets the eye: a story lives within the skin of the mask. Recently an elder was walking through a mask exhibit in Toksook Bay when he spotted the loon mask. He stopped before it and suddenly began singing—the loon song, the song of the mask itself. The mask carved the song out of him—we would say he simply remembered it. No, that's not it. It was his being in the presence of the loon again that made it possible to sing. This is more than memory; a Yup'ik would say, that mask sang through the old man.

The difference is crucial and it is monumental.

There is a remarkable convergence going on here. It is not enough, I think, to call it *art;* it is better, I think, to call it *perception.* "Even if no other inclinations give rise to the creativity of the Kuskokwim Eskimo," marveled Hans Himmelheber, a German ethnologist, in the 1930s, "the desire to describe is an unusually active stimulus. . . . An incident must be visibly illustrated, and only then does it become solidly imaginable." When Maggie Lind wanted to tell him about the storytelling sessions in the men's house, "she quickly grabbed her sketching-knife to illustrate for me the incidents by means of a sketch of the men's house: how the men lie around there on the benches, here the lamp stands." "Descriptions," he emphasizes, "are richly accompanied by gestures. Lame Jacob told a story of the carved figures on one of the rhythm-sticks in which a man found a very rare seal with a reddish head, fast asleep on an ice-block. When he came to the description of the sleeping, he laid his head to the side on one of his hands, wagged it back and forth and snored."[1]

Himmelheber has not quite grasped the radicalness of what is going on; "creativity" and "imagination" are themselves lame words. Nor will "pantomime" work, either. None of them tells us the true nature of the dynamic here; none of them—art, creativity, pantomime, mimicry—realizes that there is a field of force already contained within the thing observed.

Again, Oscar puts it best: one must "see the life" in something, implying, of course, that it has *being* already. Implying as well that the craftsman is not entirely responsible for the final outcome. The final outcome is a joint accomplishment, and is not even final, of course. The substrate, the object, has being—a voice, a story, a personality, a face. The driftwood that John Kailukiak finds on the beach in Toksook Bay and carves into his wondrous masks: is it using him to assume a different shape? Does the wood find him just as he is finding it? For the Yup'ik Eskimos know that there is a Spirit of the Driftwood; they carve its face, too. What kind of mutual intercourse, mutual perception, is happening here?

All this helps explain how Yupiit see nature: they don't. That is, they don't perceive or imagine the earth, the place, as beyond them. The

Oscar

English word "nature," by definition, is "out there." The earth, the environment, the place—all out there. An object. Yupiit don't gaze upon the earth; Yupiit, I find, don't talk about environmentalism, conservation, a land ethic, or affection for or awe of nature (unless they have been westernized); in fact, it's very rare for them to talk about nature at all. Traditional Eskimos don't acknowledge these things because they *are* nature; they are coterminous with the mind, the spirit, the being of it all. This is being a *real person*.

Consider the acorn I brought into the prison one day. I took it out of my pocket and began expounding on oakness and beauty—the marvel that the entire text of the tree, its lifespan and errand, were coded within that shell. The men immediately wanted me to pass it around; few had seen or handled an acorn. As it began its journey one of them suggested that we extract the seed and eat it.

Eat it—there it is. I have oftentimes witnessed this with Yupiit. Many of us *kass'aqs* will talk about an aspect of nature in abstract terms, even rhapsodizing about it as something beautiful, while Yupiit (like any native or non-native who lives off the land) are thinking about eating it. Birds, for instance. At the seminary late one winter I referred to the coming of spring, when the swans, geese, ducks, and cranes come back, and I made it clear that I looked forward to seeing them—as a birdwatcher. No—they were interested in eating them. That spring out in Quinhagak, Willard Church joked that whereas whites talk of preserving the Eskimo curlew, the Eskimos say that they make good eating. And as Nina jogged past a group of young pregnant women on the boardwalk one lovely spring day, she smiled and said, "Snipes," acknowledging the aerial courtship displays all around them. Their eyes lit up as they replied, "Eggs!" Eskimos speak with enthusiasm about going out and collecting wild bird eggs. Sam Berlin says that they taste great, much better than store-bought chicken eggs. I can imagine—

136

but for me personally, wild bird eggs are off limits. Indeed for many birds the law stipulates precisely that. The birds and their eggs are "out there"; I watch the nest through binoculars.

But I am neither Yup'ik nor a man of the land. The usual debate here focuses on whether these people, these Eskimos, should be "allowed" (by law) to collect these eggs, and to what degree they should be "allowed" to hunt wildlife. Government biologists and legislators argue with the natives about "subsistence," and the two sides reach no agreement on the meaning of the word. "Subsistence," "wildlife," "wildfowl": the words are wrong. It is significant that there are (or were) in fact no such words in the Yup'ik language, meaning that there is no such reality in the Yup'ik universe. The words refer to objects separate from us, and in so doing they betray a totally different reality from traditional Yup'ik practice.

Consider the Yup'ik word for "fish": *neqa,* whose base is *neqe-. Neqe-* means "fish" as well as "food." The verb base for "eat," *nere-,* is, in the fluidity of Yup'ik grammar, nearly identical to *neqe-.* The *neq/r* at the beginning of the two words marks them as coming from the same root, as two expressions of the same face. Hence, "fish," "food," and "to eat" form a unity.[2]

The issue is *ontological* (literally, belonging to the "study of being, of reality"), not moral or legal or even cultural. Not only do *kass'aqs* not "think" like Yupiit; we don't blend with the atomic structure of the earth in the way they do. This is Louis Chikoyak's and Oscar Active's message.

"You have to see the life in something": they do. They do because they *are* all life. Watching Margaret Cooke cut up king salmon at fishcamp one evening in the drizzle and mosquitoes (to which torments she is entirely oblivious), all I hear Margaret say is how joyful this is. Bending over these immense fish, her ulu knife flashing, she has been doing this for hours. It's exhausting—Tun'aq (Margaret) is smiling; in truth she is quietly rapturous. I realize that somehow this woman is the Swimmer, she is Fishing, she is the Kuskokwim; she is the human incarnation of this entire event. The world travels within such people; like a river, its errands go right through them. When Margaret died the following spring, right before her return as the Swimmer, her son put her favorite ulu into the casket. Tun'aq goes on.

This is the real world we do not perceive in this so-called New World. For me, heir to the western metaphysic, the world begins a mere hairbreadth beyond my fingertips. Like Michelangelo's famous painting in the vault of the Sistine Chapel, I reach out to touch the Spirit of the Universe outside of me. I, ego, am something else; I am not event. Though mythology and now quantum mechanics insist I am. This is a revelation, a new metaphysic; I am not prepared to step into it.

This is the New World metaphysic that Columbus trod upon in 1492 and claimed for Ferdinand and Isabella—what the physicist-philosopher David Z. Albert would call a category error.

I am brought face to face with this titanic reality on the day when a winter storm blasts in from the Bering Sea—the day when I learn that "weather" is not meteorology (object). It is personality (participatory). The seminarians, especially the men, are agitated; I have a devil of a time holding their attention. Their eyes keep wandering to the windows, just like mine did when I was a youngster. When I am done, several post themselves at windows and stare out into the maelstrom. I am wrong: they are not just like me as a child, for one of them asks as I am about to leave if I had noticed how restless they were. I had. "This blizzard," he explains. "We say *the weather is hunting somebody.*" Not like me at all.

They worry about friends and relatives: someone might be out on the tundra on a snowmobile (formerly dog-team) being stalked by the storm. I am amazed. It's not just that weather is viewed as a person; it's that their personality and its personality converge. The event is one of a piece, a whole; it is completely participatory—there are no spectators in this world of theirs.

Earlier in the winter I had witnessed a similar thing out in Toksook Bay, where I was staying at the clinic for the week. Another blizzard. Days of it. The old man walked into the empty waiting room early that morning. I am surprised that he doesn't turn on the television set, as Eskimos often do; he just stands at the window and stares out into the swirling snow and banshee wind—forever, it seems. I walk past him to go out, and he doesn't so much as glance at me. I have wondered if this was on his mind, too: the storm that hunts us.

What does it mean that John Kailukiak's eighteen-year-old son was killed on his snowmobile as he and a group of men were returning to Toksook from a basketball tournament in Newtok? Hurling himself over a bluff by the sea, the boy broke his neck—in a storm.

An accident, says western rationality.

There can be no accidents in the world constituted here, firmly corrects the Eskimo. Accidents are fiction; the very word betrays a failure of explanation—more than that, a failure of being, a failure at "seeing the life in something." Failure to see the co-mingling, the seamlessness, the possession even, of oneself by the wholeself. Accidents, like manuals, are for kass'aqs—for people who think the universe and its ways are discontinuous, like the world of Newtonian physics. The reality of nonlocality: the physicists discovered the truth of this only within my lifetime; the Yup'ik Eskimos and other Native Americans have known its truth for millennia. When I lectured on quantum theory at the seminary, Sarah Owens confided afterward that her grandparents had told her as much.

In *Qanemcikarluni Tekitnarqelartuq / One Must Arrive with a Story to*

Tell, Mike Angaiak points out that the word *ella-* means "world; out-doors; weather; universe; awareness, sense"—all of these together. *Ella-* "connotes consciousness" and "volition"; it "has a mind of its own and is capable of taking offense at callous and disrespectful remarks directed against it. On occasion, people say, it stalks men in the form of winter blizzards and attempts to kill them. Likewise, one of the names for the Supreme Being is *Ellam Yua* 'the owner [spirit] of the universe.' People also use the concept of *ella* . . . in the expression *el-langellemni* 'when I became aware,' in referring to their earliest re-membered experiences of self-awareness and an individuated per-sonality."[3]

The point is, it is *not* an automonous, separate personality that dawns upon one at a certain age: it is awareness of the wholeself.

I now understand better Susie Silook's "Mask of Post-Coloniza-tional Trauma." Made of walrus ivory, wood, sinew, baleen, and fabric, it is the flesh and very meaning of Native Alaska—it is not an object. It shows a crude Christian cross adorned at its four points with mon-strous figures, human and animal, carved in ivory. One of the grotes-queries shows an American flag projecting from its anatomy. It is an-gry, this flesh of Native Alaska; it weeps, like that Yup'ik mask outside the prison. There are two concentric hoops circling the cross, attached to it, like those that one sees on traditional shamans' masks. Rings of power, of the universe. Here, however, the outer ring is clearly broken. Discontinuous. The text scrawled on the cross is signed by Roger Silook: "They sent in their missionaries and killed us with John 3:16."

The missionaries sowed discontinuity. This, I fear, is the atom-split-ting impact of my civilization—not just the missionaries with their verses and hymns and exhortations, but the entire voice of this meta-physic that drives the west. Raven's Children, Coyote's Children, Hare's Children, Spiderwoman's Children, are struggling.

Yet "we will survive," assures a Navajo woman in the confidence of youth: "We will survive as long as the stories are wet with our breath." Still, I worry about them not making it, like that necklace in the display case.[4]

Like Oscar Active.

I met Oscar when I began teaching at the Alaska (Native) Moravian Seminary. I found him an ebullient man, and a man wrestling with something—with his life, I suppose. Determined to change it. Seemingly he was. I had read Richard Adams Carey's *Raven's Children*, about Oscar and Margaret and their family. Carey presents Oscar as a swashbuckling figure, full of life and bravado and bombast, a good-hearted boozer. In his youth Oscar was a legend throughout the delta for his prowess on the basketball court. As an adult he maintained that distinction as coach and referee. Basketball is something that moves Oscar to passion, and the Eskimos have a generous capacity to get passionate about basketball.[5]

Carey's book didn't fit my image of Oscar—too much of a caricature. I found Carey too cool, too much in control of the text—too sure of what's going on. I was living on the delta now, and his delta didn't feel like the one I knew. *Raven's Children* feels more like Carey's story: he lived with Oscar and Margaret for a year, but I think it's more surely his.

Oscar has often sought me out this winter, the winter of my writing this. He telephones whenever he's in Bethel, and sometimes from Kongiganak. I sense that he phones when he's feeling down or vulnerable to drink, which he doesn't do anymore, but he says the urge never leaves.

Oscar called again late last night. He had arrived in Bethel from Kong on a six o'clock bush flight and spent the evening grocery shopping at the Alaska Commercial. I don't know why he needed to talk, though he kept saying Bethel was a "fast" town. Perhaps the old demons were there; perhaps he called to banish them once again, for a few hours. When I met him this morning he said he had run into an old friend "under the weather," meaning the fellow was drunk and probably, too, that he offered Oscar some of his bottle, or at least whetted his thirst for the idea. Maybe this is why Oscar called so late: to be strengthened.

I wound up driving him around town to his errands before he got on a plane and flew back home: the First National Bank and the outboard marine store over by Brown's Slough. We talked much about alcohol in the lives of Yupiit. He said Elsie (his mom) won't blame her son Charlie when he comes home drunk; she blames whoever gave it or sold it to him. Or whoever threw the party. But never Charlie. Oscar had used the same logic on Margaret all those years: he would stagger in and report who gave him the booze, and she would blame the vendor. Never Oscar. Now, however, Oscar was declaring that he realized one had to take the blame for one's actions. I am reminded of eastern woodland Indians in colonial times, blaming Europeans for their drunkenness, since it was they who furnished it after all. Or even blaming the beverage itself.

The logic lives on among the Yup'ik.

Oscar illustrated with a curious analogy. He said that when a man fires up his steamhouse (which is like a sauna) and invites the other men over, and they arrive and he begins pouring buckets of water on the fire, they accuse him of "throwing them out." No! Oscar protested. "He's not grabbing them and tossing them out! It's not his fault! Think about it." His voice is earnest. "It's not that man's fault they're running out of the steam; it's the *steam's* fault! The *steam* is sending them running out the door."

Oscar could not escape traditional logic after all: western logic blames the man with the bucket, whereas Oscar calls the steam to task. With alcohol, the western mind fingers the imbiber, Yupiit blame the vendor (or the drink).

Of his own drinking career, Oscar has told me repeatedly (as he does again this morning) that he's a free man now. This through the power of Christ to transform. And he has managed to get his two brothers to surrender the bottle, too; rather, he credits this power to Christ, not himself. But they seem to be looking to him, and he's very conscious that many people are looking to him for inspiration.

Oscar didn't attend seminary this winter, so he could take the counselor's course at the Philip's Alcohol Treatment Center in Bethel. I went to his graduation in early March. He gave a moving speech, sometimes in tears, with long pauses, to the large room full of guests. Oscar is living his Christianity. He has been hired by the Association of Village Council Presidents to be an alcohol counselor in Kong and vicinity. He's getting a paycheck, and he told me he just got a raise.

Standing outside his mom's we talk about the future of the Yupiit and Oscar's role in this. I warn against the powers of western technology, the technology that Eskimos have found irresistible. Snowmobiles, motorboats, rifles, TVs and VCRs, four-wheelers—the works. And the fact that they are getting more and more hooked on a cash economy—I remind Oscar that he now has a job. I said his children would all have jobs one day (one of his daughters currently works at the Alaska Commercial Company store), and this trend will accelerate over the next few generations.

"What do you think the future of the delta will look like?" I ask. "Oh, about the same as it is now," he confidently replies. "We will still be here." No, I shake my head, it *won't* look the same. The villages will probably dry up, the smaller ones anyway, their youth drifting off (or sprinting) into Anchorage and Fairbanks. I urge him to look at the kids today: the life they see on television or in the movies and magazines and hear on the radio or hear about in school. Plus the government will not keep supporting them and, indeed, is throttling back already. They are dependent on our economy (even the oil they must have to heat their homes), and the *kass'aq* economy will insist, increasingly, that they get jobs for the cash they now cannot live without.

The boat shop: I'm surprised Oscar needs to stop by here. We walk in and he pulls out a slip from his wallet and shows it to the clerk behind the counter. It's a receipt for a brand-new forty-horse Honda outboard, the one sitting right there on the showroom floor. Oscar pats it. The tag reads $4,600. "On Sale," it announces. Oscar had been in sometime earlier and put down a deposit. He's going to borrow the rest from the bank, he tells the man, and needs the serial number off the engine to get his bank loan. I cringe inside. He's in a gay mood as he describes all this in front of the sober clerk. He is telling the clerk and me about the huge engine he bought new last summer (I remember this monster, had watched him install it on his boat); now he is buying this one, too. The big one is too fast, reserved for the trip between Kong and Bethel. The Honda will be used for the fishing, I gather. Driving from the bank to the dealership we had been talking about traditional means of transport and hunting and fishing. He said a kayak is wonderful: in a kayak you don't move too fast through the water—you notice things. He was telling me, as we clattered over the wooden bridge into Lousetown, how an old-timer could paddle down the Kuskokwim and notice every scrap of wood along the shore. But in his powerboat, Oscar concedes, he notices this scarcely at all.

Too fast.

Perception. He is singing the virtues of paddling a kayak as we walk up the steps into the Honda dealership—I wonder if Oscar ignores the irony.

I brought Oscar back to this world as we stood outside his mom's house and chatted. He and his people would become enslaved to these manufactures, and they would lose their old relationship, in truth their powers, with the land and waters. I warned, too, that the game would not give itself so readily anymore—the Gift would likely disappear.

He had as much as confirmed this when I picked him up this morning: he had been out seal hunting yesterday down in Kong and had shot at a seal, and missed. Came home with nothing. Driving to the bank he laughed: he swore those seals have been "trained" already by the other hunters this season, meaning that the seals (especially the spotted) that are around now are extremely wary of men with guns.

They keep their distance.

Oscar seemed to agree that the old relationship would disappear and said plaintively that on nice spring days like this he forbids his kids to watch too much TV—but he still has that down payment on the Honda outboard, and the bank has him in its power now.

While leaning on the counter, Oscar tells the clerk and me that the main reason he is making this quick trip to Bethel is to shop for food; the larder is nearly bare at home. Just a little walrus meat left. At the Alaska Commercial last night he bought pork chops and other grub (he calls it).

Somebody, it may have been the clerk making conversation, says something about the birds coming back. I look at Oscar and flatly declare, "Oscar, it's too soon for the birds to come back," meaning that there is still too much ice and snow. Still too cold. It's early April; I figure the birds won't be back for another two to three weeks. "No, it's not too soon! My freezer is empty and I need them!" I get the eerie sense that this man's need is somehow taken into consideration by the birds in their return; *human need* is somehow an active ingredient, a signal perhaps, in the annual cycle. That is, human need is somehow a determining force in animal behavior—which is what all the myths say. Nevertheless I am dumbfounded when I actually hear it asserted in an outboard marine shop.

The seal had eluded him. He had found a job in the *kass'aq* economy this winter and was bringing in good money. He had been given a raise. But he had to fly to Bethel to shop at the supermarket. Oscar was buying another new engine and putting himself into debt for it and happy about all that. But, again, the freezer is nearly empty of the food of the land. He tells me he sometimes gets tired of native food and craves some "sweet" western food. Like a good hamburger. In Bethel, I imagine.

Seals. Oscar called again one morning a few weeks later from Kongiganak. He needed to talk. He said things were going badly. I probed. It's the seals: he hasn't been able to get a single one this season. He has been out several times since I last saw him in Bethel and says he and his partner haven't even *seen* one. Other men in the village are getting them, but not him.

He blew up at Margaret as a result. She was away for a week in April, and while she was gone the house was clean and he did everything for himself. When she got back, though, he had "expectations" of her: to clean up and prepare food. The problem, he said, is that Margaret lets wild meat go bad out in the arctic entryway (the porch). "It gets rancid." This isn't right, he adds. He upbraids her, but she seems indifferent to his pleadings. And the cleaning up: he means chiefly the kitchen. He says that when she's at home there is junk food on the table, which bothers him.

Oscar is convinced that seals are avoiding him because his home is soiled. By which he's referring to food, mainly: the candy and chips and cookies and soda around, the spoiled meat in the entryway, the dishes not properly cleaned up. He said he's now cleaning out his bowl when he eats, that is, not leaving any food scraps when he's through. He said, too, he was going to take out that bad meat today and bury it in a shallow "grave"—tidy up, so seals will give themselves to him again. I urge him to try again once things are in proper order—not to be discouraged. He seems resolved not to lay the burden of cleaning up on Margaret; he will help.

It embarrasses me, now, to recall how Oscar told the class last winter that he had definite expectations of his wife; this was a vexing issue for him. Like the missionary, shoehorning him into my culture, I had argued against this, saying we could have no expectations of somebody else. I was a blockhead; belatedly I recognize that he was invoking tradition, as with a woman taking care of the animal flesh. Pontificating up there at the front of the class, I didn't appreciate that I was arguing with a gendered sphere of activity within a different cosmology.

Oscar's struggle is ontological—with ancient reality, the aboriginal reality of the world. Like seals watching us. I am amazed as I sit here and realize that a man, a man I know rather well, actually telephoned me to say the seals were watching his home, and it had failed their inspection. And moreover it was chiefly his wife's fault, so he got mad at her. This man is a Yup'ik Eskimo, "he lives three thousand years deep into time," and this is his real world. It is slipping through his fingers even as I write these words.[6]

It occurs to me that people so sensitive to events, to the world—so that it is not outside, but coursing within—cannot withstand perturbations as easily as we westerners do. They are thrown off balance and don't readily recover. We recognize this trait in the terrible time they have with separation or with the loss of a loved one.

It happened that another dear Yup'ik friend of ours died while we were in Alaska. In the days following Elizabeth's funeral, I occasionally visited her family, to console them. I would frequently notice Lila, Elizabeth's sister, cooking and serving food and cleaning up in the kitchen. Her kindness was striking, as was her strength and warmth at the funeral, especially to Elizabeth's children. Lila is clearly a lovely person.

One day I struck up a conversation—Lila and I were alone in the kitchen. She talked about death in her family. A little over twelve years ago she gave birth to a daughter. Her picture hangs there on Elizabeth's dining-room wall—Lila gestures with her chin. When she was three she came down with meningitis and died.

Lila told me forthrightly that she's now an alcoholic—has been assailed by alcohol all her adult life. She said that when her daughter died she began drinking with added fervor, a remark like those I had often heard from the men in jail. Grief drives them to the bottle and chains them there—either grief or fear.

Lila stares dreamily out the kitchen window, across a sink full of dishes. "You know, that was nine years ago . . . but it feels like nine months ago, . . . it feels like nine weeks ago, . . . it feels like nine days ago." She turns and looks straight at me. "It feels like nine seconds ago."

Time is a rubber band up here—as Sarah Owens told me after class, her grandparents knew Einstein's world. The death, which the calendar on the wall says happened long ago, for her did not. It clings to her like smoke. Several years later she had another daughter born to her, at one minute after two o'clock: the exact minute, Lila said, the first girl died.

Accidents, like manuals and inelastic time, are for *kass'aqs*.

Perhaps, over the years, there has been too much trauma for these extraordinarily perceptive, artistic people. The vibration of piano string and guitar, the interval of the internal combustion engine, the grain of driftwood on its way to becoming the mask, the figure leaping out of the walrus tusk: they see and hear and touch and, ultimately, participate in the "becoming" of it. Maybe it's the loss of this perception, this field of force, this "art," which is the mysterious X factor that has driven so many of them to despair, made them susceptible to drink. I don't think liquor is the fundamental problem; there is something more powerful, more profound, anterior to that. I sense they have lost something of the Story: they no longer synthesize the cosmos with their hands, their music and dance, clothing and homes and tools, their language, even their names. Living ceases to be artful, cosmically artful. The art they do now is fragmented, disconnected; it doesn't speak one seamless Story.

We discussed this in prison one day. Walter Kenegak delivered a speech on the matter—an outstanding piece of oratory, ranking with some of the finest by Native Americans over the centuries. Quietly, punctuating with silence every so often, he declares how their ancestors were laughed at for their clothing (yet it was warmer, he whispers, than what they got in return), the sod houses, their transportation (sled dogs and kayaks). They were told their beliefs were primitive and barbaric. Their spiritual code, the masks and dances—all pagan. Shamans were satanic. Everything valuable in life was discredited, scorned, held in contempt. They were shown dazzling things, hardware and such, and they coveted these. Yet these very things are strangely aloof: rifles and snowmobiles and motorboats and so on. They don't have the feel of the earth, of intimacy, about them. Something coolly artificial inheres in the new gadgets. Here in prison things are fake. The table he is leaning on, for instance—"not even real wood," he muses, feeling it, as though searching for its reality. "I can't put my feet on the ground in here." He said, in the end, that it's all like a bad dream. He tells me privately he often prays that he won't wake up in the morning.

Walter Kenegak, a celebrated artist, can no longer create the world.

When Walter had finished, Qavcicuaq described how the teachers arrived and taught them things in school. Many of them valuable, he felt. Yet they killed the soul of the language, literally smiting the children when they spoke Yup'ik—the new world order spoke a different reality. The native tongue became something private, subversive; in any case, it was not now the conversation of the real world, which *kass'aqs* now controlled.

One carved out the masks, the drums, and tools of social discourse through a different syntax, where reality itself necessarily, ominously, shapeshifted into something unfamiliar. Something aloof, incapable of "putting its feet on the ground," as Kenegak lamented.

I had this confirmed when I stopped by the Jesuit mission house in Kenegak's home village, to visit the aging priest who has been the missionary up here for years. The village is solely Roman Catholic. Father J. and I come round to the subject of Eskimo dances, which he said the missionaries now support, seeing as they're now purely recreational, he says. In the old days, he continues in his dignified manner, many of the songs and dances were composed by the shamans, and the church denounced these performances. The missionaries forbade, as well, all masks made by shamans. Back when he first arrived, people were using wooden masks, but these were difficult to carve, he said, and so the art was lost—though I don't believe him. They must have always been difficult to make, yet that had never stopped the carvers. No, the missionary *reality* is what stopped them. In time, continued the priest, wooden masks were replaced by paper-bag masks, and eventually masks just about disappeared. Today almost none are used in the dancing; when they are, it is a noteworthy exception.

Wooden masks to paper bags to nothing at all. In the two years I lived on the Yukon-Kuskokwim delta, I saw masked dancing just once.

The *kass'aq* knew nothing of *yua*—the inherent person, the spirit, of each object in this talking world. The white man was observational, icy, detached, attaching anthropological labels to everything. Western reality lacked the power to enter the inner rings of energy of the mask, that awesome realm the Yup'ik had known before the first Russian turned up, carrying the logic of the rifle, or the first missionary stepped ashore, bearing John 3:16.

"For God so loved the world, that he gave his only begotten Son, that whosoever believeth in him should not perish, but have everlasting life"—that's what it said.[7] This did not make sense. For they *were* perishing, by the thousands. It's right there in John Kilbuck's journals: the slaughter by epidemic disease. Harold Napoleon is right. Nor is Harold's post-traumatic stress disorder an unreasonable hypothesis, though no official I've met in bush Alaska pays it any attention.

What the survivors are left with (I deliberately choose the present tense) is unresolved grief. Like Lila Kamarov, who is a Christian, who is an alcoholic, who mourns for her daughter—all of these. She is also, above all, a lovely and kind person, which is what her sister Elizabeth kept tearfully telling her when visiting her in jail several years ago—like many Yupiit, Lila is also, in the *kass'aq* reality, an ex-con.

But I don't accept that. Lila is Yup'ik; she lives in a quantum world; this is her being, her *yua*, her perception. If Christianity has any hope of genuinely healing these people, Christ will have to enter that atomic ring of the shaman's mask and dance.

There was an old woman in Toksook Bay recently, Sally (Lila's other sister) told me, who was full of sorrow over the death of her daughter. She grieved for ever so long, maybe even nine years, for all I know. She was out on the tundra picking berries one day, the memory of her daughter, as always, vivid before her. And she began weeping. As she wept she began to hear singing behind her, even though she was very hard of hearing. A person, singing. The song started softly, then grew louder and louder. She turned and saw behind her, on a pond, a loon singing—singing to her. The loon was standing up on the water, flapping its wings—Sally mimicked. Loon was standing up flapping her wings and singing words the woman could understand.

Loon was telling this old woman that she had mourned long enough; it was time to stop now, sang loon. This freed her, released her from her grief. And she stopped grieving.

I learned one morning that Lila was back in prison. A several-month sentence for breaking probation—now serving time, ironically. Like the polar bear in the lobby of the Regal Alaskan, she is imprisoned by the mind that thinks in numbers. In her grief, in the travail of her life, the Eskimo has become criminal—so my *kass'aq* reality views her. I telephoned her; she wept when I said I wanted to come visit her. But, then, I teach at the seminary, and I have read Christ—"I was in prison and you visited me"—and I believe him. I believe Whitman, too—"and see myself in prison shaped like another man." Lila said she couldn't sleep last night. Lying on her cot, staring into the void, she kept asking herself, "Why was I conceived? Why was I born into this life of suffering?"

They all ask themselves that. Qavcicuaq is back in again, too, on the other side of the concrete wall, wondering about his story. Robert is locked up in Seward, and he wants to disappear, which he illustrates by closing his forefinger and thumb together. Kenegak vainly feels the table for familiar reality, and beseeches God not to wake him up into the morning. Into this nightmare.

I did, finally, see a live bear in Alaska. In June, when the red salmon were spawning up the Russian River. One day the two young men operating the weir across the river, just below Lower Russian Lake, spotted the returning Swimmer, by the thousands. When the news hit Anchorage it triggered a stampede like this state hadn't seen since Gold Rush days. Unfortunately for Nina and me it happened right when we were planning on a backpacking trip to the Russian Lakes—two magnificent glacier-fed lakes that we had camped beside just weeks before.

We went anyway, hoping to avoid the hordes of fishermen. They were lined up in their vehicles, round the clock, awaiting a signal from the harried rangers, who would admit them to the park for a strict two hours apiece. There they took up their stations, nearly elbow to elbow, on the lower stretch below the falls. The trail begins in that same park, though, happily for us, the first few miles follow a course well away from the river—we knew that once we found a parking spot, we could avoid the mob.

I spoke to a grizzly bear that night. Late, on the trail, still light (this is the Alaska summer, after all), twenty yards ahead of us, going our way. We rounded a bend and there he was. "They say they are humans," muses Alma Keyes. "Back then [say the elders] people used to transform into animals. Many things were visible when the earth was thin . . . , not the way it is today. They predicted that animals and other things that were visible at that time would no longer be visible [as people]." So with bears: they say they are still people even if one might not see one as a person. "If a person doesn't assume the bear has bad characteristics and talks to it in a normal tone, it could understand."

"Its ears moved when I talked to it," she remembered of an encounter from her childhood. "They would move, and it appeared to be listening to me. They are not to be criticized. I've seen them at close range, . . . and I've always given them the utmost respect."[8]

So did I. I told him we were not there to hunt him (so many campers carry rifles or shotguns or handguns). I told him it was okay. I asked his permission to camp in his place.

He turned and listened, just as Alma Keyes recalled. "Evidently, the bear can reveal itself to a person if it wants to. If a person wanted to see it, it will come to that person. It will reciprocate according to how people treat it. If a person mistreats it, it will mistreat that person."[9]

We follow him down the trail. He's young and he whimpers as he glides along (bears glide, they don't walk), not using one of his forepaws—my guess is that he had a fishing lure caught in it. A young man, a fisherman, catches up with us while all this is going on. He is terrified. He asks if I have a can of pepper spray to repel the bear— Dark One, who has merely looked at me, and listened. "No," I snap back at him. "All one needs is courtesy." Shotguns, rifles, handguns, pepper spray. Or courtesy. We have succumbed to fear; we have criminalized Bear. We continue walking, and the young fellow sticks close to me. He had heard other fishermen talk of this same bear, it seems, judging from its age; the Dark One, too, had been hauling in salmon over the past few days.

The Swimmer returning to its place of origin to spawn: I knew I was in the presence of a mighty force. They leaped the falls, they muscled their way up the chutes, they rested by the scores in the eddies. And when they got to the weir erected by Fish and Game, they were confounded: this was not part of their reality. The River, the beginning and ending, always gave them access. Here was a gate. My kind wanted to count them, of all things—measure them. Every so often a young ecologist with a counter (like the kind theater ushers use) emerges from a hut, climbs out onto the fence, and opens a narrow gate, allowing the Swimmer through, unmindful that they have wasted precious stored energy (for they don't eat on this journey, but live off their fat) marking time or struggling against the barricade. And with his thumb, clicks away with his number machine.

The Haida, from the Islands at the Boundary of the World, tell about the Creek Women, the Qaasghajiina. "In each of the headwaters of the major streams the Creek Woman lives. She watches over the salmon people who congregate there. Her lover is Sghaana, the Killer Whale. He cruises out to sea, just by the reef, watching the river mouth. Having knowledge of the weather, he sends the fair-weather clouds, which means the fish are coming to the headwaters. Then they will be guarded by the Creek Woman." Clearly "there is a complex web of patterns, a deep mystery going on in these rivers," observes Sean Kane, involving "a sexual relationship between a goddess of the river and her mate, the whale, a being of power in his most powerful manifestation." "All the stories," he warns, "say that you don't want to mess with these people."[10]

Although we surely do mess with them, for my society has no such organic stories. Meanwhile, the majority of us regard the native stories as mere juvenile entertainment. We, in our ontology, see no familiar or verifiable reality in these stories.

Hence the fishermen stand shoulder to shoulder along the riverbank in what they call Combat Fishing, tossing gaily colored lures and dragging murderous barbs across the back of Swimmer moving in dark clouds mere inches beneath the surface. Flesh snagged, Swimmer fights with powerful strokes against the man with the reel, either ripping out flesh or snapping the line, to carry then, for the remainder of its journey, its life, a thorn. Lime green, fluorescent orange, crimson red: the colors flicker just beneath the surface, the skin of the world, sometimes two or three to a body.

We did some counting ourselves: by our estimate, one in eight had a lure impaled, one in three had flesh ripped out of the back. "And like fishing too, you know, they hurt lot of fish like that": Elsie, Oscar's mother, shoves a finger in her mouth and pulls hard, disfiguring her face. "And it *hurts* us, you know! Even when they have meeting and people talkin', they don't listen to us. I feel like putting a hook on those men, you know, and pull, you know, how they feel, you know! Lot of fish die that way too."[11]

We encountered a man, an Englishman, on the platform above the falls, watching Swimmer power its way up. He said he was out the day before with one of the guide services down on the lower river, snagging salmon. An hour or so of this nonsense and he handed the guide's rod and reel back to him. "This isn't fishing; this is barbarism!" The incredulous guide, who had no other story but this one in his hand, regarded him as crazy.

There are no real stories for us about Creek Woman, Swimmer, and Killer Whale.

Or Bear. He was whimpering, holding up one of his forepaws. I couldn't see, but I imagined one of those lures stuck in his flesh, too. For others, caught in the throat. Elsie, that old Yup'ik in the Bethel Senior Center, knew about that. She still lived by the stories of the *real people*.

I once spoke at the Yukon-Kuskokwim Correctional Center on bears, on their meaning, their potency, and the esteem Native Americans traditionally had for them. I did this to encourage the inmates, to affirm and credit the old ways.

Forty Eskimo men and women are crammed in a small, stuffy room with no windows or ventilation. And yet they are attentive, some of them fervently so, as I speak for two hours, with a small break. We are in a bear's den, I believe. I tell them that by invoking the name "bear" I have summoned the spirit of the creature into the room, even as I speak. This, I am told later, unnerves them.

Toward the end I ask if anyone knows a bear story. I get two re-
sponses. The alcohol counselor (a young *kass'aq* woman who is sitting
in) has a joke to tell.

Question: How do you tell the difference between a brown bear
and a black bear?
Answer: If the bear chases you up a tree and shakes it, it's a black
bear. If the bear chases you up the tree, shakes it, shakes you
down, and eats you, it's a brown bear.

I smile. I ask if she has any personal story about bears. No, she says,
just this little joke.

There is a long pause. Andrew puts up his hand, and tells with a
sense of wonderment how he and some friends were out hunting one
day and spotted a large bear not far off. They shot it and watched it run
into a small alder and willow thicket, beyond which was a broad stretch
of mossy tundra. Entering the small grove to retrieve what they are certain will be a dead animal, they discover it has vanished: it is not in the
thicket, nor has it run out across the tundra. Dark One has simply disappeared. "Kopit is gone. He has been there, he has not been there.
Kopit has Power."[12]

This is the only story I hear in public. Chatting with one of the men
after class, I ask if he has had experiences with bears. He has, he answers in a low voice; he has gone bear hunting many times. When he
was a boy, out hunting with his grandfather, the old man made him
put his hand inside the hot, steaming body of a slain bear. He knows
bears, and they know him—but he wouldn't talk about it in that class-
room. "There used to be sayings of the animals: they got ears on the
tundra. . . . And that bear would know which person it is [who said
something]. The animal would hear what that person said."[13]

There is a serious difference here in cognition. On one hand is the aboriginal perception that human beings must learn to "know as we are known," by something more plastic in scope and shape and substance than mere human self can contain. And on the other, the more typical western philosophical declaration that "I, *Homo,* am the knower," and, moreover, "The world is what my knowledge pictures it to be."[14]

The cognitive center of gravity is different for the western and the Native American mind. Reality, as a result, wears a different face for me than it does for them. "We are inquisitive creatures," writes the sociologist Parker J. Palmer, searching the depths of the western intellect; we are "forever wanting to get inside of things and discover their hidden secrets. Our curiosity is piqued by the closed and wrapped box. We want to know its contents, and when the contents are out we want to open them too—down to the tiniest particle of their construction." "We are also creatures attracted by power," he continues. "We want knowledge to control our environment, each other, ourselves. Since many of the boxes we have opened contained secrets that have given us more mastery over life, curiosity and control are joined as the passion behind our knowing." He is a perceptive man. Notice that what he has summed up, here, bears an uncanny resemblance to Trickster: the creature passionate in his curiosity and his urge to control.[15]

No, say Trickster's Children; this is not the proper way of the human being. Driving with Sam Berlin around Bethel one day, I remark that I have heard he is a formidable hunter—realize, as you read this page, that I was creating a distinctly western envelope of reality in that seemingly innocent question. With my words I am casting the world and me—the world and Sam Berlin—into Martin Buber's famous I-It. But Sam does not go for my bait. No, he answers, he is not a great hunter. I try hooking him again: "Have you ever hunted bears?" (I am relentless). "Occasionally black bears," he responds, unperturbed (I am moving him into my cognitive realm, reality flickers between *his* and *mine*). "What about brown bears?" (I seize my advantage).

"No!" I have pulled Raven's Child far enough. It stops with the Brown One. He snaps the line. "They're too powerful." Sam fails to elaborate, though I know he means "too spiritually powerful."

I am quiet, chastened. But he's not done with me, this man. Like Kopit, he's going to teach me something, try to shift my cognitive reference, move me into the reality of the *real people.* "I know that if my family were starving, a brown bear would give itself to me." I-It has shifted to I-Thou. Cognition has sprung back into the Yup'ik domain, where reality wears a face that looks perilously like one's own and that of a bear at the same time.

Who, then, am I? "I can be a frog or a fox and still be a person," acknowledges Robin Ridington; "if my family is starving, a brown bear will give itself to me," insists Sam Berlin.[16]

This is exactly my fear.

Am I finally discovering Native America? And is this something I can *know* without becoming *known* in turn? This is an unsettling thought, one I take up in the following section. The implication is that "the personhood of the known enters the relation as well. The known seeks to know me even as I seek to know it." A disturbing thought indeed.[17]

Our conversation with the *real people,* as they call themselves, is both epistemological and ontological. As I continue babbling on to Sam about his hunting, he cuts me off. Sam tells me I must come caribou hunting with him next winter—the personhood of the known now joins the conversation. With that I fall silent. Not yet, Sam, I think to myself—I'm not yet ready for that.

SEVEN

A Witch's Story

Thought-Woman, Ts'its'tsi'nako, "is sitting in her room / and whatever she thinks about / appears." So begins a remarkable story of death and rebirth by Leslie Marmon Silko, a Laguna Pueblo.

> She thought of her sisters,
> Nau'ts'ity'i and I'tcts'ity'i,
> and together they created the Universe
> this world
> and the four worlds below.
>
> Thought-Woman, the spider,
> named things and
> as she named them
> they appeared.
>
> She is sitting in her room
> thinking of a story now
>
> I'm telling you the story
> she is thinking.[1]

This is consciousness far greater than ourselves, quickening us as we assent to it, and yet, notice, not our fabrication. Recall the Oglala seer

Nicholas Black Elk telling John Neihardt his vision of the Six Grandfathers. The Sixth, the Spirit of the Earth he calls him, grows younger even as he, Black Elk, beholds him—contracts backward in the cone of time until the old man finally recognizes him as himself.

The Spirit of the Earth—yet we don't give birth to it. It conceives us. To know as we are known: here, coiled within this powerful phrase, lies the template for Native American reality. From its DNA is born the host of stories that define the way of the human being, here. Where the land and sea, rivers and lakes and mountains and plains, the tundra, the sky, bid us attend to their spirit, their visage, not our own.

More than half a century ago, Aldo Leopold, troubled by his own alienation from the ways of the earth, urged in this spirit that we learn to "think like a mountain." Before him, John Muir escaped the cornfields of his father's Presbyterian farm to worship before the unplowed wind and sky of the Sierra Nevada. And well before Muir, a short, "firmly built" Concord surveyor learned to think like a pond and its encircling woods and fields and marshes. "It was a pleasure and a privilege to walk with him," Emerson declared of his friend and neighbor—Thoreau "knew the country like a fox or a bird," marveled Emerson, "and passed through it as freely by paths of his own. He knew every track in the snow or on the ground, and what creature had taken this path before him. One must submit abjectly to such a guide, and the reward was great."[2] One is not surprised to read of the dying Thoreau, asked by a zealous inquirer if he has made his peace with God, responding that in truth God and he have never quarreled. "So much knowledge of Nature's secret and genius few others possessed; none in a more large and religious synthesis."[3]

Yet even one as engaged as Thoreau could reach a point where the certainties of "who we are" grew shaky and clammy, an experience that disturbed him profoundly. It happened as he labored up the granitic flanks of Mount Katahdin in northern Maine, to stand finally at its summit, in Mosaic terror, before something more powerful and real than he had imagined. Thoreau found himself before the strange membrane of the world, and as he peered through he trembled at its implications.

Loren Eiseley describes the moment: "From the estimate of heights, of geological observation, Thoreau enters what he calls a 'cloud factory' where mist 'was generated out of that pure air as fast as it flowed away.' Stumbling onward over what he calls 'the raw materials of a planet,'" Thoreau exclaims: "It was vast, Titanic, and such as man never inhabits. Some part of the beholder, even some vital part, seems to escape through the loose grating of his ribs as he ascends. He is more lone than you can imagine. . . . His reason is dispersed and shadowy, more thin and subtile, like the air. Vast, Titanic, inhuman Nature has got him at disadvantage, caught him alone, and pilfers him of some of his divine faculty."[4]

The climber feels the mountain and its copulating mist perceiving him; the locus of knowledge, of *knowing*, has ominously shifted. "What is this Titan that has possession of me?" he cries out. "Talk of mysteries! Think of our life in nature,—daily to be shown matter, to come in contact with it,—rocks, trees, wind on our cheeks! the *solid* earth! the *actual* world! the *common sense! Contact! Contact! Who* are we? *where* are we?"[5]

Think like a mountain, Mr. Leopold? Thoreau got to the summit and discovered that the mountain thought him. "From the streaming cloud-wrack of a mountain summit," whispers Eiseley, transfixed by the scene, "the voice floats out to us before the fog closes in once more. In that arena of rock and wind we have moved for a moment in a titanic world and hurled at stone titanic questions. We have done so because a slight, gray-eyed man walked up a small mountain which, by some indefinable magic, he transformed into a platform for something, as he put it, 'not kind to man.'"[6]

Loren Eiseley's reaction is really the more interesting; his horror leapfrogs Thoreau's passing doubt, taking us into a protracted existential crisis, Eiseley's own, which in some degree speaks to all of us in western culture.

This thing "made out of Chaos and Old Night," this "force not bound to be kind to man"—this becomes Eiseley's lifelong fear: that the earth is ungracious after all. Born to a father who was often absent and who died when the boy was barely a man, of a mother who was altogether difficult and maddeningly deaf and, he was convinced, deranged, Eiseley grew up with an intractable sense of homelessness and wonder over who he was. As an adult he would live this anguish in the pages of his numerous books and essays—he became a celebrated anthropologist and historian of science and a sought-after public speaker—a quest his scholarly pursuits merely reinforced. Poring over Darwin's revelations, he warns: "We are process, not reality, for reality is an illusion of the daylight—the light of our particular day. In a fortnight, as aeons are measured, we may lie silent in a bed of stone, or, as has happened in the past, be figured in another guise." And again: "Instability lies at the heart of the world. With uncanny foresight folklore has long toyed symbolically with what the nineteenth century was to proclaim a reality—namely, that form is an illusion of the time dimension, that the magic flight of the pursued hero or heroine through frogskin and wolf coat has been, and will continue to be, the flight of all men."[7]

Eiseley felt keenly the icy indifference of the earth's evolutionary and geologic process, not to mention the unearthly chill of a doomed universe. There was a deep sorrow that clung to the man—the melancholy of a prophet. Behind the blandishments of nature Eiseley perceived a deeper force that was wholly unconcernd with man's dreams or even his welfare. In the early 1960s, at the height of his powers, he opens his autobiography with these lines: "It is the ruse of the fox; I learned it long ago. In the pages which follow I will show you fear, I will show you terror. But huntsman, let us have one thing clear: I am a man, in flight. Though I am an archaeologist by profession," there are places "that for my life I would not enter. . . . Though I sit in a warm room beneath a light and compose these lines, they are all of night, of outer darkness, and inner terrors. They are the annals of a long and uncompleted running"—the hopeless journey of our species. For nature is at heart a huntsman and mankind itself is prey. "I set . . . down" these final words "lest the end come on me unaware, as it does upon all fugitives." Before extinguishing the light, he scrawls: "There is a shadow on the wall before me. It is my own. I write in a borrowed room at midnight. Tomorrow," in geological time, "the shadow on the wall will be that of another"—the shape no longer human. "Very well, huntsman, let the hunt begin."[8]

Not kind to man: we are back in the roiling surf on the Carolina coast, where a young Frenchman is being swept off his feet and flung onto the sand at the feet of cheering savages—and he is afraid. We lie anchored at the mouth of a Newfoundland cove, all of us starving, wondering if we can feed ourselves with dignity in this godforsaken land—and we are afraid. We are with the tight-lipped sea captain about to run down and seize a swimming bear "by main force," and with the man who lifted his .338 and shot that monster now stuffed in the lobby of the Regal Alaskan—and we fear it. Like the young man who believes in assailing that grizzly bear up ahead with pepper spray, because bears and savages and the land itself, here, are "not bound to be kind to man." We stand with the missionaries who mutter a paternoster and cross themselves before the shamans, the masks, the dances, and fear them as demonic and call them so.

Altogether neglecting to realize that in our fears we kindle the wildfire of fear in others—this is the awful metaphysic. America has always been a force "out there" to the majority of us non-natives. Study carefully the corpus of Jacques Cartier's journals, all three voyages, and witness the engine of this metaphysic at work: the place is alien to him, heathenish (he recites the Gospels, he plants Christian crosses hither and yon), and he is altogether mightily fearful of it and its indigenes. His morbid fears ignite terror in them.

They are most clearly not afraid of him initially:

> The same day we visited one of these islands where we came across five Indians who were hunting for game. They came to meet our boats without fear or alarm, and in as familiar a manner as if they had seen us all their lives. And when our long-boats grounded, one of those Indians took the Captain in his arms and carried him on shore as easily as if he had been a six-year-old child, so strong and big was that Indian. . . . We asked them by signs if this was the way to Hochelaga? They made clear to us that it was, and that we had still a three days' journey thither.

> And on reaching Hochelaga, there came to meet us more than a thousand persons, both men, women and children, who gave us as good a welcome as ever father gave to his son, making great signs of joy; for the men danced in one ring, the women in another and the children also apart by themselves. After this they brought us quantities of fish, and of their bread which is made of Indian corn, throwing so much of it into our long-boats that it seemed to rain bread.

> As we drew near to their village, great numbers of the inhabitants came out to meet us and gave us a hearty welcome. . . . And we were led by our guides and those who were conducting us into the middle of the village. . . . They signed to us that we should come to a halt here, which we did. And at once all the girls and women of

the village, some of whom had children in their arms, crowded about us, rubbing our faces, arms and other parts of the upper portions of our bodies which they could touch, weeping for joy at the sight of us and giving us the best welcome they could. They made signs to us also to be good enough to put our hands upon their babies.[9]

Thus did Cartier arrive at the Iroquoian town of Hochelaga, where Montreal now stands, almost certainly the first European to reach these people. Of his first voyage, the year before, testing the Gaspé coastline, he describes having his longboat pursued by scores of Indians in large canoes,

dancing and showing many signs of joy, and of their desire to be friends. . . . But for the reason already stated, that we had only one of our long-boats, we did not care to trust to their signs and waved to them to go back, which they would not do but paddled so hard that they soon surrounded our long-boat with their seven canoes. And seeing that no matter how much we signed to them, they would not go back, we shot off over their heads two small cannon. On this they began to return towards the point, and set up a mar-vellously loud shout, after which they proceeded to come on again as before. And when they had come alongside our long-boat, we shot off two fire-lances which scattered among them and fright-ened them so much that they began to paddle off in very great haste, and did not follow us any more.[10]

First contact: this is what it was actually like.

With time, within a short time indeed, the Indians become over-whelmed by a wondrous horror of this man and his potential. Not merely his powers of artillery, though these are impressive enough (firing off a few rounds of cannon for their entertainment, they "be-gan to howl and to shriek in such a very loud manner that one would have thought hell had emptied itself there"—it had), but, more pro-foundly, his awesome capacity for sheer fear.[11]

> And on the following day . . . the Captain went ashore with a num-ber of his men to set out buoys and landmarks that the ships might be laid up with more care. We found a large number of the people of the village [Stadacona] coming to meet us, and among the rest, Donnacona [the chief], our two Indians [Donnacona's sons, whom Cartier had kidnapped the year before, taken to France, and brought back with him on this second voyage], and their friends, who kept apart on a point of land on the bank of the river, without one of them coming towards us, as did the others, who were not of their party. And the Captain, being informed of their presence, ordered some of his men to accompany him, and went towards the point of land where they were, and found Don-nacona, Taignoagny, Dom Agaya and several others of their party. After they had mutually saluted each other, Taignoagny began to make a speech and to say to the Captain, that Chief Donnacona was vexed that the Captain and his people carried so many weapons when they on their side carried none. To this the Captain replied that for all Donnacona's grief, he would not cease to carry them since such was the custom in France as Taignoagny well knew.[12]

Cartier's report of his third and final voyage exists only in fragment, in quaint translation by Richard Hakluyt, whose version is all that sur-vives. These are its last words: "And when we were arrived at our Fort, wee understoode by our people, that the Savages of the Countrey came not any more about our Fort as they were accustomed, to bring us fish, and that they were in a wonderful doubt and feare of us. Wherefore our Captaine, having bene advertised by some of our men which had bene at Stadacona to visite them, that there were a wonderfull number of the Countrey people [Indians] assembled together, caused all things in our fortresse to bee set in good order: etc."[13]

This, I think, has been our most devastating and enduring impact on this continent and its indigenes: Europeans furnished it all in fear. After the wreck of the *Santa Maria* off the coast of Hispaniola and the remarkable rescue of crew and cargo by local natives, Columbus decided to leave behind a small outpost of men and supplies till his return. La Navidad, as he called it, was a fort erected where none was needed: these people were unbelievably generous and "timorous." But the admiral was by now a firm believer in his own lurid fantasy of the man-eating Caribs who, he imagined, preyed upon these gentle, unarmed people. Thus, shortly before leaving, he shot off a cannon at the hull of the *Santa Maria*, derelict out there on the reef, to brief the natives on "how far the lombard carried, and how it pierced the side of the ship, and how the charge went far out to sea." Next, he "had the people of the ships arm themselves and engage in a sham fight, telling the cacique that he was not to fear the Caribs even if they should come. All this the admiral says that he did, that the king [chief] might regard the Christians whom he left as friends and might be frightened and have fear of them."[14]

"But they are crafty, thievish, and treacherous," sputters the French baron Jean de Poutrincourt, somewhere on the coast of northern Maine, "and, naked though they be, one cannot escape from their fingers; for if one turns away his gaze but for a moment, and they see a chance of stealing a knife, hatchet, or anything else, they will never fail to do so, and will put the theft between their buttocks, or hide it in the sand with their foot so cunningly that one will not perceive it. I have read in a book of travels to Florida that the natives of that province are of the same nature, and use the same industry in thieving"—a charge that is to be repeated all over North America. "And in truth it is no wonder if a poor naked folk be thievish, but when there is malice in the heart it is no longer excusable. These people are of such a nature that they must be worked on by fear, for if one tries friendship and gives them too easy access, they will plan some treachery, as has frequently been noticed."[15]

Ah, responds the native, "you are covetous, and are neither generous nor kind; as for us, if we have a morsel of bread we share it with our neighbor." And also, "seeing that we [French] are richer than they, we should give them liberally whatever we have." The missionary Heckewelder, thirty years resident among the Lenape, elaborates. "They think that he [the Creator] made the earth and all that it contains for the common good of mankind; when he stocked the country that he gave them with plenty of game, it was not for the benefit of a few, but of all. . . . From this principle, hospitality flows as from its source." Hospitality, he says flatly, "is not a virtue but a strict duty. Hence they are never in search of excuses to avoid giving, but freely supply their neighbour's wants from the stock prepared for their own use. They give and are hospitable to all, without exception, and will always share with each other and often with the stranger, even to their last morsel." Indeed, they would prefer to "lie down themselves on an empty stomach, than have it laid to their charge that they had neglected their duty, by not satisfying the wants of the stranger, the sick or the needy." Doubtless remembering his own experience, he emphasizes that the stranger has a special "claim to their hospitality, . . . on account of his being at a distance from his family and friends, and . . . because he has honoured them by his visit, and ought to leave them with a good impression upon his mind."[16]

"They are so generous and liberal towards one another that they seem not to have any attachment to the little they possess," confirms the Recollet priest Le Clercq, more than a century earlier, "for they deprive themselves thereof very willingly and in very good spirit the very moment when they know that their friends have need of it." Friends and strangers are treated alike: "Hospitality is in such great esteem among our Gaspesians that they make almost no distinction between the home-born and the stranger. They give lodging equally to the French and to the Indians who come from a distance, and to both they distribute generously whatever they have obtained in hunting and in the fishery, giving themselves little concern if the strangers remain among them weeks, months, and even entire years." Adding, "it would be a shame, and a kind of fault worthy of eternal reproach, if it was known that an Indian, when he had provisions in abundance, did not make gift thereof to those whom he knew to be in want and in need"— the extraordinary ontology of the Gift, free of fear, that was realized throughout aboriginal America.[17]

Some sixty years ago Gontran de Poncins wintered with the Canadian Inuit and was appalled to find them plundering his provisions— openly helping themselves to everything in his larder. He quickly discovered, however, that they understood his wish to live among them and his expressions of friendship as absolute—just as Poutrincourt encountered centuries earlier, though he didn't stay around long enough to learn the lesson—and that having redistributed his belongings they would now take care of this man *entirely:* feed him, clothe him in furs, house him, and guide him wherever he wished to go. But they would share his tea and sugar, and flour and rice—like family.

We now realize, unfortunately too late, that Europeans were being adopted.

Western practices of hospitality and private property were clearly a different order of experience from native perceptions of hospitality—read Captain James Cook's journals for a spectacular illustration of this. Once the principle is established that natives are "crafty, thievish, and treacherous," it follows easily that "these people ... must be worked on by fear"—a doctrine that cost Cook his life.

Fear. Let us not forget that it was the Christians who imported the personification of terror, Satan himself, over here. The Reverend John Eliot's "Day-Breaking If Not the Sun-Rising of the Gospell with the Indians in New-England" records their reaction, through a list of poignant questions put to him one day by a group of hopeful converts still struggling with this strange new reality:

> (1) Because some Indians say that we [Indians] must pray to the Devill for all good, and some to God; they would know whether they might pray to the Devill or no. (2) They said they heard the word humiliation oft used in our Churches, and they would know what that meant? (3) Why the English call them Indians, because before they came they had another name? (4) What a Spirit is? (5) Whether they should beleeve Dreames? (6) How the English come to know God so much and they so little?

"To all which they had fit answers," assures Eliot.[18]

Farther north, in Gaspesia (Nova Scotia), the priests catechized Micmac children in the terrors of "being burned in Hell," and, sadly, these gentle people believed them. "Our poor Gaspesians were formerly tormented by the Devil, who often beat them very cruelly, and even terrified them by hideous spectres and horrible phantoms," causing them "so much terror that sometimes they fell dead upon the spot."

On the contrary, these people had no such cosmic reality before Father Chrestien Le Clercq and his fellow missionaries, Catholic and

Protestant, arrived bearing such tidings. The missionary conjured up the very fear, the terrible phantom, he thundered against.

We detect Le Clercq smiling indulgently as he reports how one day a certain man "conceived . . . the plan of killing him who had tormented them cruelly for so long a time."

> He even assured the Indians that he had no doubt as to the success of his undertaking, and that there was nothing for them to do but to rejoice, for, he said, he knew exactly the route by which the Devil came among them. It was a little brook between two rocks, where he undertook to camp with his gun between his arms. One of our Frenchmen having found him in that posture asked him what he was doing, and whom he was awaiting. "Whom am I awaiting," answered he fiercely, "I am awaiting the Devil in order to kill him, to tear his heart from his belly, and after that to remove his scalp, in punishment and vengeance for the outrages and the insults which he has done us up to the present time. Too long has he been tormenting us, and the time has now arrived for me to deliver the Gaspesians from these misfortunes. Let him come; let him appear. I await him without stirring."[19]

This devil business was a new and dreadful pestilence upon the land—this the Micmac well knew, as did their New England brethren to the south, as did the natives throughout the length and breadth of the continent. The man who infected the Micmac story with the tale of the devil and his lake of fire blithely sailed home shortly thereafter, his scalp and heart intact.

Nevertheless, the fear would remain and multiply, in behavior not unlike the other deadly contagions transported here, though in retrospect even more damaging, grafting itself onto the land, infecting the stories and the lives of the indigenes themselves. I recognized this really for the first time when I lectured on alcohol to the Eskimos in the Bethel prison. We had a candid discussion; many in the room were alcoholics, indeed, were violent when drunk. One man volunteered that he feels he sees things clearly, and the world appears fine, when he drinks; only when drunk does he feel genuinely in control of his life. I know this man well; I have spent many hours with him in and out of jail. He is a strong person; he hints that he might even be a shaman. Yet I am struck by the fear that clings to him always, even in his native village. He seems acutely aware of the white presence in his native land, a presence that has changed the old realities of his universe—and he's deeply fearful. Fearful of the present and the future, for his children. Another man in the room said that when he drinks he feels invincible: he's strong, finally. I then asked the men if that meant they were afraid when sober. Many admitted that in truth they are.

Leaf back through the old records of European discovery and colonization and try to locate a reference to that initial, diabolical moment when the natives became hooked on alcohol. For at first they spurned it—the records, such as they are, say so clearly. Natives thought it tasted bad, and some even suspected the red wine, favored by the French, of being nothing other than human blood. Things must have become confusing indeed when the priests celebrated the mass with the blood of their God. Be that as it may, the first Europeans drank heavily, especially the fishing fleets, with captains paying the deckhands a portion of their wages in liquor. Distilled spirits and fortified (alcohol-enriched) wines, both just beginning to be mass-produced in sixteenth-century Europe, were widely acclaimed throughout the continent and British Isles as medicinal and prophylactic and highly nutritious, plus safer than urban drinking water. Indeed, the early French chroniclers in eastern Canada wrote how they and their confrères were drinking wine to ward off the Canadian *maladie du païs* (scurvy) and earnestly pressing it on the *sauvages* for the same reason (though the native diet had no need for an antiscorbutic).[20] We must bear in mind, too, that alcohol was not stigmatized then the way it is now—serious temperance movements were a thing of the future.

Against this background we see Monsieur de Poutrincourt, commander of the tiny French settlement at Port-Royal, imperiously summoning the aged Membertou, principal man of the Micmac, to a meeting to explain the charge that he has been conspiring against His Majesty's outpost. This is a man, Membertou, who said he could recall Jacques Cartier's visit some seventy years earlier, a man who had been a frequent guest of Poutrincourt's Order of Good Cheer that winter. He would have known the Frenchmen well. "At the first summons he came alone with our men without any hesitation. As a result he was allowed to return in peace, after having been well treated and given a bottle of wine, whereof he is fond, because says he: 'Quand il en a beu il dort bien, & n'a plus de soin, ni d'apprehension' [When he has drunk thereof he sleeps sound and has no further care or anxiety]."[21]

This is one of the first explanations, by a native, of why he drank. Membertou has been coping with the European fishing presence for many years; he claims to have known the formidable Cartier; and now he has a group of Frenchmen camped a matter of yards from his door. He has befriended these people, tolerated their rats eating his people's precious fish oils (yes, the Micmac complained about this), supped with them, and now is being called treacherous by them.

The man is being treated in fear and, I suspect, is learning their fear. "Bo-talee," writes Momaday, "rode easily among his enemies, once, twice, three—and four times. And all who saw him were amazed, for he was utterly without fear; so it seemed. But afterwards he said: Certainly I was afraid. I was afraid of the fear in the eyes of my enemies." Afraid of the fear in the eyes of the white man—alcohol, surely, helped alleviate this. I believe this is what the Eskimos in prison were trying to tell me.[22]

Fear. Loren Eiseley met a deer on a country walk one day—"the buck deer stepped out suddenly on the path and we met."

> He was too innocent to savor fear
> or the terror that followed him.
> He had young proud horns and was the most alive
> of anything I have ever met in the wood.
> He raised his ears gravely before me as though
> > he had heard
> > for the first time
> a sound from the dark behind him
> > unpronounced, undefined.
> "You do this twice and you won't live the season out,"
> I told him there at the forest's edge, but he only
> looked at me mildly
> > ruminating
> > considering
> the wraith from the forest floor
> suddenly confronting him.

The creature soon vanished into the dappled forest. "This is the nearest I have ever stood to the wild," to the person-who-is-deer, admits Eiseley. So, too, might Poutrincourt have confessed, and the missionaries Le Clercq and Eliot, and so too Cartier before them—each, in his own time, stood in the presence of the person who, like my friend Charlie, is Puffin, and was fearful. "The friendly and flowing savage. . . . Who is he?" Whitman's question ricochets through history, and it demands a better answer than we have given it.

"I it was who brought him the word," Eiseley confesses,

> never till then defined—
> death.
> I must have smelled of it like pine smoke.
> It is in the clothes of men
> in their voices from which everything flees.
> I was the messenger though I tried to whisper discreetly.
> He made his own definition
> and survived, I hope for a time he survived
> the word of which I smelled like a forest burning.

Fear. Europeans smelled of it like pine smoke, like a forest burning. A fear that devoured its beholders like a wildfire.[23]

Leslie Marmon Silko wrote this fear into Tayo, a young man of mixed blood just returned to the reservation from the war. Tayo is convinced he is insane. Silko has called her novel *Ceremony*, though I think she is not writing fiction.

Tayo is a profound alcoholic, a spiritually sick man. At the insistence of the grandmother, the family finally calls on the services of a medicine man. He, in turn, sends Tayo to an even more powerful healer, Betonie, a Navajo living in a hogan crammed with flotsam and jetsam, overlooking the slums and junkyards of Gallup.

"The old man was tall and his chest was wide; at one time he had been heavier, but old age was consuming everything but the bones. He kept his hair tied back neatly with red yarn in a chongo knot, like the oldtimers wore. He was sitting on an old tin bucket turned upside down by the doorway to his hogan. When he stood up and extended his hand to Robert and Tayo, his motions were strong and unhesitating, as if they belonged to a younger man."

He lives up here by choice, he tells Tayo, so he can "keep track of the people. . . . Because this is where Gallup keeps Indians until Ceremonial time. Then they want to show us off to the tourists." He gazed down "at the riverbed winding through the north side of Gallup. 'There,' he said, pointing his chin at the bridge, 'they sleep over there, in alleys between the bars.' He turned and pointed to the city dump east of the Ceremonial grounds and rodeo chutes. 'They keep us on the north side of the railroad tracks, next to the river and their dump. Where none of them want to live.' He laughed. 'They don't understand. We know these hills, and we are comfortable here.'"

"There was something about the way the old man said the word 'comfortable,'" signals the author. "It had a different meaning—not the comfort of big houses or rich food or even clean streets, but the comfort of belonging with the land, and the peace of being with these hills."[24]

Tayo, however, knows only the witchery of fear and despair. The witchery of war and being taken prisoner with his wounded cousin Rocky, and witnessing Rocky's senseless execution. Tayo feels he is suffocating in an insane story. Betonie's quiet confidence and unbounded mystery frustrate him, and at first he cannot perceive what the old man is trying to reveal to him: the huge dimensions of the fear that has him in its coils. "'We all have been waiting for help for a long time. But it never has been easy. The people must do it. You must do it.' . . . There was something large and terrifying in the old man's words."

Tayo "wanted to yell at the medicine man, to yell the things the white doctors had yelled at him" in the psychiatric hospital—"that he had to think only of himself, and not about the others, that he would never get well as long as he used words like 'we' and 'us.' But he had known the answer all along, even while the white doctors were telling him he could get well and he was trying to believe them: medicine didn't work that way, because the world didn't work that way. His sickness was only part of something larger, and his cure would be found only in something great and inclusive of everything."[25]

The horror of living in an incomprehensible, violent reality—this is Tayo's disease. Harold Napoleon speaks of it in *Yuuyaraq*—the spiritual disease of the Yup'ik Eskimos. Tiana Bighorse, at seventy-one, published her father's biography, and it, too, talks of it. "My father's name was Bighorse," she begins, building context. He was Navajo, "of the Tsé Deesh-gizhnii [Rock Gap] Clan, and his father was Tábąąhá [Edgewater] Clan. They called him Asdzą́ą́ Łį́į́' Yiishchį́į́h Biyáázh— Son-of-the-Woman-Who-Is-Expert-with-Horses." So he is defined.[26]

Like the Yupiit, Bighorse lived with much death from sickness— several of his wives died. Unlike the Yupiit, he also lived with assault by the United States Army, when the Navajos were captured by General James Carleton and driven like cattle to prisoner-of-war camp at Fort Sumner, at the Bosque Redondo, three hundred miles to the east: the Long Walk. Young Bighorse came home one day to find both his parents shot dead by soldiers outside their home. Barely into his teens, he became a warrior, and managed to escape the dragnet. "When Mr. Bighorse is a boy, he goes with his father. His father teaches everything that a boy should do to become a man. And what he shouldn't do. And his father tells him, 'You will be brave and be a warrior someday.'"

"In Navajo," carefully explains the daughter, "a warrior means someone who can get through the snowstorm when no one else can."

In Navajo, a warrior is the one that doesn't get the flu when everyone else does—the only one walking around, making a fire for the sick, giving them medicine, feeding them food, making them strong to fight the flu.

In Navajo, a warrior is the one who can use words so everyone knows they are part of the same family.

In Navajo, a warrior says what is in the people's hearts. Talks about what the land means to them. Brings them together to fight for it.[27]

Bighorse, grandfather to the people who had waved at me as I jogged alone on the dirt road and whom I had honked at in the parking lot, had witnessed genocide—the incomprehensible. And it clung to him like witchery. "I don't know why these people that went to Hwéeldi [Fort Sumner], they still don't want to talk about it—what happened there. I want to talk about my tragic story, because if I don't, it will get into my mind and get into my dream and make me crazy. I know some people died of their tragic story. They think about it and think about how many relatives they lost. Their parents got shot. They get into shock. That is what kills them. That is why we warriors have to talk to each other. We wake ourselves up, get out of the shock."[28]

How many relatives they lost . . . they get into shock . . . that is what kills them. Drowned in French brandy in New France, English rum in the Thirteen Colonies, whiskey out west—or, lately, vodka on the Kuskokwim or Yukon. Or a bullet. Or just afraid . . . and waiting. The witchery of it all is in Tayo's mind and in his dream, and is making him crazy.

"'There are no limits to this thing,' Betonie said. 'When it was set loose, it ranged everywhere, from the mountains and plains to the towns and cities; rivers and oceans never stopped it.' The wind was blowing steadily and the old man's voice was almost lost in it." Tayo is trying to tell him about his mother, a whore in Gallup, and about Rocky's death, and about his grisly friend Emo—but the old man isn't listening now. Betonie is talking about something much larger, vaster, than these particulars: he is talking now about a fear of the earth, of the Spirit of the Earth. On that windblown night a Navajo medicine man recalls the genesis of the white man's story, and it is worth listening to.[29]

It all started with a convention of witches here in Indian Country, he begins.

> Long time ago
> in the beginning
> there were no white people in this world
> there was nothing European.
> And this world might have gone on like that
> except for one thing:
> witchery.

As they show off their tricks, trying to outdo each other, one mysterious figure emerges from the shadows. "This one just told them to listen," saying merely, "What I have is a story."

> At first they all laughed
> but this witch said
> *Okay*
> *go ahead*
> *laugh if you want to*
> *but as I tell the story*
> *it will begin to happen.*
>
> *Set in motion now*
> *set in motion by our witchery*
> *to work for us.*

The story that unfolds is the horrifying tale of a strange, pale-skinned race across the ocean, who "grow away from the earth."

> Then they grow away from the sun
> then they grow away from the plants and animals.

They see no life
When they look
they see only objects.
The world is a dead thing for them
the trees and rivers are not alive
the mountains and stones are not alive.
The deer and bear are objects
They see no life.

They fear
They fear the world.
They destroy what they fear.
They fear themselves.

The wind, chants the witch, will bring those people here, blow them across the sea, by the thousands.

They will carry objects
which can shoot death
faster than the eye can see.

They will kill the things they fear
all the animals
the people will starve.

They will poison the water
they will spin the water away
and there will be drought
the people will starve.

They will fear what they find
They will fear the people
They kill what they fear.

Entire villages will be wiped out
They will slaughter whole tribes.

. . . .

And those they do not kill
will die anyway
at the destruction they see
at the loss
at the loss of the children
the loss will destroy the rest.

. . . .

They will bring terrible diseases
the people have never known.
Entire tribes will die out
covered with festered sores
shitting blood
vomiting blood.
Corpses for our work

Set in motion now
set in motion by our witchery
set in motion
to work for us.

By and by their fear will tunnel deep into the earth, to lay hold of the
very stone. Witchery "will find the rocks,"

. . . with veins of green and yellow and black.
They will lay the final pattern with these rocks
they will lay it across the world
and explode everything.

And so it is finished.

Whirling
whirling
whirling
whirling

set into motion now

set into motion.[30]

"Let's say, then, that a wind began to blow, ever so gently at first, down the corridors along which power flows." We have moved from the discomforting story of a Navajo shaman to the halls of an Ivy League university, where a celebrated scholar—Kai Erikson is his name—is struggling to comprehend the atomic bomb and the decision to drop it on the Japanese cities of Hiroshima and Nagasaki.[31]

So the other witches said
"Okay you win; you take the prize,
but what you said just now—
it isn't so funny
It doesn't sound so good.
We are doing okay without it
we can get along without that kind of thing.
Take it back.
Call that story back."

"But the witch"—Betonie's frightful words haunt me—"the witch just shook its head /at the others in their stinking animal skins, fur and feathers."

It's already turned loose.
It's already coming.
It can't be called back.[32]

I imagine Erikson, solitary, bent over a writing desk; the man works his mind to figure out, make intelligible, lay hold of this thing, this genesis, of the decision to use that terrible instrument. "Let's say, then, that a wind began to blow, ever so gently at first, down the corridors along which power flows. As it gradually gathered momentum during the course of the war, the people caught up in it began to assume, without ever checking up on it, that it had a logic and a motive, that it had been set in motion by sure hands acting on the basis of wise counsel." He comes at it again: "The decision, to the extent that one can even speak of such a thing, was shaped and seasoned by a force very like inertia."[33]

Erikson is a wise and humane man, and, like Jacob locked in struggle with the angel through the night, he too is wrestling with something immense and inchoate, perhaps even cosmic, and he knows it. I choose to call it the "ontology of fear." And I think, by the way, that the Navajo medicine man's explanation is as good as any I have yet heard.

"The best way to tell the story of those days is to say that the 'decision to drop' had become a force like gravity. It had taken life. The fact that the bomb existed supplied its own meaning, its own reason for being." Erikson then quotes the biographer of Secretary of War Henry L. Stimson: "In a process where such a general tendency has been set to work it is difficult to separate the moment when men were still free to choose from the moment, if such there was, when they were no longer free to choose."[34]

Erikson ends his essay still trying to decipher this monstrous thing, this terrible reality, that has been hatched somewhere within the imagination of history. "There was a feeling, hard to convey in words but easy to sense once one has become immersed in some of the available material, that the bomb had so much power and majesty, was so compelling a force, that one was almost required to give it birth and a chance to mature." Alongside this was "a feeling, born of war, that for all its ferocity the atomic bomb was nevertheless no more than a minor increment on a scale of horror that already included the fire bombings of Dresden, Tokyo, and other enemy cities. And there was a feeling, also born of war, that living creatures on the other side, even the children, had somehow lost title to the mercies that normally accompany the fact of being human."[35]

This thing, this inertia, this force like gravity, this witchery: what is its name?

N. Scott Momaday gives shape to this force in his "Strange and True Story of My Life with Billy the Kid," which begins with the unusual disclaimer, "all . . . of what follows is imagined; nonetheless, it is so."[36]

As a lad, remembers Momaday, "I dreamed a good deal on the back of my horse, going out into the hills alone." When he was twelve his parents moved to the Jemez Pueblo, and it was here, true to his Kiowa ancestry, that the boy fell in love with horses. "Desperados were everywhere in the brush. More than once I came upon roving bands of hostile Indians and had, on the spur of the moment, to put down an uprising. Now and then I found a wagon train in trouble, and always among the settlers there was a lovely young girl from Charleston or Philadelphia who needed simply and more than anything else in the world to be saved. I saved her." James Fenimore Cooper, all those Beadle & Adams dime novels, Owen Wister—what a splendid parody of all those Wild West thrillers. "After a time Billy the Kid was with me on most of those adventures. He rode on my right side and a couple of steps behind. I watched him out of the corner of my eye, for he bore watching. We got on well together in the main, and he was a good man to have along in a fight. We had to be careful of glory-seeking punks. Incredibly there were those in the world who were foolish enough to oppose us, merely for the sake of gaining a certain reputation."[37]

Erikson's "force like gravity" and my "ontology of fear" both fuse, in Momaday's perception, in the dreadful figure of Billy the Kid.

The man sitting across the table from me was slight of build and rather unseemly in appearance. He affected the wearing of black, which in another, more imposing figure might have been dramatic, even ominous; but in this man it was an unremarkable aspect, save that it accentuated something that lay deeper than his appearance, a certain somberness, a touch of grief. It was as if the Angel of Death had long ago found out his name. . . . At the same time I had the sense that his instincts were nearly infallible. Nothing should ever take him by surprise—and no one, except perhaps himself. Only one principle motivated him, that of survival—his own mean and exclusive survival. For him there was no morality in the universe but that, neither choice nor question. And for that reason he was among the deadliest creatures on the face of the earth.[38]

"There was no resonance in his voice," he recalls, "but it was thin and hard and flat—wood clacking lightly upon wood. . . . Notwithstanding, his speech was plain and direct—and disarmingly polite."

"Thank you for coming," he said.
"I will go with you," I replied.
And this is how it began; and this is the strange and true story of my life with Billy the Kid.[39]

It is a powerful reversal of the history books: herein the Indian travels to meet and explore the landscape of the white man's imagination. The speaker is Kiowa, although he could just as truthfully be Stadaconan or Micmac or Navajo or Yup'ik—what does it matter? He is, withal, Whitman's "friendly and flowing savage" coming to behold the vision of Jacques Cartier, which inspires such "a wonderful doubt and feare," or to countenance a Poutrincourt, swearing "these people . . . must be worked on by fear."

"Thank you for coming," he said.
"I will go with you," I replied.

And so he has: the native has traveled with fear ever since that first landfall. "For years now I have tried to understand what it was that I saw in his eyes at that moment," muses the narrator of his new companion. "There are times when it seems surely to have been something like sorrow, a faintest sadness. But at other times I realize that there was nothing, nothing at all, that Billy was the only man I have ever known in whose eyes there was no expression whatsoever."[40]

Betonie didn't know the name of the witch who "stood in the shadows beyond the fire,"

> and no one ever knew where this witch came from
> which tribe
> or if it was a woman or a man.
> But the important thing was
> this witch didn't show off any dark thunder charcoals
> or red ant-hill beads.
> This one just told them to listen:
> *"What I have is a story."* [my emphasis][41]

"Human beings," Erikson reminds us in his epilogue—and I think of children as I read this, especially the two to whom I told the story with which this book begins—"are surrounded by layers of trust, radiating out in concentric circles like the ripples in a pond." So it is. "The experience of trauma, at its worst, can mean not only a loss of confidence in the self but a loss of confidence in the scaffolding of family and community, in the structures of human government, in the larger logics by which humankind lives, and in the ways of nature itself."[42]

The ways of nature itself. "I am interested in the way that a man looks at a given landscape and takes possession of it in his blood and brain. . . . We Americans need now more than ever before—and in-

deed more than we know—to imagine who and what we are with respect to the earth and sky. I am talking about an act of the imagination
essentially, and the concept of an American land ethic." It is Billy's
Kiowa companion speaking—let us remember this.[43]

Kai Erikson has written here a book, a study, of human tragedy on
a broad scale, case after case, analyzing collective, large-scale trauma.
He, too, tells a story—one of profound witchery. As a sociologist he is
interested in the outcome, the shape of the wound, though he is clearly
interested as well in the shape of the mind, if that is what it is, that
spawns such horror. The latter image, however, largely escapes him
even as its imprint is vivid: "the sense that the universe is regulated
not by order and continuity but by chance and a kind of natural malice that lurks everywhere. It is a new and special truth." The Eskimos
in jail told me this.[44]

To think like a mountain . . . to know as we are known. Does the
mountain truly think this way: by a kind of natural malice? Does the
earth? Is this, after all, the hard reality of the universe?

No. It is, after all, the story of a reality that neither was inevitable nor
is privileged—the bizarre reality that Melville, in a brilliant insight,
called No Trust.[45] No faith in the Spirit of the Earth, in its commonwealth of grace, in the gift—Betonie's witch got it right; that's where
it must have started. The growing away from the mind of the place,
Thoreau's Common Sense, Merleau-Ponty's Common Flesh. Capitulating to the doubt, the dark itch, that our kind stands apart from the
rest of it, and it—the earth—moves its slow thighs by a consciousness
(if it has one at all) that is not kind to man. This story is as real as the
words on this page, and it is, I say, the ontology of fear.

Tayo feels it seeping back into his bones as he hunts for his uncle's
lost cattle. He has discovered them, stolen, on a white rancher's land,
and he has cut the barbed-wire fence to allow them to escape. But it's

night and he's alone and he is devoured by doubt; Betonie and his stories seem like a crazy thing to him now, in this the real world, after all. He collapses to the ground, overwhelmed by fatigue and terror at what they will do to him once the fence riders discover his crime and come hunting for him.

Then it appears, the mountain lion, almost as a phantom, emerging from an oak grove nearby.

> He did not walk or leap or run; his motions were like the shimmering of tall grass in the wind. He came across the meadow, moving into the wind. Tayo watched it with his head against the ground, conscious of pine needles tangled in his hair. . . . The eyes caught twin reflections of the moon; the glittering yellow light penetrated his chest and he inhaled suddenly. Relentless motion was the lion's greatest beauty, moving like mountain clouds with the wind, changing substance and color in rhythm with the contours of the mountain peaks: dark as lava rock, and suddenly as bright as a field of snow. When the mountain lion stopped in front of him, it was not hesitation, but a chance for the moonlight to catch up with him.

"Tayo got to his knees slowly and held out his hand."[46]

In the mountains of northern California I once saw a sign posted by the Forest Service on what to do if you met a mountain lion in this tract of wilderness. The sign said that insufficient scientific data on mountain lion encounters made it impossible to offer specific advice to the traveler. Oh, yes, the poster made it clear that one must have a healthy fear of such a meeting, but as to surviving the encounter unscathed, you were on your own—I liked that.

"'Mountain lion,' he whispered, 'mountain lion, becoming what you are with each breath, your substance changing with the earth and the sky.' The mountain lion blinked his eyes; there was no fear. He gazed at him for another instant and then sniffed the southeast wind before he crossed the stream and disappeared into the trees, his outline lingering like yellow smoke, then suddenly gone."[47]

There is absolutely no fear in this text, just the relentless beauty of full presence.

> Then he saw the bear. It did not emerge, appear: it was just there, immobile, fixed in the green and windless noon's hot dappling, not as big as he had dreamed it but as big as he had expected, bigger, dimensionless against the dappled obscurity, looking at him. Then it moved. It crossed the glade without haste, walking for an instant into the sun's full glare and out of it, and stopped again and looked back at him across one shoulder. Then it was gone. It didn't walk into the woods. It faded, sank back into the wilderness without motion as he had watched a fish, a huge old bass, sink back into the dark depths of its pool and vanish without even any movement of its fins.[48]

So, too, through the incomprehensible faith of a child, did the boy Ike McCaslin come into the presence of the deeply mythic bear in Faulkner's "The Bear."

Something looked at him, measured him, really, in trust.

Bo-talee perceived the fear in the eyes of his enemies, and it terrified him. But not here in a mountain lion. Nor did I perceive it, I swear it, in the grizzly bear I met in the Alaska summer twilight. And yet my Christian host on Kodiak Island clearly saw that fear. "Fear now screams at him to strike first. He brings rifle to his own eye and squeezes off one clean, earsplitting shot." Fear had gazed at him—the fear that he believed in, the fear that was ontological, had returned his fearful countenance. An echo, a mirror, after all. Tayo, however, who is a deeper Christian than this man will ever comprehend, knows that truth begins with trust and courtesy and kinship—call it human-scaled superposition. Tayo, like another master teacher, Hare the Trickster, knows that "someone's mind came to me just then."

"The horse was stamping her front feet and blowing her nostrils open wide to catch the mountain-lion smell that was on the wind now. Tayo stroked her neck. . . . He went into the clearing where the mountain lion had stood; he knelt and touched the footprints, tracing his finger around the delicate edges of dust the paw prints had made." Holding "his back to the wind," he "poured yellow pollen from Josiah's tobacco sack into the cup of his hand. He leaned close to the earth and sprinkled pinches of yellow pollen into the four footprints. Mountain lion, the hunter. Mountain lion, the hunter's helper."[49]

To all the missionaries who earnestly preached Christ to these people, from the Roman Catholics and Protestants on the Atlantic side to the Roman Catholics and Protestants and Russian Orthodox on the Pacific side, I say: this is true Christianity. I say to my churched Kodiak friend who, like Cartier, is afraid to go abroad without his rifle: Christ was preaching against an ontology of fear. Fear, let me be emphatic, works, it is genuine, and it is reasonable and logical and coherent and flawless: but only within its own reality.

"Mountain lion, becoming what you are with each breath, your substance changing with the earth and the sky." Perhaps there is always superposition in courtesy and kinship.

My wife, a physician and biologist, takes dead animals off the road. She has done so for years; it seems obvious to her. Watching her, once, lift a fox from a country road, I was moved to write about perception, courtesy, and kinship:

What did the fox pup cry as it was struck by the motorist in the night? And did the driver of that machinery of convenience think to stop, kneel and watch the green fire go out of its eyes I wonder?

Where do the fires of wildness go, and might they ever enter our calculations of necessity? Questions we seem loath to answer.

Death in this manner is unavoidable in this murderous place. This is the horror: the pitiless logic of atrocious acts. Evil is most monstrous when most banal—when they say it cannot be helped. What kind of dream is this civilization that makes us think so? Is man no longer sapient?

The cry it gave in death I imagine was but a universal plea for comfort. Surely our kind can will the mind into that fuller realm of compassion embracing both earth and our uncomprehended selves. I learned this when I heard, I swear it, the voice of fox come round again that morning. When I heard "We must stop" quietly, decisively, from the physician who says children most resemble animals. And we did.

I watched her lift the limp, smashed body from off the burning road to lay it by the river. There singing, she did, of beauty and trotting and sniffing for mice and moles. There to ask the keeper of foxes to rekindle the fire in yet another furnace of fox persuasion. There to leave tobacco with a softly furred trotter whose keeper I too must surely be. Ceremony of infinite innocence. "I can be a frog or a fox and still be a person," someone who knew creation's etiquette once observed. So obvious, so unavoidable.

Compassion—surely this is what the earth seeks most in us, the very thing we crave ourselves. Somewhere in man's primordial darkness away beyond intelligent grasp the shapeshifter arises consoled, requickened by the voice of the truly great physician.

EIGHT

Frogs

In "The Hidden Teacher" Loren Eiseley asks the question we all ask sooner or later in life: "What is it we are a part of that we do not see?" The question has come up repeatedly in this book. Eiseley seemed to think that he never found a satisfactory answer, although I would disagree. I believe he did, yet like Einstein, who posed a similar question, Eiseley could not bring himself to accept that answer and its implications.

"We are too content with our sensory extensions," Eiseley warns in his posthumous *Star Thrower,* "too content . . . with the fulfillment of that Ice Age mind that began its journey amidst the cold of vast tundras. . . . It is no longer enough to see as a man sees—even to the ends of the universe. It is not enough to hold nuclear energy in one's hand like a spear, as a man would hold it, or to see the lightning, or times past, or time to come, as a man would see it. If we continue to do this, the great brain—the human brain—will be only a new version of the old trap, and nature is full of traps for the beast that cannot learn."[1]

The great brain: the organ by which *Homo* had escaped the coarser chiseling by nature's hand to move now into the higher alchemies and giddy dreams of our evolving, soaring imagination. The human intel-

lect would take us, through our instruments, to the stars; it would give us both the permission and the ingenuity to survive any habitat on earth; and it would decisively subdue the fleshed and planted earth, as that oft-quoted Old Testament text said we could.

Yet in so doing it would alienate civilized man and woman from everything around them that mattered: "Then they grow away from the earth," prophesied Betonie's witch.[2] Native America clearly witnessed this in us: Is this not what those eloquent speeches are about in the journals of Cartier and Le Clercq and Heckewelder, leavening the voluminous literature of Indian and white relations right down to our own day? This is also what the current native authors—Momaday, Silko, Erdrich, Welch, Vizenor, Alexie—are trying to say: that there is something intrinsically wrong with our story.

Eiseley fretted over *Homo*'s great brain, but it was really his civilization's brain that worried him—the mind bent on seeing only "as a man sees." Here is his dilemma, the dilemma of modernity: the problem of *thought* and of *knowing* (cognition). The scientist could never fully bring himself to accept that *perception* and *knowledge* might reach humankind from something larger than ourselves, something enfolding us in its own immense imagination.

The proposition sounds absurd to modern sensibilities. Even so it is, I say, the way of the human being in Native America. And Eiseley knew this, mainly through the person of his mentor, the ethnologist Frank G. Speck, under whom he studied for his doctorate. It was through Speck's research among the Montagnais-Naskapi of Canada's north woods that the younger man encountered the world "where animals speak and their skins are easily shifted."[3]

"What is it we are a part of that we do not see?" Here, after all, was an answer, in a reality that Eiseley certainly had contemplated, though always from the safe (he thought) remove of the researcher.

"He was a member of the Explorers Club, and he had never been outside the state of Pennsylvania. Some of us who were world travelers used to smile a little about that, even though we knew his scientific reputation had been, at one time, great." With these beguilingly simple lines Eiseley opens one of his most provocative essays, "The Dance of the Frogs." In it—Eiseley has written it as fiction—he has split himself into two personalities: the detached ethnologist (who happens to be the narrator throughout) and the retired zoologist Albert Dreyer, who has stumbled into an archetypal event that has left him confounded in his faith in reason.[4]

Whose *reason* is it, after all, that moves the Spirit of the Earth in its errands?

"I used to think of myself as something of an adventurer, but the time came when I realized that old Albert Dreyer, huddling with his drink in the shadows close to the fire, had journeyed farther into the Country of Terror than any of us would ever go, God willing, and emerge alive." It is a tale of two minds—two different ways of measuring the universe, if you will—neither of which ever frees itself from the vise of fear. Eiseley's Country of Terror is my "ontology of fear."[5]

The story begins innocently enough: an evening in early spring, foggy and chilly outside, smoky and congenial in the lounge of the Explorers Club. Eiseley has been invited to speak to a small gathering on his excursion to the Canadian wilderness, where he has been investigating the spiritual beliefs of the Naskapi Indians up in the Quebec-Labrador region. All of this, so far, quite plausible. He has just alluded to the Game Boss idea (as it's known to ethnographers) when he's interrupted by "a low, halting query . . . from the back of the room." "And the game lords, what are they?" asks Dreyer. Whereupon Eiseley launches into a technical explanation: that many natives believed each species of animal was controlled in its abundance and distribution and behavior by a Being, one of its own kind though generally larger than the rest, with supernatural powers.[6]

"Are they visible?" interjects Dreyer once more—and we begin to feel the integrity of the speaker's reality itself being interrupted.

Yes—sometimes they are visible, replies Eiseley, obviously uncomfortable with the question. It is better to imagine them as archetypes, he goes on, rather than actual flesh-and-blood beings.

"Do they dance?" persisted Dreyer.

Eiseley is not amused: "'I cannot answer that question,' I said acidly. 'My informants failed to elaborate upon it.'" He tries to recover himself, go on with the talk, sidestepping Dreyer's surreal interrogations. "They believe implicitly in these monstrous beings, talk to and propitiate them. It is their voices that emerge from the shaking tent."

"The Indians believe it," pursued old Dreyer relentlessly, "but do *you* believe it?"

"My dear fellow"—I shrugged and glanced at the smiling audience—"I have seen many strange things, many puzzling things, but I am a scientist." Dreyer made a contemptuous sound in his throat and went back to the shadow out of which he had crept in his interest. The talk was over. I headed for the bar.[7]

The rest of the story belongs to Albert Dreyer. He pulls up a chair beside the young anthropologist, nursing his sherry before the fire, and begins telling him about a damp spring night, not unlike this one, when something strange befell him. "You must forgive me," Dreyer apologizes. "You touched on an interest of mine, and I was perhaps overeager."

On that particular night Dreyer had been working alone at home in his laboratory—he lived, at the time, on a country road well outside of town. His young wife had just recently died. "I had"—he paused— "things to forget. There were times when I worked all night. Or diverted myself, while waiting the result of an experiment, by midnight walks." Experiments: Dreyer specialized in amphibians and was renowned for his work with the Mexican axolotl and "remarkable tissue transplants in salamanders."[8]

Dreyer explains it all matter-of-factly: the research, his lab, the road and woods and nearby marsh. A foggy spring night. Nothing logically amiss, nothing irrational or fantastic. Except that he keeps interjecting *frogs* in an odd sort of way—Eiseley keeps picking up an extraneous signal; another topic seems to be condensing here, almost another force, pushing against space and time and routine experience. Something straining against the membrane of perception. "It could happen to anyone," admonishes Dreyer, elliptically, almost apologetically. "And especially in the spring. Remember that. And all I did was to skip. Just a few feet, mark you, but I skipped. Remember that, too."[9]

Hear Thoreau once again as he climbs Katahdin: "It was vast, Titanic, and such as man never inhabits. Some part of the beholder, even some vital part, seems to escape through the loose grating of his ribs as he ascends. He is more alone than you can imagine. . . . His reason is dispersed and shadowy, more thin and subtile, like the air. Vast, Titanic, inhuman Nature has got him at disadvantage, caught him alone, and pilfers him of some of his divine faculty."[10]

Dreyer, too, is somewhere he is not fully prepared to be. Thoreau had spent his adult life attending the habits of nature, but here, in this place, he has erupted into a consciousness that seems beyond his flesh, outside his control and possession. He perceives himself changing into something he knows not what: "*Who* are we? *where* are we?" Albert Dreyer, too, is about to step "behind the petty show of our small, transitory existence" into the full meaning of the event—the joy of full presence? No, this is not joy, not in this story: in Thoreau's words (quoting Milton's *Paradise Lost*) it is "Chaos and Old Night." For Dreyer is no Tayo.[11]

Nor is he an Eskimo. I once sent Nâlungiaq's poem to Robert Alixie:

In the very first times
there was no light on earth.
Everything was in darkness
the animals could not be seen.
And still, both people and animals lived on the earth
but there was no difference between them.
A person could become an animal
and an animal could become a human being.
There were wolves, bears, and foxes
but as soon as they turned into humans
they were all the same.
They may have had different habits
but all spoke the same tongue
lived in the same kind of house
and spoke and hunted in the same way.

That is the way they lived
here
on earth
in the very earliest times—
times that no one can understand now.

That was the time when magic words were made.
A word spoken by chance
would suddenly
become powerful
and what people wanted to happen

could happen
and nobody could explain
how it was.[12]

Alixie sent me a letter about it from jail:

> The poem you sent now, I have not seen before, but reading and understanding it truly is very powerful. Even my people believe in becoming an animal and likewise I treat animals as beings with intelligence. In fact I believe they still become humans especially when a man is in some emergency situation, they come to the aid of that man. I know some stories about men who encountered mammals like the herd of walrus, who became humans, sharing their food. I believe this with all of my heart, yet to many it is quite impossible. That mysterious Eskimo (Inuit) is truly right in what she wrote, because it is the same belief as my own tribe at home. Such blessing they are for me because I am greatly touched.[13]

Albert Dreyer is shackled by the ontology of fear.

"It was a late spring," he goes on, "fog and mist in those hollows in a way I had never seen before." And thousands of frogs, of all sorts, in migration. The night seemed animated by a primal, liquid force, something vaguely amphibian. The frogs were agitated by it, too, as the water beckoned them—"not water as we know it, but the mother, the ancient life force, the thing that made us in the days of creation"— "trilling, gurgling, and grunting, . . . hopping steadily toward the river." Dreyer felt it as well, the chthonic magnet, the urge to celebrate. "I joined them," he confesses. "There was no mystery about it. I simply began to skip."[14]

Simple enough. Except that as he skipped, lost in the charm and joy of it, he began to notice "beside my own bobbing shadow, another great, leaping grotesquerie that had an uncanny suggestion of the frog world about it. The shocking aspect of the thing lay in its size, and the fact that, judging from the shadow, it was soaring higher and more gaily than myself." Soon to be joined by at first one, and then another, companion. No, one didn't dare look, "for fear of what you might see there. . . . You do not look—you cannot look—because to do so is to destroy the universe in which we move and exist and have our transient being."

> I was part of it, part of some mad dance of the elementals behind the show of things. Perhaps in that night of archaic and elemental passion, that festival of the wetlands, my careless hopping passage under the street lights had called them, attracted their attention, brought them leaping down some fourth-dimensional roadway into the world of time.[15]

It is one thing to be in the presence of something frightful; it is quite another to perceive that he was "leaping with a growing ease." "I was changing," shapeshifting, exclaims Dreyer, horrified. "It was this, I think, that stirred the last remnants of human fear and human caution that I still possessed." Onward he plunges in the pitiless grip of some unkind force, bounding toward the verge of a wharf where he would, he suddenly realizes, fling himself into the inky tomb of the river. "In that final frenzy of terror before the water below engulfed me I shrieked, *'Help! In the name of God, help me! In the name of Jesus, stop!'*"

And so it did: it all just stopped. "In one electric instant . . . I was free. It was like the release from demoniac possession." Suddenly he was alone, hysterical but alone, while "there by my feet hopped feebly some tiny froglets of the great migration. There was nothing impressive about them, but you will understand that I drew back in revulsion. I have never been able to handle them for research since. My work is in the past."

As if to validate his tale to a doubtful listener, Dreyer slips off the black glove—the glove that he always wore, everyone had assumed, because a laboratory accident had disfigured his hand. "I turned my eyes away," recoils Eiseley. "One does not like a webbed batrachian hand on a human being."

The problem lies not with the hand, responds the older man; it's "the question of choice. Perhaps I was a coward, and ill prepared. Perhaps . . . I should have taken them and that springtime without question. Perhaps I should have trusted them and hopped onward. Who knows?"[16]

Dreyer's final words are Loren Eiseley's, and they are certainly not fantasy. Eiseley the historian of science, the cultural anthropologist, disciple of Thoreau—these are Eiseley's challenge to himself as well as us, and he could never answer them. I can imagine Jacques Cartier asking himself the same thing, Cartier and the swelling chorus who followed him: it was a question of choice. Perhaps we were cowards and ill prepared. Perhaps we should have taken them without question. Perhaps we should have trusted them. Who knows?

Scott Momaday entitled one of his early essays "The Man Made of Words," and the phrase has stuck. Here in "The Dance of the Frogs" is a root-bed of fear: both the narrator (Eiseley) and the zoologist (also Eiseley) are men whose language and thoughts are made of fear, like Cartier and Columbus and Cook and most of the rest of the discoverers and explorers and missionaries of Native America. This is Loren Eiseley's dilemma and his anguish throughout a difficult life. It is exactly the anguish of European history as it was planted in the soil and stone and waters and creatures of this land and in the soul of its inhabitants, who were not afraid to assume the shape and mind of the soil and stone and waters and creatures here. Robert Alixie, Yup'ik, imprisoned, confirms that. For Dreyer, however, it is "demoniac possession. One moment I was leaping in an inhuman company of elder things, and the next moment I was a badly shaken human being on a wharf." This is indeed possession—not by the Spirit of the Earth but by the ontology of fear.[17]

"The Dance of the Frogs" is a tale wet with the breath of Betonie's witch.

There is another voice, welling up from the ground of trust, which likewise speaks of a damp spring night, when "the tribes wake trilling." Immediately we sense that the organic nature of this is somehow different; the curious word "tribes" suggests a measurement different from Dreyer's science of newt neoteny and salamander tissue transplants—it sounds more aboriginal, more plenipotential. The voice and trust, here, are Mary Oliver's.

> You think it will never happen again.
> Then, one night in April,
> the tribes wake trilling.
> You walk down to the shore.
> Your coming stills them,
> but little by little the silence lifts
> until song is everywhere
> and your soul rises from your bones
> and strides out over the water.
> It is a crazy thing to do—
> for no one can live like that,
> floating around in the darkness
> over the gauzy water.
> Left on the shore your bones
> keep shouting *come back!*
> But your soul won't listen;

in the distance it is unfolding
like a pair of wings, it is sparking
like hot wires. So,
like a good friend,
you decide to follow.
You step off the shore
and plummet to your knees—
you slog forward to your thighs
and sink to your cheekbones—
and now you are caught
by the cold chains of the water—
you are vanishing while around you
the frogs continue to sing, driving
their music upward through your own throat,
not even noticing
you are something else.
And that's when it happens—
you see everything
through their eyes,
their joy, their necessity;
you wear their webbed fingers;
your throat swells.
And that's when you know
you will live whether you will or not,
one way or another,
because everything is everything else,
one long muscle.
It's no more mysterious than that.
So you relax, you don't fight it anymore,
the darkness coming down

called water,
called spring,
called the green leaf, called
a woman's body
as it turns into mud and leaves,
as it beats in its cage of water,
as it turns like a lonely spindle
in the moonlight, as it says
yes.[18]

Oliver's premise—"because everything is everything else,/one
long muscle"—is startlingly different from Dreyer's. She reminds us
of Tayo's vision: "Mountain lion, becoming what you are with each
breath, your substance changing with the earth and the sky." Or
Nâlungiaq's: "In the very first times . . . a person could become an animal, and an animal could become a human being . . . and there was
no difference."[19] Or Oscar Active exhorting me that one has to "see
the life" in things. All three visions, all of them aboriginal, come together in these stunning lines:

not even noticing
you are something else.
And that's when it happens—
you see everything
through their eyes,
their joy, their necessity.

"Only one principle motivated him," remembers Momaday of the
Man Made of Fear, "that of survival—his own mean and exclusive survival. For him there was no morality in the universe but that, neither
choice nor question. And for that reason he was among the deadliest
creatures on the face of the earth."[20]

"*Who* are we? *where* are we?" asks a slight, gray-eyed man of a mountain in northern Maine. The odd thing is not the question itself but the thing that it is seemingly addressed to: a mountain. Mary Oliver has asked as much of the tribes who wake trilling. She, however, is reborn into the atomic power of it, where the "song is everywhere." There is incalculable trust here; there is measurement of *something* in absolute courtesy—this, I say, is the key. As the terrors of self-consciousness vanish, "frogs continue to sing, driving / their music upward through your own throat, / not even noticing / you are something else."

"'Frogs,' I said desperately," recalls the ethnologist, trying to shift the conversation back to the safer, more predictable ground of zoology. "Always admired your experiments. Frogs. Yes."

> I give the old man credit. He took the drink and held it up and looked at me across the rim. There was a faint stir of sardonic humor in his eyes.
>
> "Frogs, no," he said, "or maybe yes. I've never been quite sure. Maybe yes."[21]

Frogs, no—this is emphatically not the issue. The real issue lies in what physicists call the problem of measurement: whether we start, as premise, in our very genesis, by measuring the world in fear or in trust. That decision, and it is ours alone, appears to usher its bearer inexorably into one realm of reality or another, mutually exclusive of one another. "There is, we know now to our sorrow, more than one world to be drawn out of nature. When once drawn, like some irreplaceable card in a great game, that world leads on to others."[22]

"My dad said that when he was a boy, about nine years old, he went into the bush alone. He was lost from his people." Merely a child, about to measure the world in trust.[23]

So begins a vision quest story heard years ago by Robin Ridington, at the time a Harvard graduate student doing fieldwork for a doctoral dissertation. Ridington was camped with a small band of Beaver Indians near the Alaska Highway as they hunted the moose for their winter supply. He met a man there who would change his premises. "His name was Japasa—'Chickadee'"—an old man dying of heart failure, although this isn't how he would have put it, surely. Japasa was dying of having lived; it was time to die.

"The next evening people gathered around the old man's fire, after the day's work of hunting and preparing meat and hides. His son told a story about how he and the old man survived the terrible flu of 1918–1919 that had killed many people. Then Japasa began speaking softly, apparently to himself, as if he were looking back into a dream to find the words. His son whispered a simultaneous translation into English for my benefit." The old man began surrendering his powers, revealing his medicine, his trust.

"In the night it rained," the old man's son went on.

He was cold and wet from the rain, but in the morning he found himself warm and dry. A pair of silver foxes had come and protected him. After that, the foxes kept him and looked after him. He stayed with them and they protected him. Those foxes had three pups. The male and female foxes brought food for the pups. They brought food for my dad, too. They looked after him as if they were all the same. Those foxes wore clothes like people. My dad said he could understand their language. He said they taught him a song. . . .

My dad said he stayed out in the bush for twenty days. Ever since that time foxes have been his friends. Anytime he wanted to he could set a trap and get foxes. When he lived with the foxes that time he saw rabbits, too. The rabbits were wearing clothes like people. . . .

The first night out in the bush he was cold and wet from the rain. In the morning when he woke up warm and dry the wind came to him, too. The wind came to him in the form of a person. That person said, "See, you're dry now. I'm your friend." The wind has been his friend ever since. He can call the wind. He can call the rain. He can also make them go away. . . .

My dad sang for the rain to come a couple of days ago. He sang for it to come and make him well. That rain came right away. This morning he called the wind and rain. They came and then he told them to go away. He told them he was too old and he didn't need their help any more. He wanted to tell them he was too old and didn't need them. He said it was time to die. He told them they could leave him now.

After he had been in the bush twenty days he almost forgot about his people. Then he heard a song. It was coming from his people. He remembered them and he went toward the song. Every time he got to where the song had been it moved farther away. Finally, by following that song he was led back to his people.[24]

The same night that Japasa sang his medicines back to the earth, "he gave me two stories, as well," remembers Ridington. "One was about how Indian people from far and wide used to gather in the prairie country near the Peace River to dry saskatoon berries. They came down the rivers in canoes full of drymeat, bear tallow, and berries. They sang and danced and played the hand game in which teams of men bet against one another in guessing which hand conceals a small stone or bone."

"The other story," writes the ethnologist, "was about frogs who play-gamble, just like people. He said he knew frogs because he once lived with them on the bottom of a lake."[25]

The way of the human being here, in America, begins with a

premise wholly different from western culture's. Japasa measured everything around him within an ontology of trust and courtesy. Reality, as a result, inevitably wore a different face—this is the stunning thing. Within days of returning his powers to their origin (which was also, of course, his own origination), the old man died, though not before the ceremony of his life was completed: the wind and rain and moose and foxes, declares Ridington, came to say goodbye—like the bears on Admiralty Island for Bernice Hansen's father. Unlike Eiseley, Robin Ridington came to believe this reality. "After Japasa's death . . . I cared less about data relevant to the language of personality theory and more about . . . understanding the stories the old man had made known to me seven days before I heard his death rattle. In the seventeen years that have passed since I heard Japasa give away his songs I have . . . listened to a wealth of Indian stories. I have studied them, dreamed them, told them, taught them, and made them my own."[26]

Knowing as he was known: this is how that Beaver Indian child entered manhood and consciously conducted his life thereafter, right up to its end. There was no Thoreauvian "Who are we?" for him. Japasa knew with uncanny confidence that he could be a "frog or a fox and still be a person." This was both his ceremony and his power, except that he didn't own it, nor did he invent it even while it filled him. All he did was merely measure the spirit of the earth in trust, like a child. "I stared at him," said Black Elk to John Neihardt, conjuring up his own vision of the Six Grandfathers. Yes, "I stared at him," the Sixth, the Spirit of the Earth, "for it seemed I knew him somehow; and as I stared, he slowly changed, for he was growing backwards into youth, and when he had become a boy, I knew that he was myself."[27]

Winter Count

"What I have is a story," said the witch. And that's all I have, too, merely a story. Tayo is healed in this story, his prisoned soul released by the knowledge that he need no longer measure himself by the narrative of the witchery.

"He lay back in the red dust on the old mattress and closed his eyes. The dreams had been terror at loss, at something lost forever; but nothing was lost; all was retained between the sky and the earth, and within himself. He had lost nothing. The snow-covered mountain remained. . . . They logged the trees, they killed the deer, bear, and mountain lions, they built their fences high; but the mountain was far greater than any . . . of these things. . . . The mountain could not be lost to them, because it was in their bones."[1]

Boundaries: there were none, not of species, not even of time. In fact "boundaries" were not even the question. For only the wholeself existed, "the deep muscle of the world," embracing everything, even the stories. And he was unquestionably a part of it, participating, even creating it, and "he was not crazy, . . . he had never been crazy." He was the whole dream of bear and of mountain lion and the mountain, too.[2]

It was night and it was winter, and "he stood on the edge of the rimrock and looked down below": "The canyons and valleys were thick powdery black; their variations of height and depth were marked by a thinner black color. He remembered the black of the sand paintings on the floor of the hogan; the hills and mountains were the mountains and hills they had painted in sand. He took a deep breath of cold mountain air: there were no boundaries; the world below and the sand paintings inside became the same that night. The mountains from all the directions had been gathered there that night."[3]

"I am," declares Scott Momaday, taking possession of it in his blood and brain, "a feather on the bright sky,"

> I am the blue horse that runs in the plain
> I am the fish that rolls, shining, in the water
> I am the shadow that follows a child
> I am the evening light, the lustre of meadows
> I am an eagle playing with the wind
> I am a cluster of bright beads
> I am the farthest star
> I am the cold of the dawn
> I am the roaring of the rain
> I am the glitter on the crust of the snow
> I am the long track of the moon in a lake
> I am a flame of four colors
> I am a deer standing away in the dusk
> I am a field of sumac and the pomme blanche
> I am an angle of geese in the winter sky
> I am the hunger of a young wolf
> I am the whole dream of these things
> You see, I am alive, I am alive
> I stand in good relation to the earth
> I stand in good relation to the gods

I stand in good relation to all that is beautiful
I stand in good relation to the daughter of Tsen-tainte
You see, I am alive, I am alive[4]

"I am the whole dream of these things": this, after all, is the deepest story of Native America. It is the way of the human being.

Years ago Barry Lopez wrote a small essay about an anthropologist from northern Nebraska. The Sand Hills—to the eye, endless, like the tundra. Like Ridington, this man has "listened to a wealth of Indian stories, . . . studied them, dreamed them, told them, taught them," and made them his own.[5]

The man is about to give a paper at a meeting in New Orleans: the annual convention of some scholarly association. He listens to the previous papers on the panel and finds them more than dull: they're dead. They're about anthropological Indians, not the *real people,* people like the Crow and Blackfoot and Lakota of the northern Plains, whom he knew from the stories ingrained in the soil and from the wind that breathed into his soul. "He tried to listen, but the words fell away like tumbled leaves. Cottonwoods," he remembers, his attention drifting—"winters so bad they would have to cut down cottonwood trees for the horses to eat. *So cold we got water from beaver holes only.* And years when they had to eat the horses. *We killed our ponies and ate them. No buffalo.*"

"Inside the windowless room . . . everyone was seated in long rows. . . . He remembered a friend's poem about a snowy owl dead behind glass in a museum, no more to soar, to hunch and spread his wings and tail and fall silent as moonlight. . . . He wished for something to hold, something to touch, to strip leaves barehanded from a chokecherry branch or to hear rain falling on the surface of a lake. In this windowless room he ached."

Now it's his turn—he gets up—they're all looking at him. He won't read from a prepared text; he tries instead to express the stark poetic anguish of the nineteenth century in the memory of these northern buffalo hunters, when the world of spirit was coming apart. Winter Counts, they are called. The problem was he felt them, too, he believed them, and he had made them his own.

1833   Stars blowing around like snow. Some fall to the earth
1856   Reaches into the Enemy's Tipi has a dream and can't speak
1869   Fire Wagon, it comes

And so on. Winter Counts. He had his own, though these he would not reveal to this audience.

1916   My father drives east for hours in silence. We walk out into a field covered all over with river fog. The cranes, just their legs are visible
1918   Father, shot dead. Argonne forest

The world becoming unstitched. He can feel their incomprehension; they seemingly have no capacity to understand, certainly not in this hotel ballroom thousands of miles away.

"The applause was respectful, thin, distracted. As he stepped away from the podium he realized it was perhaps foolish to have accepted the invitation. He could no longer make a final point. He had long ago lost touch with the definitive, the awful distance of reason. He wanted to go back to the podium. You can only tell the story as it was given to you, he wanted to say. Do not lie. Do not make it up."

He flees the room: this is not his realm. This is not his discourse. Out in the lobby he sees through the huge glass window a fantastic thunderstorm rolling in, raging, seizing both land and firmament in its purposes.

"He turned quickly from the cold glass and went up in the silent elevator and ordered dinner. When it came, he threw back the drapes and curtains and opened the windows. The storm howled through his room and roared through his head. He breathed the wet air deep into his lungs. In the deepest distance, once, he heard the barking-dog sounds of geese, running like horses before a prairie thunderstorm."[6]

It is Lopez's finest piece. He called it "Winter Count." I like it most for one line: "'Everything is held together with stories,' he thought," as the storm—its joy, its necessity—is about to possess him. "That is all that is holding us together, stories and compassion."[7]

I believe that. When I resigned my professorship recently, after more than two decades, I mentioned it to a handful of colleagues who I thought might understand.

My wife and I were living at the time on an island in the North Atlantic, off the coast of Canada. Here Willa Cather once had a cottage by the sea; it was here she breathed into and created her bishop, out of the air "on the bright edges of the world."[8] A place of herring and lobster fishermen, small communities of people caring for one another. I taught at the island high school, a seminar on "The Way of the Human Being" for a half-dozen seniors bound for college. Powerful: they were lovely kids. I wanted to impart confidence as well as release the imagination into new possibilities.

As Christmas approached we packed up and left our island and began a journey (a move, really) to the southwest. Our route took us through the Catskills, and I made a point of stopping off at the small liberal arts college where my teaching had begun years before (I was hired to replace a man who specialized in late nineteenth-century federal-Indian policy). We walked the grounds as a chilly winter evening settled in, the campus somber, students gone for the holiday. There was something lonely and melancholy in the air; this didn't feel like the proper way to end my teaching. The place felt dead.

We had already stopped in New Hampshire, where we had lived more recently. I had once taught (for a summer only) at Dartmouth, Eleazar Wheelock's *Vox clamantis in deserto*—the "voice crying in the wilderness" to prepare Indian youths for civility and the ministry. But coming through again like this, I had no feelings for the campus; Dartmouth held no power I could decipher.

South now, following the interstate down the Alleghenies—Scranton, Wilkes-Barre—and I started noticing signs for Carlisle. Something made me think of the Carlisle Indian School. More miles clicked by and I put it out of mind. Then another road sign and the thought stubbornly resurfaced. Nearing the exit ramp I rapidly began telling Nina about the school (founded by Lieutenant Richard Henry Pratt, operating 1879–1918) and suggested we stop and visit—feel the spirits of those Indian kids.

We pulled off and asked for directions.

And wound up at the Carlisle Barracks, "Home of the U.S. Army War College and the Military History Institute" (as it advertises itself). I told the officer who greeted us at the Military History Institute that we were interested in seeing whatever remained of the old Indian School. Grinning, he asked, "How many hours do you plan to spend?"

The man gave us a walking tour of the barracks, beginning with the Hessian Powder Magazine Museum built in the 1770s, with walls six feet thick. Squat and solid, it looked like a guardhouse. One enters the Nineteenth-Century Room, filled with Civil War memorabilia. Through a door to the left, the Eighteenth-Century Room: the Revolution. To the right, another door, into the late nineteenth and twentieth centuries. Arrows direct the visitor immediately to the wall exhibiting the Indian School period. Navigating the chamber clockwise, one reaches next the Medical Field Service School (which took over the barracks after the Indian era), then the post–World War II schools, and lastly the Army War College period.

The museum is laid out in a timeline, from Revolutionary War to present-day Army War College. Indians have a few feet of story along the wall in the geography of this formidable structure, as in the pages of American history.

But the officer was indifferent to the glass cases and posed photographs of shorn kids in uniform and starch—I remembered the bear in the Anchorage hotel. He was interested in a different story. He motioned us over to a low, heavy door, kept locked, with small barred window. Through the glass I spied a narrow, dim hallway, off which were four tiny cells, two to a side, each sealed by heavy, windowless door. "The school put Indian kids in there when they became troublesome." His voice was solemn. "The army doesn't like to advertise that." (A sign over the door read, "Storage Area: Authorized Personnel Only.")

> From seeing the bars, his seeing is so exhausted
> that it no longer holds anything anymore.
> To him the world is bars, a hundred thousand
> bars, and behind the bars, nothing.
>
> The lithe swinging of that rhythmical easy stride
> which circles down to the tiniest hub
> is like a dance of energy around a point
> in which a great will stands stunned and numb.
>
> Only at times the curtains of the pupil rise
> without a sound . . . then a shape enters,
> slips through the tightened silence of the shoulders,
> reaches the heart, and dies.[9]

The officer knew compassion. As we walked over to the museum he had remarked that there seemed to him to be an uncanny connection between Indian kids sent to the school and their fathers or uncles or grandfathers who were (difficult) Indian leaders at the time. Some of these kids were hostages, sort of, is what he was delicately saying. And some were stored in these cells when they didn't fit the mold that Lieutenant Pratt and his society had in mind for them.

Nina and I returned alone to the cells later that afternoon, bringing tobacco and words of apology to the ghosts of children incarcerated: this had been a painful revelation. The officer took us by the old hospital as well, and we visualized scores of children dying within its whitewashed walls during the fierce years of the tuberculosis epidemic, orphaned of home and family.

We left tobacco and condolences there, too.

The Coren Apartments were the girls' dormitory back then. Our guide chuckled when he said the building was supposedly haunted by an Indian girl. Local legend has it that the specter belongs to young Lucy Pretty Eagle, who arrived early one winter from Rosebud (Sioux) reservation and died four months later of a nameless contagion. Her English translation name was Pretty Eagle. On reaching the school, she, like the others, had been instructed to choose an English name from a list on the blackboard. Lucy, she decided—but I choose to call her Pretty Eagle. Those who had felt her presence described her as a benign spirit, as someone watching, or footsteps in the hall. When Superintendent Pratt wrote her parents with the news, the distraught father sent back word that she had died already, in a sense, a year before.

Pretty Eagle. We left tobacco for her at the base of an old maple in front of the Coren Apartments. Nina sang to her. We later read that Sioux parents were anguished that their children were not having their bodies wrapped and scaffolded in a tree after they died, as was customary among their people. Carlisle buried them in a box in the ground.

I resolved to visit that ground. Our friend had mentioned the Indian burial site and drew a map showing me how to get there. Originally the graves had been behind the athletic field, but when the army planned to build a road there, the bodies were exhumed and trucked to a new graveyard at the edge of the barracks.

Over by the southeast gate, bordered by the Post Exchange and busy Claremont Road, is that tiny Indian cemetery now, next to a traffic signal. As though guarding the gravesite, a low wrought-iron fence (low enough for any kid to hop over if she wished) encloses it. One enters through a small iron gate. The hundred or so native children buried here (many who died over the years had their bodies shipped back home) lie beneath plain military headstones, in perfect rank. A name is chiseled into each stone and beneath that a tribe and date of death. Some say merely "Alaska" for tribe, and some "Eskimo." There was an Aleut. A good many seemed to be Apaches and Plains Indians of one sort or another. There were Seminoles, Six Nations, Navajos, Chippewas, Cherokees, Choctaws, California tribes, Northwest Coast, and Pueblos. There was even a Mandan, as I recall, and a half-dozen just plain Unknown. Most seemed to have only English names. Pretty Eagle lay at the end of the first row, as "Lucy Pretty Eagle, Sioux," with the wrong month of death. Off in the rear corner were buried the children of what appeared to be white schoolteachers.

But mostly it was natives on that raw December afternoon.

We wondered at the logic that brought them here in train cars in feathers and headbands and blankets and braids, to die on this alien ground—this prison, really. The officer said that Pratt and his contemporaries had done it out of the best of intentions. Out of the best of intentions, or was it the firmest of opinions?

As we got out of the car I told Nina that I needed to say something to these children. The thought was gathering that this would be my final class and that I, a historian of Indian-white relations, was morally obliged to explain to these children what had happened. We slowly walked the rows, repeating aloud each name and tribe of the child therein. "Dennis, son of Blue Tomahawk," "Dora, daughter of Brave Bull," "Ernest, son of Chief White Thunder." Row upon row: I thought of war veterans. When we came to Pretty Eagle I patted her headstone, comfortingly—just a girl.

I took my position at the front of the class and looked around, professor for the last time. Before me, attentive students in silent formation. The last class at the Carlisle Indian Industrial School. They died before becoming blacksmiths and carpenters, shoemakers and tinsmiths, tailors, printers, harnessmakers, plumbers, bricklayers, or laundresses, cooks, and seamstresses. But they were already *real people*, I thought, as I fought back my anger—people who understood the way of the human being in this place. I was a man, a historian, standing before a cemetery created by blundering goodwill.

I paused and reconsidered. I had to leave them with something more satisfying than my bitterness. Besides, I was reminded of my own follies in Indian Country.

I apologized to these kids. I apologized not as an angry historian but simply as a sorrowful human being. What else can one possibly be, standing in a graveyard? I called some by name as I did so. I told them we were traveling west, and I invited any lingering spirits to come along. All I heard were the cars, though sometimes, more powerfully, the wind.

As we left I latched the gate as I had found it. But then thought better of it.

Winter Count: I opened it

Notes

Preface

1. Walt Whitman, *Leaves of Grass*, 1855 edition (New York: Viking Press, 1959), p. 69, lines 974–975; D. H. Lawrence, *Studies in Classic American Literature*, 1923 (New York: Viking Press, 1961), pp. 35, 52; Henry David Thoreau, *The Maine Woods*, 1864 (New York: Harper and Row, 1987), p. 248.
2. John Archibald Wheeler, "Bohr, Einstein, and the Strange Lesson of the Quantum," in *Mind in Nature: Nobel Conference XVII*, ed. Richard Q. Elvee, pp. 1–30 (San Francisco: Harper and Row, 1982), p. 6.

Chapter 1: Coming to America

1. Bill Hess, untitled article (the story of Katauq, an Inupiaq Eskimo, Point Hope, Alaska), *Uiñiq: The Open Lead*, special issue titled "The People of Tikigaq [Point Hope]," vol. 6, no. 2 (Fall 1991): 2. *Uiñiq* "is published by the North Slope Borough [Alaska], P.O. Box 69, Barrow, Alaska. . . . The magazine is photographed, written and produced by the editor, Bill Hess, of Running Dog Publications, P.O. Box 872383, Wasilla, Alaska."
2. Mircea Eliade, *Cosmos and History: The Myth of the Eternal Return*, trans. Willard R. Trask (New York: Harper and Row, 1959), pp. 139–162, especially pp. 150–151.
3. Henry David Thoreau, *Walden; or, Life in the Woods*, 1854 (New York: Holt, Rinehart, and Winston, 1948), p. 272; Douglas Kellogg Wood, *Men Against*

Time: Nicholas Berdyaev, T. S. Eliot, Aldous Huxley, and C. G. Jung (Lawrence: University Press of Kansas, 1982), p. 142.

4. W. H. Auden, "For the Time Being: A Christmas Oratorio" (1944), in *Modern Poetry,* ed. Maynard Mack, Leonard Dean, and William Frost, 2d ed., pp. 211–262 (Englewood Cliffs, N.J.: Prentice-Hall, 1961), p. 216, line 170.

5. Robert Bringhurst, *The Black Canoe: Bill Reid and the Spirit of Haida Gwaii,* photographs by Ulli Steltzer (Seattle: University of Washington Press; Vancouver and Toronto: Douglas and McIntyre, 1991), p. 17.

6. For a concise statement of this, see Jared Diamond, "The Worst Mistake in the History of the Human Race," *Discover* 8 (May 1987): 64–66.

7. Job 38:31–33 (New Revised Standard Version).

8. Ibid., 39:1–4, 9–12.

9. Ibid., 42:10, 12–13, 16–17.

10. Leslie E. Gerber and Margaret McFadden, *Loren Eiseley* (New York: Frederick Ungar, 1983), p. 123; Loren Eiseley, *The Star Thrower* (New York: Times Books, 1978), p. 183.

11. Richard Hakluyt, *The Principal Navigations, Voyages, Traffiques, and Discoveries of the English Nation,* 12 vols. (Glasgow: James MacLehose and Sons, 1904), 8:424–428.

12. Ibid., pp. 100, 120.

13. This entire account of the experience of Master Hore appears in H. P. Biggar, ed., *A Collection of Documents Relating to Jacques Cartier and the Sieur de Roberval,* Publications of the Public Archives of Canada, no. 14 (Ottawa: Public Archives of Canada, 1930), pp. 273–277.

14. Noël Bennett, *Halo of the Sun: Stories Told and Retold* (Flagstaff, Ariz.: Northland Press, 1987), p. 31; Gary Witherspoon, *Language and Art in the Navajo Universe* (Ann Arbor: University of Michigan Press, 1977), p. 152.

15. Witherspoon, *Language,* pp. 153–154.

16. Joseph Epes Brown, "Becoming Part of It," *Parabola* 7 (Summer 1982): 12.

17. Bennett, *Halo,* p. 37.

18. Michel de Montaigne, "Of Coaches" (1585–1588), in *The Complete Essays of Montaigne,* trans. Donald M. Frame, bk. 3, chap. 6, pp. 685–699 (Stanford: Stanford University Press, 1958), p. 693.

19. Ibid. H. C. Porter, *The Inconstant Savage: England and the North American Indian, 1500–1660* (London: Gerald Duckworth, 1979), p. 148, uses the word "new-fangles" in his version of the passage "We 'sold him our opin-

ions, our new-fangles, and our arts'" (from the John Florio [1603] edition of the *Essays*).

20. *The Journal of Christopher Columbus*, trans. Cecil Jane and L. A. Vigneras (New York: Clarkson N. Potter, Bramhall House, 1960), pp. 23–24.
21. Willa Cather, *Death Comes for the Archbishop*, 1927 (New York: Random House, Vintage Books, 1971), pp. 272–273.
22. Frederick Turner, *Beauty: The Value of Values* (Charlottesville: University Press of Virginia, 1991), p. 8.

Chapter 2: . . . to the Skin of the World

1. N. Scott Momaday, "The Man Made of Words," in *Indian Voices: The First Convocation of American Indian Scholars* [Princeton University, 1970], pp. 49–62, with discussion following on pp. 62–84 (San Francisco: Indian Historian Press, 1970), p. 53.
2. N. Scott Momaday, *The Way to Rainy Mountain* (Albuquerque: University of New Mexico Press, 1969), pp. 26, 34.
3. Ibid., p. 38.
4. Charlie Kilangak, Sr., Emmonak, Alaska, ms. (Fall 1994).
5. Farland Lyons, discussion (pp. 62–84) in *Indian Voices*, pp. 72–73.
6. Margaret Craven, *I Heard the Owl Call My Name* (New York: Dell, 1973), pp. 19–20.
7. Ibid., p. 159.
8. Peter Grant, "The Sauteux Indians (Written ca. 1804)," in *Les Bourgeois de la Compagnie du Nord-ouest: Récits de voyages, lettres, et rapports inédits relatifs au nord-ouest canadien, 1889–1890*, ed. L. R. Masson, series 2, pp. 303–366 (reprint ed., New York: Antiquarian Press, 1960), p. 317; John Lawson, *A New Voyage to Carolina*, 1709, ed. Hugh Talmage Lefler (Chapel Hill: University of North Carolina Press, 1967), p. 180; Samuel William Pond, "The Dakotas or Sioux in Minnesota as They Were in 1834," *Collections of the Minnesota Historical Society* 12 (December 1908): 413; James Adair, *History of the American Indians*, 1775, reprinted in *Adair's History of the American Indians*, ed. Samuel Cole Williams (Johnson City, Tenn.: Watauga Press, 1930), p. 6.
9. Ann Fienup-Riordan, *Boundaries and Passages: Rule and Ritual in Yup'ik Eskimo Oral Tradition* (Norman: University of Oklahoma Press, 1994), p. 3.

10. Robert Bringhurst, *The Black Canoe: Bill Reid and the Spirit of Haida Gwaii*, photographs by Ulli Steltzer (Seattle: University of Washington Press; Vancouver and Toronto: Douglas and McIntyre, 1991), pp. 16–17.

11. Fienup-Riordan, *Boundaries*, pp. 3–4.

12. Wallace Stegner, *The American West as Living Space* (Ann Arbor: University of Michigan Press, 1987), p. 19; Frederick Turner, *Beyond Geography: The Western Spirit Against the Wilderness* (New York: Viking Press, 1980), pp. 95, 129, and passim.

13. Chrestien Le Clercq, *New Relation of Gaspesia, with the Customs and Religion of the Gaspesian Indians*, 1691, trans. and ed. William F. Ganong (Toronto: Champlain Society, 1910; reprint ed., New York: Greenwood Press, 1968), p. 277. See a nearly identical statement in Reuben Gold Thwaites, ed., *The Jesuit Relations and Allied Documents: Travels and Explorations of the Jesuit Missionaries in New France, 1610–1791*, 73 vols. (Cleveland: Burrows Brothers, 1896–1901), 6:297: "I heard my [Montagnais] host say one day, jokingly, . . . 'The Beaver does everything perfectly well, it makes kettles, hatchets, swords, knives, bread; and, in short, it makes everything'" (Paul Le Jeune's Relation of 1634).

14. Thomas W. Overholt and J. Baird Callicott, *Clothed-in-Fur and Other Tales: An Introduction to an Ojibwa World View* (Washington, D.C.: University Press of America, 1982), pp. 74–75.

15. Francis Parkman, *The Oregon Trail*, 1849 (New York: New American Library, 1950), p. 13.

16. Ibid., pp. 171–172.

17. Ibid., p. 172.

18. Ibid.

19. Steven A. Jacobson, comp., *Yup'ik Eskimo Dictionary* (Fairbanks: University of Alaska, Alaska Native Language Center, 1984), appendix 7, p. 670.

20. James W. Henkelman and Kurt H. Vitt, *Harmonious to Dwell: The History of the Alaska Moravian Church, 1885–1985* (Bethel, Alaska: Moravian Seminary and Archives, 1985), pp. 76, 86. See Genesis 35:1.

21. Genesis 28:17.

22. Loren Eiseley, *The Star Thrower* (New York: Times Books, 1978), pp. 106–115.

23. Fienup-Riordan, *Boundaries*, pp. 3–4.

24. Theodora Kroeber, *Ishi in Two Worlds: A Biography of the Last Wild Indian in North America* (Berkeley: University of California Press, 1971), p. 237.

25. N. Scott Momaday, "The Colors of Night," in *The Gourd Dancer*, pp. 44–47 (New York: Harper and Row, 1976), p. 45.

Chapter 3: Cartier's Bear

1. H. P. Biggar, ed., *The Voyages of Jacques Cartier*, Publications of the Public Archives of Canada, no. 11 (Ottawa: F. A. Acland, 1924), pp. 6–9, 31.
2. Gontran de Poncins, *Kabloona*, 1941 (New York: Carroll and Graf, 1968), pp. 256, 324–325.
3. Biggar, *Voyages*, p. 260; Biggar, ed., *A Collection of Documents Relating to Jacques Cartier and the Sieur de Roberval*, Publications of the Public Archives of Canada, no. 14 (Ottawa: Public Archives of Canada, 1930), pp. 77, 79.
4. Biggar, *Documents*, pp. 76–78.
5. John Heckewelder, *History, Manners, and Customs of the Indian Nations Who Once Inhabited Pennsylvania and the Neighbouring States*, 1818 (Philadelphia, 1876; reprint ed., New York: Arno Press, 1971), pp. 254, 255, 249; "a Clam, a Dog . . . " Ruth Holmes Whitehead, *Stories from the Six Worlds: Micmac Legends* (Halifax: Nimbus, 1988), p. 4.
6. Knud Rasmussen, *The Netsilik Eskimos: Social Life and Spiritual Culture*, Report of the Fifth Thule Expedition, 1921–1924, vol. 8, nos. 1–2 (Copenhagen, 1931; reprint ed., New York: AMS Press, 1976), p. 208; Waldemar Bogoras, "Ideas of Space and Time in the Conception of Primitive Religion," *American Anthropologist*, n.s., 27 (April 1925): 236.
7. Loren Eiseley, *The Star Thrower* (New York: Times Books, 1978), p. 53; Heckewelder, *History*, pp. 252–253.
8. Heckewelder, *History*, p. 252.
9. Ibid., pp. 263–264.
10. Ibid., p. 253.
11. Paul Radin, *The Trickster: A Study in American Indian Mythology* (1956; reprint ed., New York: Schocken Books, 1972), p. 91; Robert Bringhurst, *The Black Canoe: Bill Reid and the Spirit of Haida Gwaii*, photographs by Ulli Steltzer (Seattle: University of Washington Press; Vancouver and Toronto: Douglas and McIntyre, 1991), p. 49.
12. Bringhurst, *Canoe*, p. 49.
13. Radin, *Trickster*, p. xxiii.
14. Stanley Diamond, "Job and the Trickster," introductory essay in ibid., pp. xi–xxii.

15. Radin, *Trickster*, pp. xxiv, 169.
16. Ibid., p. 87.
17. Ibid., p. 88.
18. Whitehead, *Stories*, pp. 9–10.
19. Ruth Murray Underhill, *Singing for Power: The Song Magic of the Papago Indians of Southern Arizona* (Berkeley and Los Angeles: University of California Press, 1938), p. 49.
20. Radin, *Trickster*, p. 83.
21. Whitehead, *Stories*, pp. 10–11.
22. Radin, *Trickster*, p. 88.
23. Ibid.
24. Ibid., pp. 89–90.
25. James Mooney, "The Sacred Formulas of the Cherokees," *Seventh Annual Report of the Bureau of Ethnology, 1885–1886*, pp. 301–397 (Washington: Government Printing Office, 1891), pp. 319–320.
26. Frank G. Speck, Leonard Broom, and Will West Long, *Cherokee Dance and Drama* (Norman: University of Oklahoma Press, 1951), p. 87.
27. Robin Ridington, "Beaver Dreaming and Singing," in *Pilot Not Commander: Essays in Memory of Diamond Jenness*, ed. Pat Lotz and Jim Lotz, pp. 115–128, special issue of *Anthropologica*, n.s., 13, nos. 1–2 (1971): 123.
28. Frank G. Speck, *Naskapi: The Savage Hunters of the Labrador Peninsula* (Norman: University of Oklahoma Press, 1935), p. 94; Mooney, "Sacred Formulas," p. 373.
29. Whitehead, *Stories*, pp. 50–52.
30. Ibid., p. 74.
31. Ibid., pp. 67–68.
32. Peter Grant, "The Sauteux Indians (Written ca. 1804)," in *Les Bourgeois de la Compagnie du Nord-ouest: Récits de voyages, lettres, et rapports inédits relatifs au nord-ouest canadien, 1889–1890*, ed. L. R. Masson, series 2, pp. 303–366 (reprint ed., New York: Antiquarian Press, 1960), pp. 323–324; Chrestien Le Clercq, *New Relation of Gaspesia, with the Customs and Religion of the Gaspesian Indians*, 1691, trans. and ed. William F. Ganong (Toronto: Champlain Society, 1910; reprint ed., New York: Greenwood Press, 1968), p. 91; John Lawson, *A New Voyage to Carolina*, 1709, ed. Hugh Talmage Lefler (Chapel Hill: University of North Carolina Press, 1967), p. 210.

33. Thomas W. Overholt and J. Baird Callicott, *Clothed-in-Fur and Other Tales: An Introduction to an Ojibwa World View* (Washington, D.C.: University Press of America, 1982), pp. 76–78.

34. Rasmussen, *Netsilik Eskimos*, p. 208.

Chapter 4: Einstein's Beaver

1. Ruth Holmes Whitehead, *Stories from the Six Worlds: Micmac Legends* (Halifax: Nimbus, 1988), p. 72.

2. Ibid.

3. Ibid.

4. Ibid.

5. Ibid.

6. Ibid.

7. Ibid., p. 73.

8. Ibid.

9. Samuel Hearne, *A Journey from Prince of Wales's Fort in Hudson's Bay to the Northern Ocean, 1769, 1770, 1771, 1772, 1795*, ed. Richard Glover (Toronto: Macmillan, 1958), pp. 219–220. Hearne ends the story with this Supreme Being leaving the woman with instructions that sound suspiciously like Jehovah's to Adam and Eve, in both wording and ethic. My guess is that a Chipewyan myth had become adulterated with a biblical punch line sometime before Hearne recorded the story.

10. John Dunn, *The Oregon Territory, and the British North American Fur Trade; with an Account of the Habits and Customs of the Principal Native Tribes on the Northern Continent, 1844* (Philadelphia: G. B. Zieber, 1845), pp. 60–61.

11. Gontran de Poncins, *Kabloona*, 1941 (New York: Carroll and Graf, 1968), pp. 175–178.

12. Whitehead, *Stories*, p. 73.

13. Ibid.

14. Ibid., p. 50.

15. Ibid.

16. Ibid.

17. Ibid., pp. 50–52.

18. Ibid., p. 73.

19. Ibid., pp. 73–74.

20. Ibid., p. 74.

21. Ibid.

22. Knud Rasmussen, *The Netsilik Eskimos: Social Life and Spiritual Culture*, Report of the Fifth Thule Expedition, 1921–1924, vol. 8, nos. 1–2 (Copenhagen, 1931; reprint ed., New York: AMS Press, 1976), p. 208.

23. Alan Lightman, "Inside the Box," *New York Review of Books* 39 (February 13, 1992): 38.

24. Ibid.

25. Ibid.

26. Ibid.; John Archibald Wheeler, "Bohr, Einstein, and the Strange Lesson of the Quantum," in *Mind in Nature: Nobel Conference XVII*, ed. Richard Q. Elvee, pp. 1–30 (San Francisco: Harper and Row, 1982), p. 18.

27. Wheeler, "Bohr," pp. 17–18.

28. David Z. Albert, *Quantum Mechanics and Experience* (Cambridge: Harvard University Press, 1992), pp. 15, 38; Albert, "Bohm's Alternative to Quantum Mechanics, *Scientific American* 270 (May 1994): 61.

29. Albert, *Quantum*, p. 38.

30. Ibid., p. 79 (see also n. 6).

31. Albert Einstein and Leopold Infeld, *The Evolution of Physics: The Growth of Ideas from Early Concepts to Relativity and Quanta* (New York: Simon and Schuster, 1938), p. 294; Wheeler, "Bohr," p. 18.

32. Wheeler, "Bohr," pp. 7, 13.

33. Ibid., pp. 6–7; Albert, *Quantum*, pp. 61, 64.

34. Albert, *Quantum*, p. 69; Albert, "Bohm's Alternative," p. 67; Wheeler, "Bohr," p. 6.

35. Lightman, "Inside the Box," p. 38; Wheeler, "Bohr," pp. 6, 22.

36. Wheeler, "Bohr," pp. 26–27.

37. Einstein and Infeld, *Evolution of Physics*, p. 258.

38. Sean Kane, *Wisdom of the Mythtellers* (Peterborough, Ontario: Broadview Press, 1994), pp. 50, 34–35.

39. Ibid., pp. 116–117.

40. Robert Bringhurst, trans., "Sapsucker," in Kane, *Mythtellers*, p. 29.

41. Wheeler, "Bohr," p. 7; Kane, *Mythtellers*, pp. 45, 50.

42. Albert, *Quantum*, pp. 144–145; Albert, "Bohm's Alternative," pp. 63, 66.

43. Albert, "Bohm's Alternative," p. 67; Mary Oliver, "The Sea," in *American Primitive* (Boston: Little, Brown, 1983), p. 69.

Chapter 5: Raven's Children

1. Noël Bennett, *Halo of the Sun: Stories Told and Retold* (Flagstaff, Ariz.: Northland Press, 1987), p. 37.

2. Rainer Maria Rilke, "The Panther," in *Selected Poems of Rainer Maria Rilke*, trans. Robert Bly (New York: Harper and Row, 1981), p. 139.

3. Paul Radin, *The Trickster: A Study in American Indian Mythology* (1956; reprint ed., New York: Schocken Books, 1972), p. 89.

4. Matthew 25:35–40 (New Revised Standard Version).

5. Walt Whitman, *Leaves of Grass*, 1855 edition (New York: Viking Press, 1959), pp. 62–63, 67 (lines 827, 840–841, 941–943); Mary Oliver, "The Chance to Love Everything," in *Dream Work* (Boston: Atlantic Monthly Press, 1986), pp. 8–9.

6. John W. Andrew ("Trapper John"), "Brown Bear Study a 'Slap in the Face,'" *Bethel (Alaska) Tundra Drums*, May 27, 1993, p. A4; Andrew, "Respect of Bears Left Hunters Safe," ibid., June 3, 1993, p. A3.

7. Transcribed interview with Maxie Altsik and Charlie Kilangak, Sr., February 5, 1996, used with permission.

8. Transcribed interview with Charlie Kilangak, Sr., February 5, 1996, used with permission.

9. Ibid.; Ann Fienup-Riordan, ed., *Agayuliyararput/Our Way of Making Prayer: Yup'ik Masks and the Stories They Tell*, trans. Marie Meade (Seattle: Anchorage Museum of History and Art, University of Washington Press, 1996), p. 43.

10. Transcribed interview with Carrie Anvil and Charlie Kilangak, Sr., February 1, 1996, used with permission.

11. William Faulkner, "The Bear," 1942, in *Bear, Man, and God: Eight Approaches to William Faulkner's "The Bear,"* ed. Francis Lee Utley, Lynn Z. Bloom, and Arthur F. Kinney, 2d ed. (New York: Random House, 1971), p. 7.

12. Transcribed interview with Elsie Active, February 5, 1996, used with permission; Whitman, *Leaves of Grass*, p. 63, lines 841–842.

13. Letter to Martin, May 5, 1996, used with permission.

14. Harold Napoleon, *Yuuyaraq: The Way of the Human Being*, ed. Eric Madsen (Fairbanks: Center for Cross-Cultural Studies, University of Alaska Fairbanks, 1991), pp. 8, 10–11.

15. Ibid., p. 12.
16. Knud Rasmussen, *The Netsilik Eskimos: Social Life and Spiritual Culture*, Report of the Fifth Thule Expedition, 1921–1924, vol. 8, nos. 1–2 (Copenhagen, 1931; reprint ed., New York: AMS Press, 1976), p. 208.
17. Napoleon, *Yuuyaraq*, p. 14.
18. Ibid., p. v.

Chapter 6: Oscar

1. Hans Himmelheber, *Eskimo Artists*, 1938 (Fairbanks: University of Alaska Press, 1993), p. 12.
2. Steven A. Jacobson, comp., *Yup'ik Eskimo Dictionary* (Fairbanks: University of Alaska, Alaska Native Language Center, 1984), pp. 261–263.
3. Eliza Cingarkaq Orr and Ben Orr, eds., *Qanemcikarluni Tekitnarqelartuq/ One Must Arrive with a Story to Tell: Traditional Narratives by the Elders of Tununak, Alaska* (Fairbanks: Lower Kuskokwim School District and the Alaska Native Language Center, 1995), p. 366.
4. Barre Toelken to Martin, personal communication, January 1996.
5. Richard Adams Carey, *Raven's Children* (Boston: Houghton Mifflin, 1992).
6. Henry David Thoreau, *The Maine Woods*, 1864 (New York: Harper and Row, 1987), p. 106.
7. John 3:16 (King James Version).
8. Ann Fienup-Riordan, ed., *Agayuliyararput / Our Way of Making Prayer: Yup'ik Masks and the Stories They Tell*, trans. Marie Meade (Seattle: Anchorage Museum of History and Art, University of Washington Press, 1996), pp. 39, 45.
9. Ibid., p. 45.
10. Sean Kane, *Wisdom of the Mythtellers* (Peterborough, Ontario: Broadview Press, 1994), p. 47.
11. Transcribed interview with Elsie Active, February 5, 1996, used with permission.
12. Ruth Holmes Whitehead, *Stories from the Six Worlds: Micmac Legends* (Halifax: Nimbus, 1988), p. 74.
13. Transcribed interview with Charlie Kilangak, Sr., February 5, 1996, used with permission.
14. See Parker J. Palmer, *To Know as We Are Known: Education as a Spiritual Journey* (San Francisco: HarperCollins, 1993), pp. 20–21.

15. Ibid., p. 7.

16. Robin Ridington, "Fox and Chickadee," in *The American Indian and the Problem of History*, ed. Calvin Martin, pp. 128–135 (New York: Oxford University Press, 1987), pp. 133–134.

17. Palmer, *To Know*, p. 58.

Chapter 7: A Witch's Story

1. Leslie Marmon Silko, *Ceremony* (New York: Viking Penguin Books, 1977), p. 1.

2. Aldo Leopold, *A Sand County Almanac and Sketches Here and There* (New York: Oxford University Press, 1949), pp. 129–133; Ralph Waldo Emerson, "Thoreau," in *The Portable Emerson*, ed. Mark Van Doren, pp. 567–589 (New York: Viking Press, 1974), pp. 574, 579.

3. Emerson, "Thoreau," p. 581.

4. Loren Eiseley, *Francis Bacon and the Modern Dilemma* (1962; reprint ed., Freeport, N.Y.: Books for Libraries Press, 1970), pp. 88–89. Eiseley neglected to put quotation marks around "was generated . . . flowed away." I have supplied them. See Henry David Thoreau, *The Maine Woods*, 1864 (New York: Harper and Row, 1987), pp. 84–86.

5. Thoreau, *Maine Woods*, p. 95.

6. Eiseley, *Francis Bacon*, p. 90.

7. Thoreau, *Maine Woods*, p. 94; Eiseley, *The Star Thrower* (New York: Times Books, 1978), pp. 175–176.

8. Kenneth Heuer, ed., *The Lost Notebooks of Loren Eiseley* (Boston: Little, Brown, 1987), pp. 140–141.

9. H. P. Biggar, ed., *The Voyages of Jacques Cartier*, Publications of the Public Archives of Canada, no. 11 (Ottawa: F. A. Acland, 1924), pp. 147, 150, 162–163.

10. Ibid., pp. 50–51.

11. Ibid., p. 135.

12. Ibid., p. 129.

13. Ibid., p. 259.

14. *The Journal of Christopher Columbus*, trans. Cecil Jane and L. A. Vigneras (New York: Clarkson N. Potter, Bramhall House, 1960), pp. 132–133.

15. Marc Lescarbot, *The History of New France*, 1609, trans. W. L. Grant, 3 vols. (Toronto: Champlain Society, 1911), 2:326–327.

16. Reuben Gold Thwaites, ed., *The Jesuit Relations and Allied Documents: Travels and Explorations of the Jesuit Missionaries in New France, 1610–1791*, 73 vols. (Cleveland: Burrows Brothers, 1896–1901), 1:173; Lescarbot, *History*, 3:214; John Heckewelder, *History, Manners, and Customs of the Indian Nations Who Once Inhabited Pennsylvania and the Neighbouring States*, 1818 (Philadelphia, 1876; reprint ed., New York: Arno Press, 1971), p. 101.

17. Chrestien Le Clercq, *New Relation of Gaspesia, with the Customs and Religion of the Gaspesian Indians*, 1691, trans. and ed. William F. Ganong (Toronto: Champlain Society, 1910; reprint ed., New York: Greenwood Press, 1968), pp. 245, 117.

18. John Eliot, "The Day-Breaking If Not the Sun-Rising of the Gospell with the Indians in New-England," 1647, *Massachusetts Historical Society Collections*, 3d ser., 4 (1834): 3.

19. Le Clercq, *New Relation*, pp. 312, 224–225.

20. Lescarbot, *History*, 2:569.

21. Ibid., pp. 355, 576.

22. N. Scott Momaday, "The Fear of Bo-talee," in *The Gourd Dancer* (New York: Harper and Row, 1976), p. 25.

23. Eiseley, "The Deer," in *Another Kind of Autumn* (New York: Charles Scribner's Sons, 1977), pp. 76–77; Walt Whitman, *Leaves of Grass*, 1855 edition (New York: Viking Press, 1959), p. 69, line 974.

24. Silko, *Ceremony*, p. 117.

25. Ibid., pp. 125–126.

26. Tiana Bighorse, *Bighorse the Warrior*, ed. Noël Bennett (Tucson: University of Arizona Press, 1990), p. xxv.

27. Ibid., p. xxiv.

28. Ibid., pp. 81–82.

29. Silko, *Ceremony*, p. 132.

30. Ibid., pp. 132–138.

31. Kai Erikson, *A New Species of Trouble: The Human Experience of Modern Disasters* (New York: W. W. Norton, 1994), p. 189.

32. Silko, *Ceremony*, p. 138.

33. Erikson, *New Species*, p. 189.

34. Ibid., pp. 199–200.

35. Ibid., p. 202.

36. Momaday, *In the Presence of the Sun: Stories and Poems* (New York: St. Martin's Press, 1992), p. 43.

37. Ibid., p. 47.
38. Ibid., pp. 51–52.
39. Ibid., p. 52.
40. Ibid., p. 63.
41. Silko, *Ceremony*, pp. 134–135.
42. Erikson, *New Species*, p. 242.
43. Momaday, "The Man Made of Words," in *Indian Voices: The First Convocation of American Indian Scholars* [Princeton University, 1970], pp. 49–62, with discussion following on pp. 62–84 (San Francisco: Indian Historian Press, 1970), p. 53.
44. Erikson, *New Species*, p. 241.
45. Herman Melville, *The Confidence-Man: His Masquerade*, 1857 (New York: Holt, Rinehart, and Winston, 1964), p. 247. See chaps. 42 and 43.
46. Silko, *Ceremony*, pp. 195–196.
47. Ibid., p. 196.
48. William Faulkner, "The Bear," 1942, in *Bear, Man, and God: Eight Approaches to William Faulkner's "The Bear,"* ed. Francis Lee Utley, Lynn Z. Bloom, and Arthur F. Kinney, 2d ed. (New York: Random House, 1971), p. 16.
49. Silko, *Ceremony*, p. 196.

Chapter 8: Frogs

1. Loren Eiseley, *The Star Thrower* (New York: Times Books, 1978), p. 120.
2. Leslie Marmon Silko, *Ceremony* (New York: Viking Penguin Books, 1977), p. 135.
3. Gale E. Christianson, *Fox at the Wood's Edge: A Biography of Loren Eiseley* (New York: Henry Holt, 1990), p. 142.
4. Eiseley, *Star Thrower*, p. 106.
5. Ibid.
6. Ibid., p. 107.
7. Ibid., pp. 107–108.
8. Ibid., pp. 106, 108–110.
9. Ibid., p. 110.
10. Henry David Thoreau, *The Maine Woods*, 1864 (New York: Harper and Row, 1987), pp. 85–86.
11. Ibid., pp. 94–95.

12. Knud Rasmussen, *The Netsilik Eskimos: Social Life and Spiritual Culture,* Report of the Fifth Thule Expedition, 1921–1924, vol. 8, nos. 1–2 (Copenhagen, 1931; reprint ed., New York: AMS Press, 1976), p. 208.

13. Letter to Martin, October 10, 1996, used with permission.

14. Eiseley, Star Thrower, pp. 111–112.

15. Ibid., p. 113.

16. Ibid., pp. 114–115.

17. N. Scott Momaday, "The Man Made of Words," in *Indian Voices: The First Convocation of American Indian Scholars* [Princeton University, 1970], pp. 49–62, with discussion following on pp. 62–84 (San Francisco: Indian Historian Press, 1970); Eiseley, *Star Thrower,* p. 114.

18. Mary Oliver, "Pink Moon—The Pond," in *Twelve Moons* (Boston: Little, Brown, 1979), pp. 7–8.

19. Silko, Ceremony, p. 196; Rasmussen, *Netsilik Eskimos,* p. 208.

20. Momaday, *In the Presence of the Sun: Stories and Poems* (New York: St. Martin's Press, 1992), pp. 51–52.

21. Eiseley, *Star Thrower,* p. 109.

22. Eiseley, *Francis Bacon and the Modern Dilemma* (1962; reprint ed., Freeport, N.Y.: Books for Libraries Press, 1970), p. 73.

23. Robin Ridington, "Fox and Chickadee," in *The American Indian and the Problem of History,* ed. Calvin Martin, pp. 128–135 (New York: Oxford University Press, 1987), p. 130.

24. Ibid., pp. 129–131.

25. Ibid., p. 132.

26. Ibid.

27. Ibid., p. 134; John G. Neihardt, *Black Elk Speaks: Being the Life Story of a Holy Man of the Oglala Sioux* (New York: Simon and Schuster, Pocket Books, 1972), p. 25.

Winter Count

1. Leslie Marmon Silko, *Ceremony* (New York: Viking Penguin Books, 1977), pp. 135, 219.

2. Mary Oliver, "Crows," in *New and Selected Poems* (Boston: Beacon Press, 1992), p. 220; Silko, *Ceremony,* p. 246.

3. Silko, *Ceremony,* p. 145.

4. N. Scott Momaday, "The Delight Song of Tsoai-talee," in *The Gourd Dancer* (New York: Harper and Row, 1976), p. 27.

5. Robin Ridington, "Fox and Chickadee," in *The American Indian and the Problem of History*, ed. Calvin Martin, pp. 128–135 (New York: Oxford University Press, 1987), p. 132.

6. Barry Holstun Lopez, "Winter Count 1973: Geese, They Flew Over in a Storm," in *Winter Count*, pp. 51–63 (New York: Avon Books, 1981), pp. 58–63.

7. Ibid., p. 62.

8. Willa Cather, *Death Comes for the Archbishop*, 1927 (New York: Random House, Vintage Books, 1971), p. 273.

9. Rainer Maria Rilke, "The Panther," in *Selected Poems of Rainer Maria Rilke*, trans. Robert Bly (New York: Harper and Row, 1981), p. 139.

Acknowledgments

Portions or all of the following works are reprinted herein by permission.

"The Fear of Bo-talee," "The Delight Song of Tsoai-talee," and "The Colors of Night," from *The Gourd Dancer*, by N. Scott Momaday. Copyright © 1976 by N. Scott Momaday. Reprinted by permission of N. Scott Momaday.

"The Panther," from *Selected Poems of Rainer Maria Rilke*, ed. and trans. Robert Bly. Copyright © 1981 by Robert Bly. Reprinted by permission of HarperCollins Publishers, Inc.

"The Deer," reprinted with the permission of Scribner, a Division of Simon and Schuster, from *Another Kind of Autumn*, by Loren Eiseley. Copyright © 1976 by Loren Eiseley. Copyright © 1977 by the Estate of Loren Eiseley.

"Pink Moon—The Pond," from *Twelve Moons*, by Mary Oliver. Copyright © 1978, 1979, by Mary Oliver. First appeared in *The Western Humanities Review*. Reprinted by permission of Little, Brown and Company and the Molly Malone Cook Literary Agency.

"Ts'its'tsi'nako, Thought-Woman," "Jean-Pierre," from *Ceremony*, by Leslie Marmon Silko. Copyright © 1977 by Leslie Marmon Silko. Reprinted by permission of Viking Penguin, a division of Penguin Putnam, Inc.

"Puffin" reprinted by permission of Charlie Kilangak, Sr.

"Sapsucker," translated by Robert Bringhurst, reprinted by permission of Robert Bringhurst.

"The Loom," from *Halo of the Sun: Stories Told and Retold*, by Noël Bennett. Copyright © 1987 by Shared Horizons. Reprinted by permission of Noël Bennett, Director, Shared Horizons, Inc.